S0-ASV-277

Deviant Behavior

Patterns, Sources, and Control

Deviant Behavior

Patterns, Sources, and Control

Stuart Palmer

University of New Hampshire
Durham, New Hampshire

and

John A. Humphrey

University of North Carolina
Greensboro, North Carolina

Plenum Press • New York and London

Library of Congress Cataloging in Publication Data

Palmer, Stuart Hunter, 1924.
  Deviant behavior: patterns, sources, and control / Stuart Palmer and John A. Humphrey.
     p.   cm.
  Bibliography: p.
  Includes index.
  ISBN 0-306-43285-4
  1. Deviant behavior. 2. Crime and criminals. I. Humphrey, John A. II. Title.
HM291.P2723   1989   88-23264
302.5'42—dc19   CIP

We gratefully acknowledge permission to reprint the following:

The Twelve Steps (New York: Alcoholics Anonymous World Services, Inc., 1939, pp. 71–72).

Clellan S. Ford and Frank A. Beach, *Patterns of Sexual Behavior* (New York: Harper & Row, Inc., 1951, pp. 125–133). Copyright renewed 1979 by Ford and Beach.

Laud Humphreys, *Tearoom Trade* (New York: Aldine de Gruyter, pp. 6–8; 12–13) Copyright 1970, 1975 by R. A. Laud Humphreys.

© 1990 Plenum Press, New York
A Division of Plenum Publishing Corporation
233 Spring Street, New York, N.Y. 10013

Printed in the United States of America

TO OUR FAMILIES

Preface

This book is for the student in the introductory course on deviant behavior and in related courses. A wide range of ideas and facts is set forth in a way that should be comprehensible to the student without prior knowledge of this area of study. In Chapter 1, "The Nature of Deviance," various ways of defining deviance are explored and one is settled upon: Deviance is behavior that is unusual, not typical, in a society or group.

Chapter 2 is devoted to a preliminary consideration of several main currents of social thought that seek to explain why deviance comes about and is perpetrated. These explanations fall into four broad theoretical categories. First, there are those theories that view the major sources of deviance as having to do with the extent to which individuals are bound into or dissociated from the group; these are termed social integration theories. Second, there are the cultural support theories, which specify that there are subcultures of deviance, that is, bodies of customs and values that advocate a given form of deviance and are socially transmitted from one person to another through the learning process. Third, there are social disorganization and conflict theories, which focus on the ways in which a lack of group organization and the presence of broad social and cultural conflicts bring about deviance. Fourth, there are those theories that center on how society reacts to the future possibility of deviance, on how social controls can in fact beget deviance; these are quite appropriately named societal reaction theories.

Toward the end of Chapter 2, the various theoretical approaches to deviance are drawn together, synthesized as much as is possible without forcing them into one mold and so destroying them. In some respects the various theories share common ground; in other respects they complement each other. This is as it should be, for the field of deviance covers a multitude of behaviors. While these behaviors all have in common the fact that they are not typical of the members of a society, they vary greatly from one another.

Chapters 3 through 10 each deal with one or several closely related forms of deviance. These chapters are concerned with the major forms of violent behavior: homicide, assault, rape, and robbery; property or theft crimes and white-collar crime in business settings; prostitution and homosexuality; the various forms of mental illness; suicide; and alcohol and other drug abuse.

Yet the question remains: Why study deviance? Most individuals find the analysis of various forms of deviant behavior to be intrinsically interesting. It should also be kept in mind that there can be broader reasons for studying deviance. Human behavior is either conforming or deviant or in some cases a combination of the two. An understanding of deviance sheds light on the nature of conformity and vice versa. We all conform much of the time and we all deviate some of the time. If behavior were closely conforming, if there were no deviations from prescribed norms, societies would quickly atrophy and die. For it is through deviance, particularly but not only in its positive forms, that innovation—new ways of solving problems—comes about. Without innovation human social organizations would lack the capacity to change. And absence of that capacity means a very short lifetime for either societies or individuals.

Thus the study of deviant forms and processes has universal applicability: It helps us to understand deviant behavior and the individuals who manifest such behavior. It also helps us to understand our relationships to others and ourselves. Finally, it helps us to comprehend the nature of society, not only our own society, but human societies everywhere.

Stuart Palmer
Durham, New Hampshire
John A. Humphrey
Greensboro, North Carolina

Contents

1

The Nature of Deviance

DEFINING DEVIANT BEHAVIOR

Introduction

There is great diversity of deviant behavior ranging from crime, mental illness, and suicide to minor rule breaking in school or at home, to excessive behaviors such as overeating and overdrinking, to such positive forms as invention. Deviance implies nonconformity, doing things differently from the everyday routines. This makes the study of deviance intrinsically interesting to most people. But deviance is also a highly useful field of study. It helps us to better understand the nature of conformity and of human social life in general, since all human behavior is, after all, in varying degrees, either conforming or deviant. Further, the analysis of deviance helps us to understand the nature of social change. Without deviance there would be little change, and without change societies atrophy and die out.

There are in everyday life many preconceptions, misconceptions, uncertainties, and differences of view about what does and does not constitute deviance. Is the behavior of a president of the United States who lies to the country deviant? Of a physician who commits euthanasia or mercy killing? A scientist who invents a new vaccine which prevents the spread of disease? An engineer who invents a "burglar-proof" safe? A person who finds a new way to crack that safe?

Are those who are "different" because of their physical characteristics deviant, such as the blind, the deaf, the obese, the very short, the very tall? Are those who hold to values different from that of the majority deviant? Members of religious sects such as the Amish and the Hutterites? Political radicals and conservatives? What of those whose economic conditions of life are quite apart from the mainstream—the very poor and the very wealthy? Finally, what of behavior that is from certain standpoints conforming and yet socially disapproved? Professional theft is an apt example. Those who make their living through

1

thievery hold to a close set of rules of their own, are often quite conforming in gaining their livelihood, yet are considered deviants by society at large.[1]

What is deviant and who is a deviant are, then, complex questions
that often inspire ambiguous answers. Most of us would agree that
conforming behavior is not deviant, that the conformist is not a deviant
person. Deviance is nonconformity. But what standard is to be used to
decide what is conformity? Culture and social organization help to provide answers.

Culture and Social Organization

Societies are organized groupings of interdependent individuals.
Some societies, such as the United States, are large, composed of millions of individuals. Others are small; for example, certain Eskimo societies contain but 200 or 300 persons. Regardless of size, the members
of each society possess a culture and a system of social organization.
A *culture* is a body of widely shared customs and values which provide
general orientations toward life and specific ways of achieving common
goals.[2] Much of a culture consists of ways of solving problems that
have been passed on through learning from one generation to the
next. Culture is sometimes briefly defined as a society's storehouse of
knowledge.

Cultural customs provide the basis for the social organization of a
society. A society's system of *social organization* is made up of the norms
and roles that guide interaction among its members.[3] *Social norms* take
two parallel forms: behavioral and expectational. *Behavioral norms* are
the patterns of actual behavior that individuals typically follow when
interacting under given conditions. It is common practice in the United
States for store clerks to give customers the correct change when a
purchase is made. Some do not for one reason or another. Since most
clerks, do, however, this practice constitutes a behavioral norm.

Expectational norms are what people typically expect each other to
do under given conditions. Most of us in the United States share the
expectation that store clerks will give us, the customers, the correct
change. The patterned expectations are so strong that many of us do
not carefully count our change. Since the same expectations are widely
shared, this pattern constitutes an expectational norm.

Often expectational norms demand a little more than behavioral
norms deliver. In many situations when individuals interact, we expect, as it were, a little more than we know will occur. We expect store
clerks to be honest and avoid mistakes, yet we know that in practice
some will either attempt to be dishonest or will err occasionally.

Some sociologists view the behavioral and expectational norms which are the smallest units of a system of social organization as distinct from culture. Others see them as a part of culture.[4] Without trying to resolve this difference in viewpoints, we can note that cultural practices and values certainly determine in considerable measure the specific nature of norms. Through norms, cultural prescriptions are translated into patterns of interaction. Thus our cultural customs and values having to do with the distribution of economic goods and with honesty bear directly on the nature of expectational and behavioral norms for the store clerks' behavior in the above example.

Social roles are clusters of norms which individuals follow when occupying given positions or *statuses* in the society's system of social organization.[5] As with single norms, roles may involve patterns of typical expectations as to how individuals in a given position should act, or they may involve patterns of typical actual behavior that people do in fact act out when occupying a particular position. Most if not all of us have age and sex roles and familial roles such as wife, husband, mother, father, son, or daughter. Many of us have work and educational roles. There are also political, religious, even recreational roles. And there may be social class, racial, and ethnic roles.

Social roles are usually acted out through other roles. There are no parents without children, no husbands without wives, no teachers without students, and vice versa in each case. Roles and the norms which they comprised make interaction predictable. They make it possible for us to predict each other's behavior in given types of situations and so to anticipate each other's actions and to carry out our own actions accordingly. These reciprocal predictions and actions lend stability to social situations, making them recognizable over time. It is mainly in this way that roles and norms contribute to social organization.

Because of our need for predictability in human affairs as a basis of social organization, we often become annoyed, upset, or angry when people deviate unexpectedly from norms and roles. Such deviation can threaten group organization and us as individuals because we are dependent on that organization for our existence.

Defining Deviant Behavior

Deviant behavior is frequently defined as behavior which does not conform to norms and roles.[6] This is the *normative approach* to deviance. Some sociologists prefer to use expectational norms and typical role expectations as the criteria of deviance while others prefer to use behavioral norms and typical role behavior. For certain types of analysis, one or the other may be more suitable. We think that the criterion of behavior is usually the more useful. Here, one can measure the extent to which the behavior of individuals under given circumstances conforms to or deviates from what people in general typically do under those circumstances. Expectations are often set more stringently than behavioral norms in order to ensure that people "measure up" to those behaviors. Hence individuals may typically fall short of an expectational norm. If, in such instances, one used the expectational norm as the standard, one would conclude that most individuals were deviating. Yet actually most of them might be conforming to a behavioral standard different from the expectational standard.

Sociologists who favor the behavioral criterion and those who favor the expectational criterion are, in any case, in agreement that deviance is behavior which does not conform to social norms. There is, however, still another group of sociologists who take a fundamentally different view. Those sociologists stress the idea that deviance actually occurs only when other people react to norm violations by a given individual, take action, and label him or her as a deviant.[7] This is the *societal reaction approach.*

The first approach to defining deviant behavior, the normative, applies well where there are firmly established taboos in society against certain serious transgressions. The second approach, that of societal reaction, does not apply well in such instances. As an example, almost all societies have strong taboos against murder. They specify that it is an extremely serious wrong or deviation to kill another person except in clear self-defense or in the line of culturally prescribed duty.[8] An example of the latter is a prison guard killing an escaping inmate. The issue here is whether or not someone has killed another except in self-defense or the line of duty. It is not necessary to determine precisely who committed the act, or to label the offender, in order to conclude that deviance has occurred.

On the other hand, the societal reaction approach, which holds that deviance is in the eye of the beholder and the mouth of the labeler, is especially applicable to ambiguous situations where norms are unclear. Here there will be differing views as to whether a deviant act has been carried out and, if so, who is the deviant. In the United States, euthanasia or mercy killing is such a case. So is homosexuality between adults. So is prostitution. The police may arrest some prostitutes and thereby label them as lawbreakers. Others may be ignored. Frequently, the higher the social status of the person—the call girl in the case of prostitution—the less the likelihood of being labeled.

In a very real sense, then, the societal reaction and normative approaches are not mutually exclusive and can be reconciled. What is typical behavior or typical expectations for persons in given positions in certain types of situations is not always clear. In other words, when norms are not well established, it is exceedingly difficult to know which behaviors are deviant and which are not. It is at this point that from a scientific standpoint the societal reaction approach becomes especially relevant. It allows us to see that in situations where what is conforming or deviant is ambiguous, the group attempts to resolve this ambiguity by sometimes labeling behavior as deviant, sometimes not. This is one of the processes by which behavioral and expectational norms are established.

Therefore, suppose that relatives who help a family member to die are prosecuted, but physicians who help patients to die are not. Prostitutes on the street are prosecuted; those in fashionable apartments are not. It may then gradually come about that euthanasia by physicians is conforming and by others deviant; prostitution by call girls conforming, by streetwalkers deviant. It is true that there may be a tendency for group members to react to the behavior of individuals in such a way that those with less power and prestige are labeled as deviant. And this may lead to the development of norms such that what the less powerful do is more likely to constitute deviation than what the more powerful do. While we do not condone this, we note that it is often a part of the social process in everyday life.

DIMENSIONS OF DEVIANCE

Institutionalized versus Individualistic Deviance

Deviance varies along a number of dimensions: the degree to which it is socially patterned and therefore institutionalized or individualistic and not institutionalized; the extent to which it is innovative or not; and the degree to which it is socially evaluated as positive or negative behavior. There is also the question of the extent to which deviance can involve physical characteristics of individuals.

As to whether deviant behavior is *institutionalized* or *individualistic:* we have said that those who follow the normative approach define deviance as behavior which does not conform to expectational or behavioral norms. There is, however, a partial exception to this. Behavioral and expectational patterns—that is, norms and the roles composed of them—may be ones which are approved by one or more small groups within a society and disapproved by the larger society. Thus in the example used earlier, there are norms and roles for professional theft. Those involved in professional theft expect each other to follow patterned behaviors; and in fact they tend to do so. The wider society disapproves of conformity to professional theft norms and approves of deviation from them. In such instances we say that deviant behavior is *institutionalized.*

At the opposite extreme is highly *individualistic* deviance. Here the person deviates from conventional norms and roles in ways which are not patterned and institutionalized but are peculiar to him or her. A vivid example is a recent case in which someone placed a live rattlesnake in a man's roadside mailbox. The rattlers had been removed so there would be no warning signal. The man came home, opened the box and reached in, was bitten, and was hospitalized in serious condition. There are no expectational and behavioral patterns or norms for this form of deviance. Hence it is very individualistic and not at all institutionalized. All deviant behavior ranges between individualistic and institutionalized extremes.

Why do deviant norms arise, that is, why does deviance become institutionalized rather than remain individualistic? If an individualistic form of deviance—some new type of behavior only one or a few people exhibit—satisfies a widespread need in a group to solve some problem, then it is likely to be taken up by group members. Then deviant behavioral and expectational norms and roles will arise. A variety of related norms and roles that help to solve a broad, general problem for a group and that are negatively evaluated by the larger society constitute what is sometimes called a *deviant subculture.*[9]

Thus certain forms of theft can become institutionalized and a subculture of professional thieves may arise. Individuals first develop ways of solving the problem of how to steal regularly without being apprehended, convicted, and punished. There are ways not only of theft per se but also of developing relationships with police, lawyers, and fences who retail the stolen goods, such that the whole enterprise is expedited. These ways are taken up by considerable numbers of thieves and become patterned. Criteria for the selection of recruits to the professional theft subculture are instituted. This is to ensure a steady flow of new blood, of individuals who will perpetuate the theft subculture but who will not undermine and disrupt it, not flood the market with stolen goods and so reduce their value. The professional theft subculture serves a wider goal of providing an occupation which is lucrative and within criminal circles prestigious.

From the point of view of professional thieves, a person who follows their norms is a dependable conformist. From the standpoint of our society at large, both are deviant. Here it is the prevailing, socially acceptable customs, values, norms, and roles of the overall or general culture of a society that form the standards as to what constitutes deviant behavior.

Over time, institutionalized deviance may become so widespread in a society that it is no longer negatively evaluated. Alternately, the value system of the society may shift over time and embrace behavior that was once deviant. Thus, in the United States, wearing a scanty bathing suit was deviant behavior in the earlier part of this century, but because values have changed and wearing of scanty suits has become commonplace, this is no longer deviant.

Innovative Deviance

Innovation is the process of putting together in a new way two or more existing ideas or material forms so that a problem is solved. Invention is a form of innovation. So is creativity in the arts and sciences.[10] And so too are new solutions to problems that people devise in everyday life. Innovation ranges from inventing a new paper clip to the development of a new airplane engine to the creation of a symphony to the formulation of a theory of the universe.

By its very nature, then, innovation is deviant behavior, and it is individualistic. It diverges from the tried-and-true ways of behaving of the larger society or of institutionalized subcultures of deviance. Yet much individualistic deviance is not innovative. It often takes the form of random behavior which does not solve a problem, of repeating over and over an action which does not achieve an intended result, or even of freezing up in a given situation and taking no direct action which might lead to a new solution.

In sum, deviance varies in the extent to which it is institutionalized or individualistic, and individualistic deviance varies in the degree to which it is or is not innovative. Innovation is a form of deviance that is the lifeblood of social and cultural change. Without it there would be little possibility of shifting the traditional ways of solving the problems of a society in order to cope with changing conditions and therefore with new problems. If it serves a widespread need of the society at large or of a group within the society, an innovation will tend over time to become a patterned part of the general culture, or of the accepted norms and roles of the society in general, or of an institutionalized deviant subculture.

Negative versus Positive Deviance

It is usual both in social science and in everyday life to conceive of deviant behavior as socially unacceptable and *negative*. Often it is. Yet a considerable amount of deviant behavior is actually defined by society's members in *positive* fashion.[11] They view it as socially acceptable and reward those who are deviant. The members of a society are likely to define a form of deviant behavior in a positive rather than a negative way if it seems to be helpful for them, to solve a problem for them. If it seems not to do that but rather to threaten their existence in some way, they are likely to define that deviant behavior negatively.

Thus innovative deviance may be defined positively by others if they perceive that it solves a problem they want solved. If it solves a problem they do not want solved or if the solution is likely to cause other larger problems for them, then they will be prone to define that form of innovation as negative deviance. Consequently, the engineer who invents a new burglar-proof safe is applauded. The professional criminal who invents a new way of cracking that safe is not applauded but is punished if possible.

Sometimes the social reception of innovative deviance will be mixed. If a new military weapon is invented, some may see it as diabolical, others as a patriotic contribution to national defense. If new ways of conceiving of humanity are set forth by a creative thinker, some may define those conceptions as heretical and threatening, others as significant contributions to understanding. Darwin's ideas on evolution and Freud's on personality are excellent examples.

Some institutionalized, that is, subculturally patterned, deviance may be positively defined by society's members. An example is the "think-tank." Here scientists or artists live for a year or more, work, and discuss their work in an atmosphere designed to facilitate innovation and creativity. Think-tanks are, sociologically speaking, places of institutionalized deviance, deviant subcultures designed to further individualistic deviance which takes the form of innovation. Generally they are defined positively by society's members because they are thought to provide opportunities for positive scientific breakthroughs and artistic expression.

However, institutionalized subcultures of deviance that are positively defined by others are rare. This is in part because if they are viewed positively, they are likely to be integrated into the mainstream of the culture and lose their identity as deviant subcultures. Hence most positive deviance is both individualistic and innovative in nature.

Along with varying according to whether it is institutionalized or individualistic and innovative or not, then, deviant behavior is evaluated by the members of society along a continuum from extremely positive to extremely negative. These are dimensions of deviance which will be referred to repeatedly in the chapters which follow.

Physical Deviance

Physical characteristics of individuals are sometimes considered deviant if they diverge from what is typical. As with behavioral deviance, this can have unfortunate consequences: the individual may be labeled or singled out in a negative way. In any case, some individuals possess unusual, atypical physical characteristics. These can cover a wide range, such as shortness, tallness, obesity, extreme thinness, brain damage, facial disfigurement, facial beauty, missing limbs, blindness, deafness, speech defects, or very long fingernails.[12]

Certain forms of physical deviance are present from birth, while others occur only after birth. Some, once present, can later be corrected or otherwise changed. This is one of the uses of cosmetic surgery. Others cannot: a missing limb can never be replaced except by an artificial device. Again, some forms of physical deviance are the conscious result of the actions of others. Thus, negative deviants in some societies have been branded, have had their limbs cut off, their eyes gouged out, as punishment and as a means of attempting to deter others.

While most forms of physical deviance are visible, some are invisible. Certain invisible forms have visible behavioral manifestations. An invisible brain defect may lead to low intelligence as manifested in poor learning and problem-solving ability. Other invisible forms have little outward consequence. Thus, a person with one kidney is atypical yet may appear and function as one with two kidneys.

There are forms of physical deviance which do not necessarily alter the individual's behavior directly but do alter the behavior of others. In some groups if a person with a badly disfigured face enters a roomful of people, the interaction will be different than if a person without disfigurement enters. Obviously, when a person's atypical physical characteristics affect the behavior of others, this is likely to have an indirect effect on his or her behavior. For example, a child with a scarred face may become reclusive in order to avoid the hostile reactions of others.

Those who have in common physical characteristics of an unusual nature may be voluntarily or involuntarily segregated. For example, there are towns where very short people have chosen to live, with everything constructed to scale.[13] There are hospitals for the mentally retarded, colonies for those with leprosy. In some instances, segregation leads to the institutionalization of deviant behavior; residents of a home for the blind may develop patterns of dependence that they would be less likely to develop if they were "out in society."

In any event, many forms of atypical physical characteristics are positively or negatively evaluated by society, often the latter. A person considered to be of great beauty, according to the prevailing cultural standards, may be applauded and much rewarded. Frequently, however, physical deviance is negatively evaluated by others because it is a threat, a reminder of what could be their lot. For example, a person badly disfigured by burns may be a reminder that this can happen to almost anyone. Physical deviance may be a threat to others because it directly disrupts ongoing interaction—the person with the facial scar entering the crowded room—or because it affects the individual's behavior in ways that disrupt interaction. The blind person, for example, is likely to slow up and complicate everyday interaction patterns.

Physical deviants, because they constitute threats to individuals and to interaction processes, are sometimes hounded, discriminated against, especially in employment, or ostracized. They are in some settings labeled as morally inferior because of physical incapacity or behavioral inability over which they may have no control. By ascribing to them moral inferiority, the labeler attempts to gain moral superiority. There will be less common instances of the opposite tendency: those physical deviants with socially approved atypical characteristics, such as beauty, may be labeled as morally superior. They may be esteemed by labelers as heroes.

Finally, it is certainly the case that much marked physical deviance can lead to a "damned-if-you-do-and-damned-if-you-don't" situation for both the individuals and those with whom they interact. They and others may have to recognize the fact of their physical deviance if interaction is to be shifted so that it proceeds in a new but smooth way. In so doing, the fact of physical deviance is singled out; attention is drawn to it. Thus blind persons must in many circumstances draw different reactions from those to the sighted. This in itself implicitly labels them as different and in need of special treatment.

THE RELATIVITY AND SPECTRUM OF DEVIANCE

The Relativity of Deviance

What is deviant in one society is not necessarily as deviant in another. What was deviant once may not be so now. Cultural customs and values, behavioral and expectational norms, vary from one society to another and change over time, as do the ways in which the members of various societies react to behavior by labeling it as deviant or not.

Those who act according to the culture in which they were brought up when they later find themselves in a different cultural setting are likely to face severe difficulties.[14] This is well illustrated by the emigration of young men from rural Poland to the United States around the beginning of this century. Sexual customs in rural Poland were such that what constituted rape here in the United States did not there. Many of these young men found themselves in criminal court, bewildered at having been charged with forcible rape.

There are certain forms of deviance that are nearly universal.[15] Murder and primary incest are two. Even here the definitions of what constitutes murder or incest vary from one society to another. Core definitions are similar but socially acceptable exceptions vary. Thus in nearly all societies, killing of other members of the society except in self-defense or in the line of culturally prescribed duty is seen as murder, but what constitutes self-defense or duty can vary considerably across societies. Again, almost all societies have strong taboos against sexual relationships between mother and son, father and daughter (primary incest). Yet some societies exempt male rulers and in fact demand sexual relationships between them and their daughters in order to maintain royal lineage.

What is negative deviance in one society may be positive deviance in another. The athlete who wins again and again is applauded in contemporary United States society but was disparaged in traditional Hopi society. Homosexuality, although never the prevailing form of sexual orientation in a society, is rewarded in some societies and punished in others. Regarding physical deviance, wide variations also exist. Thus, in Germany, facial dueling scars on males have been defined as symbols of honor while the same scars in the United States are negatively evaluated disfigurements. Extreme obesity in females is a criterion for beauty in some African societies where "fattening houses" are used to create beauty.

A Spectrum of Deviance

Deviance constitutes a rich, varied, inherently interesting panorama of behavior. It includes murder and the failure to dot an *i* or cross a *t*; suicide and automobile parking violations; high intelligence and low intelligence; making an everyday social gaffe and bank robbery; corporate white-collar crime and petty shoplifting; movie stardom and violence on skid row; overeating and psychosis; prostitution and artistic creativity.

Most of the chapters in this book are organized to sample major forms of deviance across a spectrum ranging from those very negatively evaluated to those positively evaluated in the United States. Certain forms of deviance described in the chapters ahead are largely individualistic; others are mainly institutionalized. While some are clearly innovative, most have little of the innovative component. A few involve physical deviance in varying degrees, but many do not.

At the most negative extreme of the spectrum are crimes of personal violence such as murder, which in most societies are evaluated as especially negative. At the other extreme are creative scientific and artistic acts. Not all of the latter are given high approval by society but in almost all societies, including the United States, some such creative acts are approved.

Between the two extremes is a host of behaviors. We have selected for analysis in this book those that are especially prevalent and of special interest in the United States. "Victimless" crimes, such as homosexuality and prostitution, and juvenile delinquencies are negatively evaluated although not as much so as crimes of violence. Members of our society are in relative agreement as to which crimes are the most serious and which the least serious. Mental illness and suicide are further forms of negative deviance. Next, some extreme behaviors, such as alcoholism and drug abuse, are seen by the society as negative. Some, like overexercise, are evaluated neutrally. On the other hand, overwork is often viewed positively despite its potential for damaging health.

Finally, there are those forms of problem solving and of scientific and artistic achievements that meet with approval. The suggestion of a plant employee on how to cut production costs or the development by an elementary school teacher of a new way to teach children mathematics are examples of problem solving on an everyday level. Scientific breakthroughs in the fields of energy, transportation, and pollution control are likely today to meet with high public evaluation. Artistic creativity, on the other hand, is slower to gain widespread attention in the United States; such artists as Picasso and Faulkner, for example, while now acclaimed, were originally viewed with puzzlement or disdain.

THE LATENT FUNCTIONS OF DEVIANCE

Individuals understand that certain innovations contribute to the welfare of the group. This is the main reason that some forms of deviance are defined positively. Negative deviance, whether innovative or not, whether institutionalized or not, is usually seen by the members of a society as unwanted problem behavior carried out by difficult, or incompetent, or incapacitated individuals. Seldom is it understood in a society at large that negative deviance can contribute to the perpetuation of the society.

The sociologist Robert Merton wrote in the 1940s of the manifest and latent functions of social phenomena, including deviance.[16] *Manifest functions* are those consequences of patterned social relationships that are intended, recognized, and understood by a society's members. *Latent functions* are those consequences which are unintended and little, if at all, recognized or understood by members. The purpose of this section is to enumerate a number of latent functions of deviant behavior, most of which contribute in one way or another to social organization.

Group Cohesion and Defining the Moral Code

One important latent function of deviance is that it contributes to *group cohesion*. Various forms of negative deviance, especially crime, are a threat to the more or less law-abiding members of society, who tend to draw together in common defense against criminal violators. They form law-and-order groups and include the "war on crime" as part of political ideology. Simultaneously, criminal violators to some extent organize themselves to protect their interests. Some form smaller or larger professional crime organizations. Further, these two types of groups, the law-abiding majority and the law-violating minority, are to a degree organized in relation to each other. Gambling, drug, and prostitution syndicates cannot, for example, continue to exist without a considerable measure of cooperation between them and the supposedly law-abiding public, including politicians and police officers. In these ways, then, negative deviance has the positive consequence of contributing to the organization of a society.

Second and relatedly, negative deviance has the latent function of helping to define and *clarify the moral code* of a society. Just as we can know the nature of light in terms of dark, and cold in terms of hot, so can we know the nature of what is right in terms of what is wrong. Negative deviance such as crime, by the very recognition of it, tends to strengthen the rightness of noncriminal behavior. This is related to the first function in that the possession of a strong common moral code strengthens group solidarity.

Scapegoats and Escape Valves

Third, negative deviance can have the latent function of providing *scapegoats* for the aggressive tendencies of some of society's members. Thus negative deviants are stigmatized, ostracized, imprisoned, physically and psychologically tortured, and sometimes killed in the name of deterrence and rehabilitation. This allows society's nondeviant members to make legal these forms of aggression, to legitimize violence. At the same time, some individuals will gain satisfaction through identifying with negative deviants and their behavior, through vicariously "living" with them as they carry out their transgressions and even as they undergo punishment. One may not view this as a positive consequence of deviance. It is, in any case, an unintended and largely unrecognized consequence.

Fourth, deviance can directly serve as an escape or *safety valve* for the tensions that individuals experience because of the pressures of the social system. These pressures are likely to take the forms of demands to conform, or of social and economic deprivation of various kinds. Deviance can be a means of expressing individuality as a way of countering conformity, especially when innovation is involved. Deviance can also be a way of rebelling against the established social order and the frustrations that are its consequences. It is, in a word, a way of "throwing over the traces." This last may in some instances of deviance be recognized by society's members and in others not.

Social Change

A fifth and related function is that sudden increases in negative deviance can serve as *warning signals* that social change is necessary.[17] Large rises in crime, mental illness, alcoholism, and suicide are indicators that social pressures on individuals to conform, to achieve, or to accept failure are beyond tolerable limits and that discontent is becoming widespread. Initially a society's members may react with hostility and demand conformity from deviants. Over time, however, the threat of ever-increasing negative deviance is likely to lead to a consideration of the need for change.

Sixth, deviance can function as an actual *means of effecting social change* as well as a warning signal that change may be needed. If all behavior always conformed closely to cultural customs and values, to conventional norms and roles, the society would not have the capacity for change. Deviance which takes the form of innovation, even if negatively evaluated, can be a major source of social change. If a society cannot respond to change, it atrophies and dies out.

On the other hand, too much change in too short a time spells disorganization for a society. Individuals do not know what to expect of each other. They are unclear as to how to work together toward common goals. Long-range needs go unmet. Chaos threatens. For most societies social life is a blend of conformity and deviance: organization is maintained while change is accommodated.

Achievement, Identity, and Employment

Seventh, deviance can be a means of *achievement* and of gaining *self-identity*.[18] For the dispossessed and the socially excluded, for outsiders, negative deviance, especially crime, can spell achievement. Well-executed criminal behavior can lead to the approval of the offender's peers and to self-esteem as well. This is the case in many adult professional thieving rings and adolescent gangs. Amateur crimes, especially violent ones, can serve much the same function. The person who kills another often in retrospect views the crime as one of decisiveness and action. While that person may experience remorse, he or she may also feel more effective. The man who commits rape may in his own eyes validate his sexual prowess. In the prestige hierarchy of prison inmates, violent offenders rank high. Also, the public often shows its admiration as well as revulsion in response to efficient or bizarre crimes. Notoriety attaches to some offenders; they become despised heroes. Innovative deviance, both positive and negative, can lead to a sense of self-fulfillment, of having expressed oneself individually rather than as a cog in a social machine. Positive innovation in the form of socially valued inventions may bring much social applause and monetary rewards as well. This too can greatly enhance self-identity.

Finally, an eighth function of negative deviance is one so obvious that it is even more unnoticed than the other latent functions. The various sets of social-control apparatus that a society uses in its attempts to respond to negative deviance can be enormous economic enterprises. They provide *employment.*[19] In the United States this is especially true of the criminal justice and mental health systems. At any one time, several million individuals are in prisons, jails, and mental hospitals. Millions more are receiving mental health treatments outside of hospitals or, if criminal offenders, are on probation or parole. Several millions of persons are employed as police officers, judges, and other court personnel, in correctional work as probation and parole officers and as prison and jail guards and administrative personnel, or as social workers, psychologists, psychiatrists, and hospital attendants.

Society's organized ways of attempting to control negative deviance are big business. They make possible a significant proportion of jobs in the total work force. Thus a very real function of deviance is to provide jobs through employment of agents of social control. It is understandable, then, that social-control systems, especially criminal justice and mental health systems, seldom function "effectively," rarely achieving the results for which they were consciously, manifestly intended. Even though without conscious design, those who work as agents of social control are unlikely to be so effective that they reduce the problem of deviance with which they were employed to deal. If they were fully effective, many would be out of jobs. Thus ineffective control means employment, and it simultaneously allows the other aforementioned latent functions of crime to operate.

SOCIAL CONTROL AND SOCIALIZATION

Informal and Formal Social Control

Social control is the process by which individuals are induced to follow cultural customs and values in their behavior, to conform to norms and roles. It involves learning, often teaching as well, and the administering of rewards and punishments.[20] Social control is threaded through all of social life and through all stages of an individual's life. In the family, in school, on the job, out in the community, efforts are continually made to teach and to induce people to behave in conforming, nondeviant ways. Generally, we are rewarded by others for conformity and punished for deviation. The main exception is the rewarding of adults for innovation that others evaluate positively.

The social-control process ranges along a continuum from the very informal to the highly formalized. The more control involves close personal interaction without written rules and without clearly specified rewards and penalties, the more it is *informal*. Conversely, the more control occurs in impersonal, bureaucratic settings with written rules and legalistically specified rewards and punishments, the more it is *formal*. Thus, a mother teaching and a child learning how to eat "properly" involves very informal control. Basic training of new recruits in large military organizations is highly formalized social control. Elementary school teaching and learning are between these two extremes.

Small societies have traditionally depended on informal social control to bring about conformity and minimize deviance. Social approval and disapproval of parents, friends, and other community members are powerful rewards and punishments in personal, small-group settings where everyone knows everyone else. But in large mass societies, these informal controls do not work as well. The approval or disapproval of one's neighbors or the community simply does not have the impact it does in a small society. Often in the large society, there are few if any real neighbors and little sense of community.

Therefore in mass societies, formal control systems come into being in order to replace the informal controls of the smaller societies. Bodies of law, police organizations, judicial systems, and such institutions as prisons and mental hospitals develop. These will be discussed in a following section.

While social control ostensibly aims at inducing people to conform, in fact it may serve to increase negative deviant behavior. This is because the social reaction to deviant behavior on the part of an individual may be such that he or she is labeled as deviant, treated as a deviant, made to feel a deviant, given the role of a deviant. Additionally, the individual may be either informally segregated with other deviants in the community or segregated in institutions for negative deviants such as prisons and mental hospitals. Segregation of deviants tends to increase the intensity of deviant behavior because they reinforce one another's deviance.

Socialization

Socialization is the process by which individuals learn to behave in socially approved ways, to follow cultural customs and values and social norms and roles.[21] It is therefore integral to the process of social control. Socialization is what makes us social beings who perpetuate culture and participate in the social organizational system. It occurs especially in the family and in school during childhood and adolescence. But it also takes place in many areas of adult life, notably on the job.

Socialization is a learning process that may be formal or informal. Sometimes teaching is involved, sometimes not. Individuals are expected to make their behavior under certain circumstances match what is typically done by others in similar situations and positions. The young child is expected to learn the given language, to eat properly, and so on. A little boy is expected to learn to act and dress like a little boy. A little girl is expected to act and dress like a little girl. The new worker is expected to learn how to carry out properly his or her particular job. Thus, socialization is in large measure a matter of learning social roles, that is, bodies of norms which typify how those who hold certain positions in recurring social situations are to act.

Imitation of role models is a common means of socialization. Another individual may consciously act as a role model. The mother demonstrates to her little girl how to act like "a lady" in such and such a situation. The athletic coach acts out for the player the movements required in a given football play or demonstrates how to execute successfully a particular tennis shot. Again, a person may observe another who is performing a certain role although the other is not consciously acting as a model. In either case, the more an individual's imitative behavior matches that of an acceptable role model the more his or her behavior is likely to be rewarded, and the more it diverges from that of the role model the more likely is punishment. Rewards and punishments can take the form of social approval and disapproval, of physical warmth or coldness, of giving or withholding money or material goods, of allocating or withdrawing prestige. Of course, corporal punishments of various kinds are often used.

Socialization can occur without role models. Individuals learn from *information* that comes to them through word of mouth, through reading, and through general observation. Most formal education is socialization without role models. Teachers transmit culture by telling students about it and by directing them to written sources, but they seldom act out roles other than that of teachers. And on-the-job training is likely to involve being told what to do rather than shown. Of course, new employees often do observe other workers who without conscious intent serve as role models.

In the early stages of a given form of socialization there is often a formally defined or informally understood *probationary period*. Certain mistakes, that is, deviant behaviors, are tolerated. Gradually or abruptly tolerance decreases. Probation may be simply a matter of a period of time when certain kinds of mistakes are allowed, or it may involve a series of stages, each more demanding of conformity than the last. Almost always, however, certain behaviors are not tolerated from the outset. Thus, the military recruit on the firing range is given time for practice before his scores are used to determine whether he meets minimum proficiency standards. If he shoots the instructor, this is another matter.

The socialization process may go awry for a number of reasons. Inadequate socialization is a major source of deviance. Individuals may imitate role models who are inadequate from the standpoint of society's members. For example, children may imitate slovenly, ill-mannered parents. When the children exhibit the "manners" of their parents, the community responds with rebuffs and ridicule. Or individuals may receive from others, or from written sources, misleading information as to how to behave in a given circumstance. Again they lack information relevant to socially acceptable behavior in certain situations. As a consequence, socialization may simply not occur. The person's behavior may then randomly be appropriate or inappropriate.

Finally, others may with or without conscious intent reward the individual for socially unacceptable behavior and punish him or her for acceptable behavior. Those others may simply be confused as to what is appropriate. They may reward behavior that meets their needs regardless of society's customs, values, and norms. Still others may consciously induce the individual to carry out deviant behavior as when the criminal parent rewards criminality on the part of the child and punishes legitimate activity.

Deviant Socialization

The socialization process pertains to learning to conform to the cultural customs and values and the norms of society. But customs and values of deviant subcultures and the norms of the social organization of deviant groups are also learned.[22] That is, there is also *deviant socialization* to institutionalized forms of deviance. Although this can apply to positive deviance, it is much more common in regard to patterns of negative deviance; negative deviance is much more frequently institutionalized than positive deviance.

Examples of deviant subcultures are those of violence, professional theft, corporate white-collar crimes, homosexuality, drug use, and "think tanks," the last being positive deviance. Rather than displaying individualistic behavior, individuals conform to the customs and values of the deviant subculture. As we noted earlier, "honor among thieves" and general cooperation in professional theft requires much conformity to the subculture of theft even though the behavior of all who follow that subculture is defined as deviant by the wider society.

Individuals become socialized to customs and values of deviant subcultures; they can learn deviant norms and roles, just as others are socialized to customs and values of the general culture and learn socially acceptable norms and roles. Deviant socialization may occur in childhood. For example, the child in a criminal family may be socialized to crime by his parents. Much deviant socialization takes place, however, in adolescence and adulthood, especially early adulthood. Juvenile reformatories and jails and prisons for adults are institutions where criminal subcultures flourish and deviant socialization is common. Mental hospitals are thought by some students of deviance to be places where those incarcerated become socialized to mental illness, learn the role of the mental patient. Homosexual networks in some urban areas may provide the means to socialization in subcultures of homosexuality.[23]

The process of deviant socialization proceeds in the same fashion as socialization to the general culture. Individuals are told or shown by others the requisite customs and norms or they observe role models. They are rewarded by others within the deviant subculture for meeting expectations, for conforming to the behavior patterns of that subculture. They are punished for failure to do so. One difference between much deviant socialization and socialization to the general culture is that in the former case social stigma often, although not always, attaches to the learning of deviant roles. Individuals who learn in criminal or homosexual subcultures realize that they are becoming negatively defined by the wider society at the same time that their behavior within the deviant subcultures earns the approval and reward of their peers. Thus socialization to deviant subcultures comes to mean self-definition as an outsider whereas socialization to the general culture means self-definition as an insider.

Tolerating Deviance

Some negative deviance is tolerated by the group some of the time. Individuals seldom insist that the behavior of others conform very, very closely to typical behavior under given conditions. Similarly, individuals tend to tolerate in others some degree of divergence from expectations.[24] They expect others *not* to meet their expectations exactly. This is a recognition that everyone is not the same as everyone else and that individuals cannot under most circumstances behave as closely calibrated machines. However, any broad deviation in behavior will likely result in a "once-only" warning or a recognition that the individual is a deviant person and so can only be expected to act in a deviant fashion. The once-only warning is just that: don't do it again or punishment will be forthcoming. Recognition that a person is a deviant does not necessarily imply tolerance. More often it involves placing restrictions on him or her as long as the deviant behavior continues: "If he acts crazy, put him in a mental hospital." "If he persists in assaulting people, put him in prison."

THE POLITICS OF DEVIANCE

Power and Deviance

There is a political dimension to much if not all of social life in that individuals attempt to use power to achieve their ends. *Power* means the ability to control the behavior or life condition of others. The more powerful may institutionalize social arrangements such that the less powerful enter into negative deviance and are prosecuted for it. The more powerful have much to say about what is officially designated as negative deviance. They are either the makers of laws and regulations or they influence the lawmakers. The powerful are likely to legislate in their own favor, to make laws and regulations against certain behavior of others rather than against their own. Thus laws against common theft—burglary, robbery, shoplifting—are stringent, whereas laws against white-collar crime—crime in business settings such as price fixing and embezzlement—are less so.[25]

The less powerful may be exploited by the powerful in other ways that may lead them to commit negative deviance. The powerful influence the distribution of wealth in their own favor. By and large it is the powerless who steal from stores and homes and who commit criminal homicide. This is in part because of the more severe social pressures under which they live. They have fewer resources—less money, influence, education, medical care, recreation—to cope with everyday problems of life.

The powerful also influence the agents of social control, such as police, who enforce laws and regulations.[26] And, once accused of a crime or violation of a regulation, the powerless are less able than the powerful to demonstrate innocence and escape punishment whether they are innocent or guilty. Here again they have fewer resources—less money to hire able lawyers, for example.

The powerful do not continually and consciously conspire to exploit the powerless in these ways, but individuals are naturally self-interested and tend to use power for personal rather than altruistic ends. This applies where negative deviance is concerned as it does elsewhere in life.

The Manufacture of Deviants

The tendency for the powerful members of a society to determine what constitutes positive and negative deviance, and the strong punitive reaction to negative deviance, play a part in the creation of deviance and the assumption of negative deviant roles and careers. The social-control mechanisms of the police, the courts, and institutions such as prisons and mental hospitals sometimes aid in this process. Individuals are officially labeled as negative deviants, often publicly displayed as such, and are segregated with others who have been similarly designated within institutions or in the community, where opportunities for further learning of negative deviance—for deviant socialization— are increased.

The assembly line processing of individuals into career deviance has been designated by some analysts as "the manufacture of deviants."[27] This idea helps to reconcile two opposite social processes, that is, while society professes to abhor certain forms of deviant behavior, deviance in fact contributes to the organization and perpetuation of society.

While the notion of the manufacture of deviants is a useful one, it is dangerous to conclude that all individuals who persist in negative deviance are so manufactured. Many simply are not processed in this way. They progress into deviant careers quite independently of the formal control process. On the other hand, the idea of manufacturing deviants has not been used in conjunction with positive deviance. Yet there are social processes at work which formally label individuals as positive deviants, reward them for being such, and process them through institutions which tend to segregate them, allow ample opportunity for positive deviant socialization, and launch them on positive deviant careers. The undergraduate and graduate schools of our colleges and universities and their processes or recruitment of students and faculty to some extent exemplify this.

PROBLEMS IN RESEARCH ON DEVIANCE

Ethical Issues

There has been much scientific analysis of deviant behavior. Yet the difficulties of studying deviance are formidable, mainly because much negative deviance is clandestine in nature. Those who act in deviant ways may be fearful of embarrassment if found out and so will be reluctant to provide information. Others may fear prosecution if discovered. Still others will be concerned that knowledge of what they do and how they do it will be of great personal cost to them.

Thus the professional fence who receives and sells stolen goods may well be concerned that his business will suffer if the "wrong" people know what he is doing. He is far less likely to fear prosecution because he has usually arranged a "live-and-let-live" accommodation with officials. There will also be those who are reluctant to provide information for fear that others who engage in that deviance will consider them "squealers" and seek to punish them.

For those and other reasons, researchers of deviance face a number of ethical and legal problems. They must take care not to cause grief to subjects or their relatives and friends. They must be careful not to violate the law. For example, if citizens know that crimes have been committed or are being planned, they have a legal obligation to report that to law enforcement authorities. This applies to researchers as well as others. Yet if researchers are to observe crime firsthand, this problem is likely to arise. After having gained information from those who violate the law, researchers may later be called as witnesses in a court trial. This is rare but it does occur. Do researchers then have a primary obligation to confidentiality with their subjects or to the demands of a court?

While there are some informal and formal guidelines and codes for the conduct of research and for answering such questions, these are sometimes unclear or contradictory. Generally speaking, researchers agree that information is to be gained from subjects only after the nature of the research has been explained and the subjects have agreed. This is termed "informed consent." But the matter is complicated by the fact that subjects are not always in a position to make purely voluntary judgments. They may fear retribution from authorities if they do not cooperate, in the case of, say, prison inmates who fear their paroles will be withheld. Although they may be incorrect in their assessment of the situation, it may nonetheless affect their decision to consent. Or some subjects, such as mental patients, may be unable to reach a decision.

Even when subjects decide without any coercion to participate in research on deviance, they may be subject to harmful effects. If this happens, it is often because the research process creates unresolved anxiety in subjects. An example is research in which an investigator interviews young women regarding incestual relationships with their fathers when they were children or teenagers. The young women are actually part of a large group who answered written questionnaires about sexual experience. They reported that they had incestual relationships and volunteered to be interviewed. Very likely they are unaware that discussion of their earlier involvement in incest may trigger severe anxiety, which continues after the interview. The investigator has a responsibility to see that this does not occur. If subjects experience anxiety during the interviews, then provision must be made to allow them to resolve their anxiety. In some instances this can be done by turning the fact-finding interview into a therapeutic session during its later stages. If carried out competently, this may provide benefits to subjects that they would not have gained had they not participated in the research.

In certain instances, researchers may believe that their known presence will destroy the validity of their observations. Thus a male sociologist might wish to observe certain aspects of prison life. He might believe that if inmates knew he was a researcher, they would act differently than if they did not. Therefore he might arrange to have himself falsely committed to prison. Prison officials and inmates might believe he was a bona fide offender. Only a judge and a few others outside the prison setting might be aware of the ruse. Obviously, this would violate the privacy of inmates and prison personnel. Is such an invasion of privacy justified on the grounds that increased knowledge about the nature of prison life will be of much social value?

These are unresolved issues. Much as it may be desirable to have clear-cut rules, regulations, and laws to guide research behavior, they do not exist. At present each researcher must decide for himself or herself the proper balance between individual rights and the social need to understand human behavior and institutions.

SUMMARY

The diversity of deviance is limited only by the variety of conformist behaviors. Deviance occurs within a sociocultural context and varies widely along a number of dimensions. Social organization is structured by norms and roles that guide interaction. Culture is formed by the customs and values that provide general orientation toward life and ways of achieving common goals. There are two types of social norms: behavioral and expectational. Behavioral norms are the patterns of actual behavior that individuals typically follow when interacting under given conditions. Expectational norms are what people expect each other to do in certain situations. Social roles are clusters of norms that individuals follow when occupying given statuses in the society's system of social organization. Together, social organization and culture make interaction predictable. The survival of society depends on such predictability.

Three approaches to the definition of deviant behavior have been common. The first two involve the normative approach: deviant behavior may be defined as a departure from either behavioral or expectational norms. The third focuses on societal reaction: deviance may be said to exist only when an individual's behavior is so labeled by others.

Dimensions of deviance include institutionalized versus individualistic and negative versus positive. Institutionalized deviance is carried out in a patterned normative way; occupants of deviant roles—professional thieves, for example—may change but the role persists. Individualistic deviance does not follow preestablished norms; it is particular to the individual. Individualistic deviance may be innovative in nature, that is, it may involve the process of putting together in a new way two or more existing ideas or material forms so that a problem is solved. And physical deviance may be either institutionalized or individualistic. Typically we think of deviance as negative, but it may have positive consequences as well. Breakthroughs in science and art depart from the traditional ways of viewing reality and are often evaluated positively by society's members.

Latent functions of behavior are those consequences, while unintended, which tend to contribute to social organization. Latent functions of deviance serve to (1) enhance group cohesion and define the moral code; (2) provide scapegoats and (3) escape valves; (4) provide warning signals that social change is needed; (5) actually bring about social change; (6) enhance achievement and self-identity; and (7) provide employment.

Social control consists of both formal and informal means of inducing individuals to follow cultural customs and values in their behavior, to conform to norms and roles. The more social control relies on impersonal, legalistic rewards and punishments, the more formal it is. Informal social control occurs in the course of daily interaction and is not dependent on codified rules that are officially enforced. Socialization is part of the process of social control. It is itself the process by which individuals learn, either formally or informally, to behave in socially approved ways, to follow cultured customs and values, social norms, and roles. Socialization commonly occurs by the imitation of role models or by the accumulation of information. Socialization to institutionalized forms of deviance also occurs in the same ways.

Political considerations greatly affect the generation and control of deviance. Political influences refer to power or the ability to control the behavior or life conditions of others. The more powerful segments of society are likely to be in a position to influence legislation in their own favor. The powerful disproportionately control wealth and resources by exploiting the powerless and making the latter more prone to commit acts of deviance. The powerful also influence the judicial processing of deviants. The powerless are more apt to be arrested, convicted, and sentenced than are the powerful.

Much deviance is by necessity carried out in a clandestine manner. Research on deviant behavior must carefully protect the anonymity and integrity of the deviants and their victims. Every effort should be made to gather accurate data on forms of deviance. The National Crime Survey was a recent effort to increase the validity of data on criminal behavior. Precise data must be collected and interpreted as independently of cultural bias or political motive as possible. Those involved in deviance should not suffer as the result of participation in research on their behavior.

REFERENCES

1. See Edwin H. Sutherland, *The Professional Thief* (Chicago: University of Chicago Press, 1937); also, Carl B. Klockars, *The Professional Fence* (New York: Free Press, 1974).
2. For general discussion, see Ralph Linton, *The Tree of Culture* (New York: Knopf, 1955).
3. For a cogent discussion, see Arnold Birenbaum and Edward Sagarin, *Norms and Human Behavior* (New York: Praeger, 1976).
4. Talcott Parsons, *The Social System* (New York: Free Press, 1951), p. 206.
5. Bruce J. Biddle and Edwin J. Thomas, eds., *Role Therapy: Concepts and Research* (New York: Wiley, 1966).
6. For an excellent brief discussion, see Alex Thio, *Deviant Behavior* (Boston: Houghton Mifflin, 1978), pp. 3–7; also, Birenbaum and Sagarin, *op. cit.*
7. Edwin M. Schur, *Labeling Deviant Behavior* (New York: Harper and Row, 1971).
8. For various relevant studies, see Marvin E. Wolfgang, ed., *Studies in Homicide* (New York: Harper and Row, 1967).
9. Edwin M. Lemert, *Human Deviance, Social Problems, and Social Control* (Englewood Cliffs, NJ: Prentice-Hall, 1967); also, Marshall B. Clinard, *Sociology of Deviant Behavior*, 4th ed. (New York: Holt, Rinehart, and Winston, 1974).
10. Leslie T. Wilkins, *Social Deviance* (Englewood Cliffs, NJ: Prentice-Hall, 1965); also, Frank R. Scarpitti and Paul T. McFarlane, eds., *Deviance: Action, Reaction, Interaction* (Reading, MA: Addison-Wesley, 1975), pp. 5–6.
11. Scarpitti and McFarlane, *Deviance*; also, Wilkins, *op. cit.*
12. Erving Goffman, *Stigma* (Englewood Cliffs, NJ: Prentice-Hall, 1963); also, Leslie Fiedler, *Freaks* (New York: Simon and Schuster, 1978).
13. Fiedler, *ibid.*
14. Thorsten Sellin, *Culture Conflict and Crime* (New York: Social Science Research Council, 1938).
15. George Peter Murdock, "The Common Denominators of Culture," in *The Science of Man in the World Crisis*, ed. Ralph Linton (New York: Columbia University Press, 1945).
16. Robert K. Merton, *Social Theory and Social Structure*, rev. ed. (New York: Free Press, 1968).
17. Lewis A. Coser, *Continuities in the Study of Social Conflict* (New York: Free Press, 1967), Chap. 4.

18. *Ibid.*
19. Stuart Palmer, *The Prevention of Crime* (New York: Behavioral Publications, 1973).
20. For an excellent discussion of deviance and social control, see Albert K. Cohen, *Deviance and Control* (Englewood Cliffs, NJ: Prentice-Hall, 1966).
21. Peter I. Rose, ed., *Socialization and the Life Cycle* (New York: St. Martin's Press, 1979).
22. Lemert, *Human Deviance;* also, Howard Becker, *Outsiders: Studies in the Sociology of Deviance* (New York: Free Press, 1963).
23. Thomas J. Scheff, ed., *Mental Illness and Social Processes* (New York: Harper and Row, 1967); also, Evelyn Hooker, "The Homosexual Community," in *Sexual Deviance,* eds. John H. Gagnon and William Simon (New York: Harper and Row, 1967).
24. Ralph Linton, *The Study of Man* (New York: Appleton Century, 1936).
25. Richard Quinney, *The Social Reality of Crime* (Boston: Little, Brown, 1970).
26. Jerome H. Skolnick, *Justice Without Trial: Law Enforcement in a Democratic Society* (New York: Wiley, 1975)
27. Thomas Szasz, *The Manufacture of Madness* (New York: Dell, 1970).

2

Explanations of Deviance

This chapter discusses four main types of explanations or theories of deviant behavior. These four types—social integration, cultural support, social disorganization and conflict, and societal reaction—are used throughout the book to analyze the various forms of deviance. The chapters that follow clarify why the given types of explanation are or are not especially useful in understanding a specific form of deviant behavior. How certain of these theories can be modified or extended to explain deviance more fully is discussed. Further, there is emphasis on how the theories can in some instances be combined and synthesized to increase their explanatory power.

This chapter has two related functions. First, it provides an overview of the social forces which do and do not generate deviance and conformity. Second, it serves as a resource chapter for the rest of the book. Put differently, the student new to the study of deviance should first conceive of this chapter as a broad introduction to the explanation of deviance. Second, the student should return to this chapter from time to time for a fuller treatment of theories of deviance than the chapters which follow can provide.

THE NATURE OF CAUSE, EXPLANATION, AND THEORY

We tend to think that any given occurrence has a cause. This is wrong in the sense that most things happen for multiple reasons. We say, for example, that we contract the flu because a certain viral strain "is going around." This is true in a limited way. Another major factor is the bodily resistance level of the given individual. One person "comes down with" the flu and another does not although both are exposed to the virus. Many factors influence the resistance level of the body. Causation is almost always a complicated set of forces which produces some occurrence.

So it is with deviance. Any form of deviance is likely to be the

result of multiple factors, many of which may in some degree counteract each other. Moreover, the forms of deviance are highly diverse.
Hence the sets of factors that lead to one form of deviance may not
lead to another.

An *explanation* is a description of the set of forces which brings
about, or at least precedes, a given occurrence. A *theory* is a formal
statement of the relationships that are believed to obtain among certain
sets of forces and certain occurrences. A theory, then, is really a tentative descriptive map that attempts to describe what leads to what. All
formal explanations are essentially theoretical, that is, no explanations
are seen in science as eternal verities or iron-clad laws. They are all
subject to change as new evidence and understanding occurs. Therefore, at bottom all explanations have a tentative, theoretical character.

In everyday life we tend to denigrate theory. We say such-and-
such a theory is just abstract words, does not apply to the real world.
All theories are abstractions. As maps, they are abstractions of reality.
If a map were not an abstraction, it would be a duplicate of what it
attempts to describe; it would be of the same scope and complexity
and hence of no use. We all use informal theories much of the time.
We have a theory about how to get to a certain city, about how to
become an adult, whatever. Since these are personal, since they are
our own, we do not label them useless abstractions as we sometimes
do formal theories.

There is no single, overarching theory of deviance. This is as it
should be. As we discussed in Chapter 1, deviance varies along many
dimensions. Certain explanations will be more useful for understanding some forms of deviance than others. Further, if we had a single
theory of deviance we would really have a single theory of all behavior.
In the broad sense, deviance and conformity are the two sides of the
coin of social interactions. If we could explain one side with one set of
forces, then by implication at least we could explain the other side.

The factors that lead to deviance are a complex web of biological,
psychological, social-psychological, and sociological components. In the
nineteenth century much attention was given to biological factors in
deviance. From time to time during the present century, there has been
a resurgence of interest in the biology of deviance.[1] Overall, however,
attempts to explain deviance in biological terms have not been fruitful.
While biology no doubt plays some part in the occurrence of some
deviance, it is seldom a large part and little attention is given to it here.

The role of psychological factors in deviance has received much
investigation since the early days of Freud's work and before.[2] While
there can be little doubt that psychological factors play a significant
part in much deviant behavior, this is not to say that deviance is necessarily a result of psychological disorders. Psychological disorders are

forms of deviance. When we speak of psychological explanations of deviance, we are usually referring to the ways in which social experience is interpreted by individuals and translated into behavior.

The theories of deviance stressed here are sociological, that is, based on aspects of the social system and culture, and social-psychological, which is to say, based on patterns of interaction among people. While emphasis is not predominantly placed on psychological factors per se, their connection to sociological and social-psychological factors is clear. It is from the interrelationship of those sociological and social-psychological factors and the individual organism that a person's social experience and psychological makeup result, which in turn influence whether behavior is conforming or deviant.

Sociological and social-psychological theories of deviance fall into four broad groups. In the main each of these four groups has sociological and social-psychological dimensions rather than some being purely sociological and others entirely social-psychological. The four groups of theory are:

1. *Social integration* theories which focus on the extent to which individuals are or are not bound to and regulated by groups.
2. *Cultural support* explanations which stress the social learning of deviant behavior patterns.
3. *Social disorganization and conflict* theories which emphasize cultural and social conflicts of one form or another.
4. *Societal reaction* theories which have as their main concern the ways in which a society's members in their reaction to real or presumed deviance actually bring about the deviance they are ostensibly attempting to control.

This chapter is devoted to a consideration of these four groupings of theoretical explanations of deviance. In each chapter which follows, these four types of explanations are considered in terms of their relevance to the given form of deviance being analyzed.

SOCIAL INTEGRATION THEORIES

Durkheim: Social Integration

Emile Durkheim, the great French sociologist, wrote in 1895 that deviance was integral to and necessary for modern social life and provided social organization and other functions for society.[3] Durkheim argued that two related processes were especially relevant to the existence of deviant behavior in groups.[4] The first of these was *social inte-*

gration or the extent to which individuals were bound into, or isolated from, social groups. While Durkheim was not fully clear about the meaning of social integration, he stressed consensus about basic life values as a criterion of integration. The more individuals shared values about critical concerns in life, the greater was social integration. Conversely, the more divergent were values and attitudes, the greater was social isolation.

The second process emphasized by Durkheim was *social regulation* of individuals' behavior. While Durkheim saw a basic distinction between regulation and integration, for practical purposes we can say that social integration and social regulations go hand in hand. When one is high, so is the other; and the less effectively that regulation operates, the greater is social isolation. This concept of *anomie*, critical to Durkheim's work, refers to social conditions of low regulation, low integration and therefore high isolation, and relative normlessness. It was Durkheim's contention that, given certain limited exceptions, deviance especially in the forms of crime and suicide increased as anomie became greater.

In 1897, Durkheim's landmark work, *Suicide*, was published.[5] In that book Durkheim argued that certain social conditions lead to high incidences of three forms of suicide. *Egoistic suicide* resulted from low levels of social integration and high levels of isolation. *Altruistic suicide* was a consequence of the opposite conditions: very high social integration and low isolation. Here, individuals were so bound to the group, the society, that they killed themselves for "the good of the state." The third form, *anomic suicide*, was brought about by a sudden decrease in social regulation of individuals' behavior. Actually, anomic suicide is in many respects a special case of egoistic suicide: it is generated by sudden social changes that involve decreased social integration, increased isolation, and decreased social regulation of behavior.

On the one hand, then, we have Durkheim's contention that low integration and anomie produces suicide. On the other hand, there is his recognition that the opposite conditions, overintegration and close regulation of behavior, lead to a form of deviance—altruistic suicide. This is a significant perception on Durkheim's part. Its value as an explanation of deviance will recur at later points.

Merton: Anomie

Robert Merton's essay "Social Structure and Anomie" was published in 1938 and has since been extended and revised several times.[6] Merton attempted to give the concept of anomie new, explicit meaning and to apply it to both conforming behavior and a variety of forms of deviance. The result has been a theoretical formulation which has had great impact on the study of deviance and, more broadly, on sociology in general.

The heart of Merton's theory is the extent to which individuals are unable to attain the legitimate, *institutionalized means* to achieve socially approved *cultural goals* that connote success. Merton distinguished between culture and social structure. Culture is composed of the customs, values, and norms related to socially approved success goals. Social structure denotes the roles, norms, and relationships among roles, which provide the means for achieving those success goals. Placement or location of individuals in the social structure—in social class, educational, occupational, and other roles—determines in large measure whether they can gain cultural goals that connote success. The greater the disparity between goals and the means of attaining them, the more a condition of anomie exists, and individuals are then more likely to turn away from conformity and to illegitimate deviant means.

Merton specified four broad forms of deviance: innovation, ritualism, retreatism, and rebellion. Which form of deviance occurs depends on whether individuals accept, reject, or replace goals and, separately, means. *Innovation* refers to deviance which results from individuals' acceptance of cultural success goals and their rejection of the socially accepted and institutionalized means. They reject the legitimate means because they are unable to gain access to them. This is usually because individuals have lower socioeconomic statuses and roles in the social structure. They then substitute illegitimate or negative deviant means for legitimate ones. They do not necessarily actually innovate these means. They may simply imitate someone else. Therefore, Merton's use of the term *innovation* is not similar to the usual meaning of the word as discussed in Chapter 1. By innovation, Merton refers to various deviant means of a socially disapproved criminal nature which are used to attain cultural goals.

Ritualism is the second form of deviant behavior analyzed by Merton. Ritualism occurs when cultural goals are rejected while the institutionalized means are accepted. Ritualism is essentially overconformity and in that sense constitutes deviance. Individuals compulsively act out in extreme form the approved institutionalized means. In so doing they largely lose sight of the cultural success goals for which they were earlier striving. In this sense they reject the goals and accept, overaccept really, the means. This form of deviance is common among middle-class persons who can attain means only sufficiently adequate to achieve success goals to a very limited extent. They work and strive, harder and harder, at the same task without increasing success. The means become the goals, that is, the ends. The librarian who is so intent on proper shelving of books that he or she seeks to dissuade others from removing books from the shelves and reading them is a ritualist. So is the admissions clerk at the hospital who insists on having all forms filled out according to regulations while the patient dies. And so is the person with several routine jobs who spends all waking hours working and has no time and energy for use and enjoyment of whatever meager success goals accrue as a result. Overconformity—ritualism—is a form of deviance that is frequently socially defined as mildly negative but seldom criminal.

Retreatism is Merton's third form of deviance. Individuals are unable to achieve cultural success goals through legitimate means and do not, for whatever reasons, turn to illegitimate means. They reject or turn away from both cultural goals and institutionalized means. They withdraw, retreat, from much of social life, often in apathy. The behavior of some drug addicts, hermits, "dropouts" fits this category of deviance. The deviance involved is usually negatively defined by society although more often than not to a moderate rather than severe degree.

Merton's final form of deviant behavior is *rebellion*. Again, individuals are unable to acquire the legitimate means to cultural success goals. They reject both but, instead of retreating, seek to create new goals and means to replace the prevailing ones. This is almost always a group enterprise in which deviance becomes institutionalized. Examples range from some juvenile gangs to political revolutionary movements. Rebellion is always defined by the general society as negative, usually severely so, at the outset. In certain instances the rebellious movement becomes widely accepted in the society. Its goals then become the cultural success goals and its means the socially approved, legitimate ones for pursuing those goals.

Merton's formulation is valuable because it explicates very well the condition of anomie as the result of a disjuncture between institutionalized means and cultural goals. It shows how place in the social structure predisposes individuals to deviance. The formulation is also valuable in that it specifies four different broad forms of deviance. Its major deficiency, and a large one, is that it does not deal with the question of why one form of deviance rather than another comes about; that is, why means are rejected rather than accepted or replaced rather than merely rejected is simply not explained. Also, the distinction between cultural goals and institutionalized means is not always clear. What is a goal from one standpoint may be a means from another. For example, is obtaining a college education a goal or a means?

Henry and Short: External Restraint

Andrew F. Henry and James F. Short, Jr., developed in the mid-1950s a theory of criminal homicide and suicide which built in part on Durkheim's concepts of social integration and regulation.[7] These authors viewed homicide and suicide as extreme forms of aggression, as alternate responses to frustration. They gave central attention to three variables: *status, strength of the relational system,* and degree of *external restraints.* By status, Henry and Short meant prestige. By strength of the relational system, they referred to the degree to which individuals are involved in social or cathectic relationships with others. By external restraints, they meant the extent to which individuals are required to conform to the demands and expectations of other persons:

> A person of low status is required to conform to the demands and expectations of persons of higher status merely by virtue of his lower status. A person involved in intense "social" interaction with another person is required to conform to the demands and expectations imposed as a condition of the relationship. These observations may be summarized in the following proposition: the strength of external restraint to which behavior is subjected varies positively with the strength of the relational system and inversely with position in the status hierarchy.[8]

Henry and Short went on to suggest that homicide varies positively with the strength of external restraint over behavior. Persons of lower status are subjected to one-sided restraints. They must conform to the expectations of those of higher status while the latter need not conform to their expectations. This leads low-status individuals to blame others for the frustration they consequently experience. They tend to aggress outwardly toward others rather than toward themselves.

Henry and Short suggested that suicide, on the other hand, is characteristic of high-prestige groups. They argued that as prestige increases, there is a decrease in the strength of the relational system, that is, in the extent to which individuals are involved in social or cathectic relationships with others. Further they held that as prestige increases, there is a decrease in the strength of external restraint—the degree to which behavior is required to conform to the demands and expectations of others. In summary, their position was that as prestige of individuals becomes greater and external restraints and the strength of the relational system decrease, suicide increases; conversely, as prestige becomes lower and restraints and strength of the relational system increase, homicide also increases.

> When behavior is subjected to strong external restraint by virtue either of subordinate status or intense involvement in social relationships with other persons, it is easy to blame others when frustration occurs. But when the restraints are weak, the self must bear the responsibility for frustration.[9]

Strong external restraints mean conflict among individuals whereas weak restraints imply an absence of conflict.

As with many theories of deviance, the Henry and Short thesis was confined to crime—in fact to one form of crime, homicide—and to suicide. It has implications, however, for several forms of aggressive behavior toward others and for various forms of self-aggressive behavior as well, of which suicide is the most extreme. The Henry and Short formulation is admirable in that it brings together into one unified theory sociological, psychological, and economic factors. A major drawback is that the concept of strength of the relational system was used in such a way as to be contradicted by the facts. As we shall see in Chapter 9, suicide tends to predominate at both the high and low ends of the social class spectrum. Henry and Short saw the relational system as weak in the higher social classes and strong in the lower while hypothesizing that it is a weak relational system which predisposes individuals to suicide. And their hypothesis that high homicide rates are characterized by strong relational systems seems not to fit the facts regarding homicidal offenders who tend to be "outsiders," that is, not bound at all closely to the social system (see Chapter 3).

Straus and Straus: Reciprocity and Integration

Jacqueline and Murray Straus reformulated Durkheim's original ideas concerning social integration in a 1953 research report.[10] Based on their analysis of homicide and suicide in Ceylon, they concluded that a major social condition related to those two forms of deviance was *closeness or looseness of structuring* of a society. A society is closely structured, that is, integrated, to the extent that reciprocal rights and duties are stressed and enforced. In a society that is closely integrated, the emphasis on reciprocity in carrying out roles and norms (rights and duties) operates to preclude violence toward others. This is because individuals are helping each other play out their roles effectively and hence see little reason to blame each other for whatever severe frustrations they experience. Hence, Straus and Straus predicted low homicide rates and high suicide rates in closely integrated societies.

On the other hand, in loosely structured or loosely integrated societies, reciprocal rights and duties are stressed and enforced relatively little. Individuals are not helping each other to carry out their roles and hence find it easy to blame each other for the frustrations they feel. Thus Straus and Straus predicted high homicide and low suicide rates in loosely integrated societies. Their formulation and Durkheim's theory are congruent in this sense: Durkheim predicted altruistic suicide (for the good of the state) when social integration was high. Straus and Straus predicted suicide *in general* under conditions of high integration. Where they predicted homicide under conditions of low integration, Durkheim predicted egoistic suicide. However, Durkheim did in passing suggest that homicide would also be high when integration was low.[11]

As for the relationship between the Straus and Straus thesis and

Henry and Short's formulation, the latter predicted that when strength of the relational system was weak (low integration), suicide would be high; and when strength of the relational system was great (high integration), homicide would be high. Thus Straus and Straus and Henry and Short took opposite positions on the conditions which generate homicide and suicide. This need not lead the student of deviance to throw up hands in exasperation. Opposing theories are subject to analysis in light of the facts. Chapters to follow, especially 3 and 9, will bring the facts to bear on these opposing views. Meanwhile, we believe that the introduction by Straus and Straus of reciprocity in the everyday carrying out of social roles adds an important dimension to the idea of social integration.

Hirschi: Social Control Theory

Another attempt to understand the effects of social integration on deviant behavior was set forth by Travis Hirschi.[12] Hirschi sought to explain not why individuals engage in deviant behavior, but why they do not. To Hirschi, integration refers to the bonds the individual forms with society. The stronger the bonds or adherence to the conventional social norms, the less the likelihood of deviant behavior.

These bonds have four essential elements: attachment, commitment, involvement, and belief. Durkheim's dictum[13] that "we are moral beings to the extent that we are social beings" helps us understand the element of *attachment*. Becoming a social being implies the willingness to conform one's behavior to the expectations of others. Attachment then refers to the degree of closeness of the individual's ties to normative behavior.

Commitment refers to the extent of the individual's involvement in conventional activity, for example, going to school, working, or raising a family. The greater the investment in the activities of everyday life, the less the time, energy, and inclination for deviant behavior.

Involvement is closely related to the element of commitment and means, simply, the intensity of participation in conventional activity. An individual's time and energy are expended on legitimate pursuits. The likelihood of aberrant behavior is thereby significantly reduced.

The final element is *belief*. Hirschi's control theory depends on the existence of a common value system, that is, belief in the conviction that this value system is equally valid for all members of society and that everyone is morally obligated to adhere to it. However, all persons believe that conventional morality is valid or that it applies to them. The less credence the individual gives to the belief in a common value system, the greater the chances of deviant behavior.

Attachment, commitment, involvement, and belief, the elements of the bond between the individual and society, provide a measure of social integration. The stronger the bonds, the more the individual is integrated into society and, as a consequence, the greater the societal control over individual action. To Hirschi, the stronger the social control, the less probable is deviant behavior.

CULTURAL SUPPORT THEORIES

Cultural support explanations stress the social learning of deviant behavior. That is, they are concerned with how customs, values, and behavioral and expectational norms for given forms of deviance and learned by individuals through association with one another. Essentially this body of theory holds that deviant behavior is learned through the same process as conforming behavior. Whether the outcome is deviance or conformity depends on whether customs and norms are components of a subculture socially defined as deviant or of the widely approved overall culture and social system.

The cultural support explanation, which could equally well be termed normative support, was first formally set forth by Edwin Sutherland in his *differential association* theory in the late 1930s.[14] Decades later, other sociologists brought together Sutherland's ideas and Merton's work on anomie and deviance. The first of these was Albert Cohen who in the mid-1950s suggested an elaboration of differential association theory through a special use of the concept of anomie.[15] Following that, Richard Cloward and Lloyd Ohlin in 1960 provided a variation on the Sutherland and Cohen approaches with their formulation of *delinquent opportunity structures*.[16]

The specific cultural support theories just mentioned and soon to be discussed in some detail were concerned mainly with explaining criminal behavior. This is true of quite a number of other theories of deviance. Criminal behavior has long been a major focus of research on deviance in the United States and Western Europe. To some extent, however, theories which were originally presented as applicable to crime may be relevant to other forms of deviance such as mental illness and suicide. Interestingly, there are no formal theories of positive deviance. This, as we have seen, is a neglected area in the analysis of deviant behavior.

Sutherland: Differential Association

In the nineteenth and early twentieth centuries, crime and most other forms of deviance were seen by most scholars as individualistic forms of behavior. Edwin Sutherland, an American criminologist, sought to correct this interpretation. He saw crime as largely the outcome of learning customs, values, and norms conducive to the violation of laws, regulations, and roles. Certainly, he was correct in perceiving that some forms of crime are in fact institutionalized rather than idiosyncratic. However, Sutherland failed to see that there are indeed forms of crime that are not institutionalized. As will be true with the other theories of deviance discussed here, Sutherland's *differential association* theory has definite advantages for explaining certain forms of crime and types of deviance and distinct drawbacks in regard to others.

Sutherland and Donald Cressey outlined the differential association theory in nine steps in numerous editions of their widely used textbook, *Criminology*[17]:

1. *Criminal behavior is learned*, not inherited, and not individualistic or innovation behavior.
2. The learning of criminal behavior occurs largely through *communication with others*.
3. Learning takes place mainly in *informal, primary group settings*. The mass media are distinctly less important.
4. Learning includes *specific techniques, motives, drives*, and *attitudes* for committing crimes.
5. The nature of motives and drives is learned from *other persons whose definition of the legal codes are favorable or unfavorable to violation of those codes*.
6. An individual becomes criminal or delinquent because of *an excess of exposure to definitions favorable to the violation of legal codes* over definitions unfavorable. This is *differential association*: the individual associates in small groups differentially with persons who define laws as rules to be violated or followed, and consequently learns from them techniques, motives, drives, and attitudes which are either criminal or law abiding.
7. *Differential associations vary along four dimensions: frequency*, that is, how often they occur over individuals' life histories; *duration*, or the actual length of time of the association; *priority*, which emphasizes that the earlier in life the associations occur, the more impact they have; and *intensity*, which stresses that the more the association with another person is in a general, overall way rewarding, the greater will be its impact on learning. In sum, the greater the frequency, duration, priority, and intensity of an association, the stronger its consequences in producing learned behavior of a criminal or noncriminal nature.
8. Learning criminal behavior through differential association *involves all of the processes that are found in other forms of learning:* imitation, reinforcement, transfer, and so on.

9. *Criminal behavior is not explained by general needs and values* such as striving for social status or as a reaction to frustration since noncriminal behavior results from the same needs and values.

Before considering which forms of deviance seem most and least explained by Sutherland's theory, one methodological problem of a severe nature should be specified. It is extremely difficult to measure the frequency, duration, priority, and intensity of differential association over the life histories of individuals. This is especially true of the last, intensity, since the reward value of associations is a subjective matter: that which is pleasurable to one person maybe painful to another.

This methodological drawback aside, Robert Burgess and Ronald Akers suggested that the Sutherland formulation does not really account for why criminal behavior patterns are actually learned once the differential associations have occurred.[18] In an attempt to remedy this, they introduced the idea of *differential reinforcement*. In psychological learning theory, differential reinforcement refers to the reward value of carrying out various behaviors (as opposed to the intensity or reward of *associations* per se in Sutherland's thesis). The more a form of behavior leads to reward rather than punishment, the more it will be repeated. Thus Burgess and Akers suggest that the missing element in differential association theory is the extent to which criminal behavior, once performed, is actually learned or not learned because it either does or does not bring reward.

With or without the Burgess–Akers modification, Sutherland's theory obviously is of most value in explaining institutionalized crime. When he spoke of definition favorable to the violation of rules and laws, Sutherland referred essentially to the existence of a criminal subculture or body of customs, values, and norms which could be learned by individuals who had contact with it. Patterned criminality, especially professional theft, requires subcultural learning. The aspiring professional thief must learn the customs and values of his desired profession if he is to be successful.

The less patterned, less institutionalized, and more individualistic the criminal behavior, the less useful is differential association as an explanatory device. The innovative lawbreaker obviously does not follow the customs of a criminal subculture. At the same time, little criminality is innovative as is true of most other forms of behavior. Much criminal behavior follows customs to some extent, and to that degree Sutherland's theory is relevant.

Differential association has the potential for explaining other institutionalized forms of deviance than crime. When the conceptions of definitions favorable and unfavorable to rule and law violation are extended to embrace definitions favorable and unfavorable to deviance of various kinds, we have the beginning of a general theory of institution-alized deviance. However, a major problem with Sutherland's formulation, whether as originally set forth or extended to deviance in general, is that there is no explanation whatsoever as to why definitions favorable to rules and law violation, or deviance more generally, exist. Albert Cohen attempted to remedy this deficiency in his reaction-formulation theory of delinquent subcultures.

Cohen: Delinquent Subcultures

In Sutherland's formulation, the body of customs, norms, and values conducive to law violation is in effect a criminal subculture. Fifteen years later, Cohen proposed the question, Why does a delinquent subculture exist?[19] He was interested in juvenile crime and so focused on the delinquent subculture of male adolescents, a subculture parallel to Sutherland's criminal subculture.

In an attempt to answer the above question, Cohen drew on the concept of anomie as formulated by Merton. Cohen argued that lower-class boys in America learn to want middle-class status or prestige as symbolized by culturally approved symbols of success, that is, material goods and money. The position of these boys in the lower socioeconomic strata of the social structure makes it unlikely that they will be able to achieve the institutionalized means, especially education and occupation, which make achievement of those goals possible.

This is where the psychological concept of *reaction formation* is brought to bear. The concept refers to the tendency for individuals to denigrate that which they want and cannot achieve, to react against it. Cohen suggested that those lower-class boys who experienced the greatest status frustration would tend to have a reaction formation to the values of the middle class for honesty, thrift, delayed gratification, and utilitarianism. To adapt to this common problem of status deprivation brought about by anomic conditions, they would in interaction with each other develop behavior patterns and values diametrically opposed to those of the middle class to which they aspired: customs, norms, and values conducive to theft and assault. These customs, norms, and values constituted the *delinquent subculture*. They provided the boys with common solutions to the shared problem of *status deprivation*. Involvement in the delinquent gang conferred status, and theft could lead to the illegitimate achievement of at least some symbols of success such as material goods and money.

Thus Cohen was able to explain how differential association became possible—through reaction to certain anomic conditions. This is the major value of Cohen's theory. Serious drawbacks revolve around the assumptions that delinquency is largely a lower-class, male phenomenon. Certainly adjudicated delinquency has traditionally been so. But studies in which youthful subjects disclose in confidence to researchers their illegitimate activities (self-report studies) indicate that middle- and upper-class adolescents may be as delinquent as those in the lower class.[20] Moreover, female adolescents are increasingly being apprehended by police and brought into juvenile court for theft, assault, and other crimes.[21]

Cloward and Ohlin: Delinquent Opportunity Structures

Richard Cloward and Lloyd Ohlin, several years after Cohen, formulated the idea of *differential illegitimate opportunity.*[22] They accepted Merton and Cohen's conceptions of anomie and status frustration as a result of a disparity between goals and means. They tacitly accepted Sutherland's formulation of differential association, but they questioned whether lower-class youth could easily turn to delinquency as a solution to status problems.

Cloward and Ohlin's answer was that access to law-violating patterns of the delinquent subculture is by no means automatic. There are in their formulation three segments of the delinquent subculture: *criminal, conflict,* and *retreatist.* These they call *illegitimate opportunity structures.* Lower-class adolescents, deprived of status, have differing likelihoods of gaining access to these three opportunity structures; thus Cloward and Ohlin's central concept—differential illegitimate opportunity.

The *criminal opportunity structure* of the overall delinquent subculture is the most preferred of the three segments that compose it. This segment involves customs, norms, and values for theft. If it is absent from a neighborhood, it will be exceedingly difficult for lower-class youth to engage systematically in theft and so gain some of the material symbols of status. Moreover, if this structure is at hand, admission is not automatic. Youth must satisfy "recruitment requirements," they must learn the role of thief, they must demonstrate that they can cooperate successfully with such others as professional thieves and fences who are "old hands" in the structure. These others, then, restrict admission to the structure, to recruits who seem to be able to work with them, who will not spoil "a good thing."

The second illegitimate opportunity structure in Cloward and Ohlin's formulation is termed *conflict* or violence. This has to do with activities of violent gangs. Here, too, admission is not automatic. Status-deprived youths must meet recruitment requirements and learn the requisite roles if they are to be accepted members. They must have fighting prowess, be willing to take great risks, and be able to function as team players.

There remains, Cloward and Ohlin hold, the *retreatist* opportunity structure. This refers largely to the use of drugs as a way of life. Those youths, who have been unable to gain the legitimate means to achieve middle-class status and success goals and who have also been unable to gain access to the criminal and conflict illegitimate structures, seek a final acceptance here. While admission to the retreatist structure is not difficult, even in this case one must be able to cooperate with others to a considerable degree in the procurement and use of drugs if one is to be accepted. Rejection means solitary wandering in a cultureless no-man's land between legitimate and illegitimate structures. Although Cloward and Ohlin do not pursue the matter at length, in fact admission to a jail for some individualistic transgression or to a mental hospital because of apparent or real symptoms of mental illness are two final solutions. Suicide is also a final solution.

The great value of Cloward and Ohlin's approach is that they draw attention to the fact that access to illegitimate opportunity structures is far from automatic and requires satisfying criteria for recruitment and role learning. On the other hand, a severe shortcoming is that, like Cohen, they for the most part confine their analysis to lower-class male youth, largely ignoring criminal deviance by females and by middle- and upper-class adolescents.

Wolfgang and Ferracuti: Subcultures of Violence

In the mid-1960s, Marvin E. Wolfgang, a sociologist, and Franco Ferracuti, a psychologist, set forth a *subcultural* explanation of violent crime.[23] This was really a return to Sutherland's position but confined to such forms of deviance as homicide and assault and, to a lesser extent, rape and robbery. The two researchers suggested that in some locales—certain neighborhoods of urban areas, certain regions of a country, and certain countries—there existed bodies of customs, norms, and values that favored violence as a solution to life problems. Individuals, especially males, learned and practiced violence, that is, violent crime was seen as an institutionalized form of deviance. Violence was, in the Wolfgang–Ferracuti formulation, a customary form of response in certain social settings. A subculture of violence is characterized by a

> Quick resort to physical combat as a measure of daring, courage, or defense of status appears to be a cultural expression, especially for lower socioeconomic class males of both races. When such a culture norm response is elicited from an individual engaged in social interplay with others who harbor the same response mechanism, physical assaults, altercations, and violent domestic quarrels that result in homicide are common.[24]

Wolfgang and Ferracuti do not give sustained attention to how and why *subcultures of violence* develop. They do, however, suggest in passing that such subcultures are likely to arise when relative deprivation for economic goals is great, that is, in the lower socioeconomic strata.[25] Now, it is clear that in some parts of the United States—some urban areas, some whole states especially in the South—resorting to violence is more common than elsewhere. Violence does indeed *tend* to be more institutionalized in some locales than in others. Moreover, there is in United States culture as a whole some degree of reliance on and respect for aggressive behaviors which are lesser forms of violence. (To the extent that this is so, aggression and violence are conforming rather than deviant behaviors.)

The facts seem to be that in the United States and various other countries, some violence is culturally induced, some subculturally induced, and some quite individualistic. Often a combination of the three is at work. Certainly in the United States many persons who commit violent crimes have had virtually no contact with a subculture of violence. And many, while they may have been influenced somewhat by the overall culture's emphasis on aggressiveness, do not value violence as a way of coping with life's problems although on rare occasions they have used it. Chapters 3 and 4 deal with these matters.

The Wolfgang and Ferracuti thesis verges on the tautological. Subcultures of violence are to be found where customs of violence and values which advocate it exist in full-blown form. Violent behavior is caused by such concentrations of customs and values. To be sure, this is so in the sense that where there is a subculture of violence, there *must* be relatively high incidences of violent crime. However, where such a subculture is not to be found, there may be considerable violent crime. The subculture of violence thesis is but one explanation of such forms of serious negative deviance as homicide, assault, rape, and robbery. It is necessarily consistent with institutionalized violence but leaves much room for other forms of explanation where more individualistic violence is concerned. Its major value lies in explicitly directing attention to the fact that violence is not necessarily an individual, psychological phenomenon but can be a subculturally induced, sociological one.

SOCIAL DISORGANIZATION AND CONFLICT THEORIES

The Chicago School: Social Disorganization

In the 1920s and 1930s the "Chicago School" of sociology arose, which stressed the critical role of *social disorganization* in producing numerous forms of negative deviance. Researchers, many of them faculty members of the University of Chicago such as Louis Wirth and Clifford Shaw, became fascinated with the urban slum as a generator of crime, delinquency, mental illness, suicide, and alcoholism.[26] The main contention of these analysts was that in the core areas of our large urban concentrations, personal, primary group relationships tended to disappear and to be replaced by impersonal, secondary group relationships. Conduct norms were no longer clear. The informal controls of social disapproval, ridicule, and the like which characterize life in primary groups broke down. Formal laws and rules replaced unwritten but well-understood conduct norms. Police, courts, and jails succeeded informal control processes and were far less effective. Moreover, the ethnic "melting pot" nature of our urban slums introduced a confusion of cultural customs and values imported from other countries, mainly European, around the world.

The Chicago School researchers found high rates of the various forms of negative deviance just mentioned in the "socially disorganized" areas of Chicago and other American cities. As we now see, there turned out to be severe problems in interpreting these findings. There was a tendency for people already negatively deviant to gravitate to slum areas. In some instances residents of slum areas were more readily caught up in official statistics on deviance. And in certain respects the economically depressed urban areas were well organized. "Skid rows" where vagrants congregate have indeed been shown to be well organized in an informal fashion. Residents have their codes of conduct and help each other in myriad ways, but in ways different from those economically more fortunate.[27]

Sellin: Culture Conflict

Thorsten Sellin in 1938 published his significant book, *Culture Conflict and Crime.*[28] He argued that when individuals were exposed to and learned *conflicting conduct norms*, crime was likely to result. Individuals might first learn the norms of one culture, then move to another where what constituted crime was defined differently than in the first. They might be located at the borders between cultures and could then be caught between, *conflicting definitions* of crime. Again, changes over time within a given culture might mean that individuals behaved on the basis of earlier norms which conflicted with later definitions of what constituted crime. Finally, differing ethnic, social class, urban-rural, and other subcultures within a given culture might at any time have conflicting conduct norms and criminal definitions. If individuals moved from one subcultural setting to another, they could be trapped, as it were, into crime. Also, one subculture might be dominant over another and so use its standards for judging the behavior of those socialized in the other and persecute them for negative deviance. Although Sellin's formulation had no political bias in the usual sense, it provided in some respects the theoretical basis for social-class conflict explanations of deviance which were later to evolve.

Miller: Lower-Class Subculture

Walter Miller wrote in 1958 of *lower-class subculture* as "a generating milieu of gang delinquency."[29] His thesis was that lower-class customs, values, and norms in the urban areas in the United States demanded that lower-class boys act in ways defined as criminal by the overall culture, usually involving violence and theft. There were, Miller said, *six focal concerns* of lower-class subculture:

1. *Trouble,* or behavior such as violence or theft, which can lead one to "get into trouble" with middle-class authorities. This is viewed in lower-class life as something to be avoided but also as something that can confer status, a "rep."
2. *Toughness,* or the value placed on physical strength, masculinity, bravery in combat.
3. *Smartness,* or the ability to outwit others and to avoid being fooled by them.
4. *Excitement,* or the concern with relieving the humdrum nature of everyday life with risk-taking thrills, especially through drinking, brawling, sexual adventuring, and gambling.
5. *Fate,* or the belief that one's life is controlled by forces over which one has no control, a combination of luck and the coercive power of the affluent to affect one's life.
6. *Autonomy,* a surface concern with avoiding controls (in the face of the forces of fate) and with independence together with an underlying desire to seek restrictive environments, such as jails, prisons, and mental hospitals, on which one can be dependent.

It was Miller's view that these six focal concerns either directly or indirectly lead to criminal behavior patterns, especially violence and theft. These patterns are *customary* in lower-class subcultures, part of the way of life of the urban poor. They are seen as deviant by lower-class persons only in the sense that middle-class authorities define them as deviant and react to them with hostility and punishment.

Miller was essentially providing an alternative to the cultural support explanation of crime and delinquency provided by Sutherland, Cohen, and Cloward and Ohlin. Cohen posited a subculture of crime set up *outside* lower-class subculture by boys of that class who were thwarted in their strivings for legitimate success goals. Miller argued in effect that there did not exist a separate criminal subculture. Rather, behavior patterns which the middle-class defined as criminal were threaded through the subculture of the lower class and were a functional part of lower-class everyday life.

However, Miller was not centrally concerned with the issue of political conflict between the upper and lower strata of the class system in America. He did not explicitly insist that the lower class was the inevitable loser in a power struggle with the middle and upper classes, one in which the higher classes defined behavior of the lower as criminal for political purposes. This position was later to be explicated by Richard Quinney.

Quinney: Political Conflict

Richard Quinney in 1970 presented his *social reality* theory of crime. This went further than previous formulations in attempting to show that *political and class power factors* were the root explanations of crime. Quinney's central thesis was that the politically powerful created one form of negative deviance—crime—and gave it its "social reality" as a means of social control:

> Criminal law is used by the state and the ruling class to secure the survival of the capitalist system, and, as capitalist society is further threatened by its own contradiction, criminal law will be increasingly used in the attempt to maintain domestic order.[30]

Quinney presented his argument in six statements. In his view,

1. Crime is "a definition of human conduct that is created by authorized agents in a politically organized society."[31] There was for Quinney no such phenomenon as intrinsic crime. It is what people say it is. But not everyone has a voice in this.
2. "Criminal definition describes behavior that conflicts with the interests of the segments of society that have the power to shape public policy."[32] Powerful capitalists (or, in some societies, totalitarian leaders) see to it that laws are formulated which make criminal and punishable behavior (theft and assault mainly) that may threaten their hold on power, money and prestige.
3. "Criminal definitions are applied by the segments of society that have the power to shape the enforcement and administration of criminal law."[33] Through their formal agents of control—police and the judiciary—the powerful apprehend and punish the weak who transgress the laws.
4. "Behavior patterns are structured in segmentally organized so-

ciety in relation to criminal definitions, and within their context persons engage in activities that have relative probabilities of being defined as criminal."[34] Quinney's meaning is that some of the norms of the lower classes are formally defined as criminal by the powerful. Thus lower-class persons necessarily learn criminal patterns. Moreover, they are then defined as criminal and learn to take on the role of criminal. This is how the institutionalization of crime is perpetuated.

5. "Conceptions of crime are constructed and diffused in segments of society by various means of communication."[35] The powerful communicate an *ideology* of crime, emphasize its threat, and so reinforce the process of defining crime, enforcing criminal law, and creating criminals.

6. A summary statement: "The social reality of crime is constructed by the formulation and application of criminal definitions, the development of behavior patterns related to criminal definitions, and the construction of criminal conceptions."[36] *The powerful, through communication and to serve their interests, create the idea of crime, define it in terms of behavior patterns followed by the powerless, coerce the powerless to take on criminal roles, and punish them for doing so.* This exerts social controls on the powerless designed to keep them from usurping the power of the powerful. It also allows the powerful to carry out undetected self-serving exploitative business practices. Such practices often go undetected because they are not defined as crime while attention is focused on the criminally defined behavior of the powerless.

This is radical criminology and, like many theories, has positive and negative qualities. It does reflect the undisputed fact that in most systems of justice the powerful exert more influence, and to their own benefit, than the powerless. It is especially useful as an explanation of how the powerful cover up their own exploitative behaviors. It helps to explain the ebb and flow over time in defining and prosecuting as crimes certain "victimless" activities such as homosexuality and drug abuse. It reminds us that the powerful may use and pervert the criminal justice system to silence their enemies. As we shall soon see, it has relevance to the general process of labeling individuals as negative deviants. What Quinney's theory does not do well is explain certain behavior—murder, assault, rape are primary examples—that is abhorred and defined as criminal by most individuals regardless of their power in many societies including ours. Relatively powerful, affluent persons commit these crimes although less often than the powerless and the poor.

Thio: Power Theory

Alex Thio in 1978 outlined his power theory of negative devi-ance.[37] This theory attempts a broader explanation of deviance than Quinney's since it applies to a wider range of deviance than crime and to societies everywhere, not only capitalistic and totalitarian societies. Thio contends that life is always unequal, that all do not possess the same power, that is, all are not equally able to control the behavior of others.

Thio sets forth three propositions:

1. "The more power people have, the more likely they will engage in lower-consensus deviance—the 'less serious,' more profita-ble, or more sophisticated type of deviance—with lower proba-bility of being labeled deviant."[38] Lower-consensus deviance is that which has relatively little societal-wide recognition as seri-ous negative behavior. The powerful control to a considerable degree which behaviors gain widespread recognition as seri-ously negative and as punishable. Thus they arrange to have less consensus about the more profitable forms of deviance. These forms are less often punished and if they are, they are punished less harshly. Conversely, the powerful arrange to have more consensus about the less profitable forms of deviance. Thus higher-consensus deviance, which tends to be harshly pun-ished, is left to the powerless.

2. "It is more likely that the powerful will engage in lower-consen-sus deviance than the powerless will commit higher-consensus deviance."[39] That is, the powerful are more seriously negatively deviant, more criminal, than the powerless. The powerful, Thio reasons, have more opportunities: the range of possibilities for negative deviance is greater. It is easier for a businessman to defraud his customers or the Internal Revenue Service than it is for a lower-class person to rob a bank. Also, the powerful have a greater likelihood of feeling subjectively deprived than the powerless. The powerful person's goals are virtually unlimited. "The more power one has, the higher one's aspirations are, and the greater one's subjective deprivation is," Thio contends.[40] The powerless, in contrast, do not expect much. Further, there are fewer social controls on the powerful. They are less vulnerable to exposure and punishment than the powerless and this en-courages them in their negative deviance.

3. "Deviance by the powerful induces deviance by the powerless that, in turn, contributes to deviance by the powerful."[41] In brief, the powerful influence the powerless to be deviant by leading

them into illegal activities, by setting poor examples, and by
reinforcing inequality in the society. The powerless aid and abet
the negative deviance of the powerful by an unwillingness to
prosecute them for their crimes. (Agents of social control, being
the tools of the powerful, are themselves without power and
fear losing their jobs if they prosecute the powerful.) The fact
that the powerless commit "heinous" crimes makes the powerful self-righteous and tolerant of their own deviance. The powerless direct their criminal activities against themselves. The poor
are largely the victims of violence and theft by the poor. This
only compounds their oppression and perpetuates inequality,
contends Thio.

A major drawback of Thio's approach has to do with the definition of
negative deviance. The powerful habitually engage in lower-consensus
deviance, Thio contends. This means that there is little agreement in
the society as to whether these customary actions of the powerful are
to be defined positively or negatively. It is Thio who is making this
judgment. True, many of us might agree that certain exploitative activities of the powerful are indeed harmful and negative. But if enough
of us agree, then those actions would no longer constitute lower-
consensus deviance.

A further criticism is similar to that which applies to Quinney's
social reality of crime theory: Thio's formulation does not actually answer the question of why certain "traditional" violent behaviors, such
as murder, assault, and rape, are defined as serious crimes and of why
they are committed. The powerful also commit these crimes, less frequently than the powerless but they commit them. When they do, the
powerful may be punished less harshly than the powerless but they
have still committed higher-consensus deviance, contrary to Thio's as-
sertion. As with Quinney's approach, Thio's theory best explains certain political and business activities such as "abuse of power," the sale
of defective and dangerous products, and so forth.

SOCIETAL REACTION THEORIES

The Dramatization of Evil and Symbolic Interaction

In 1967 Edwin M. Lemert wrote that

> older sociology . . . tended to rest heavily upon the idea that deviance
> leads to social control. I have come to believe that the reverse idea, i.e.,

social control leads to deviance, is equally tenable and the potentially richer premise for studying deviance in modern society.[42]

This idea, that *social control begets deviance*, is the heart of the societal reaction explanation. The *reaction* of society to presumed or actual negative deviant behavior tends to bring about the very behavior it is ostensibly designed to reduce or prevent.

One of the first students of deviance to give sustained attention to this form of explanation was Frank Tannenbaum. In 1938 in *Crime and the Community*, Tannenbaum argued that in its attempts to curb unlawful behavior by juveniles, society seeks to *dramatize* the nature of this "evil."[43] They young person acts—often for adventure, excitement, fun—in ways society defines as threatening. Tannenbaum describes society's reaction in this way:

> The process of making the criminal . . . a process of tagging, defining, identifying, segregating, describing, emphasizing, and evoking the very traits that are complained of.[44]

The social definition of behavior as evil is attached to the person who behaves in that way. In the process the person is induced to take on the role of negative (evil) deviant.

The societal reaction approach to deviance developed in good measure out of such ideas as Tannebaum's and the *symbolic interaction* school of social psychology. Symbolic interactionists such as Herbert Blumer emphasize that the individual is an active organism attempting to cope with an environment composed of other persons, relationships, and "things."[45] The individual *interprets* the behavior of others with whom he or she is interacting, that is, the individual makes a determination as to the *meaning* of the behavior of others. In addition, the individual attempts to *define* and convey to others how they are to act. This process of individuals reading the meaning of, and defining, each other's behavior is called *symbolic interaction.*

The societal reaction explanation, that social control leads to deviance, is thus based in good part on Tannenbaum's ideas of creating negative deviants by reacting to them as such and on the ideas of Blumer and others about the symbolic nature of social interaction, that is, the central place of interpretation, definition, and *meaning*, in interaction. Society, in reacting to negative deviance, conveys its sense of the evil meaning both of the behavior and of the actor; the latter internalizes this meaning, attaches it to the self, and learns the role of deviant.

Societal reaction is not so much a theory in the usual sense as it is a broad orienting, or sensitizing, concept. Above all it focuses attention on the social-control process as an intrinsic aspect of much deviance.

Labeling, an important component of societal reaction, is also essentially an orienting concept rather than a theory.

The Labeling Process

A number of sociologists, among them John Kitsuse, Thomas Scheff, and Edwin Schur, have stressed the centrality of the *labeling process* in the analysis of deviance.[46] Labeling is an integral part of the broader process of societal reaction although it is sometimes construed as a separate process. *Societal reaction* is the general process by which the group responds to actual or presumed deviant behavior of its members. Labeling is a more specific process within societal reaction by which attention is verbally brought to individuals because of their behavior, physical characteristics, or other attributes. It often serves to precipitate further reaction by the group to deviance: a judgment, through the judicial process, as to whether the person is deviant and punishment, exemplified by imprisonment.

We label each other throughout life and not only with respect to negative deviance. We label in regard to conformity. We say so-and-so "does everything by the book." We label in relation to positive deviance. We say that Jones is a creative person and Smith is a genius at figuring out how to solve a tough problem. But we are of course especially prone to label others for their negative deviance. This may be deviance that has actually be manifested or deviance of which someone has wrongly been accused. Thus we say that a youth is a thief because he allegedly engaged in shoplifting. We say that a girl is a prostitute because she allegedly took money for a sexual relationship. We say that someone is crazy or insane or psychotic because he or she acted in a way that seems otherwise incomprehensible.

When a person is labeled, those who do the labeling set up expectations that some of the person's future behavior will match the deviant role in which he or she is being cast. They and others are likely to reward the person for behavior which does conform to the deviant role and to punish for that which does not. Thus when a person is labeled as delinquent or as mentally ill, he or she is likely to be rewarded for behavior which conforms to the deviant label. The person is expected to accept the label and the role it implies, and to take on a self-image which reflects the label. The person who does is often held to be "cooperating" while the person who does not is thought to be "difficult."

Labeling varies along several dimensions. We have already said that it can be applied to positive deviance and to conformity as well as to negative deviance. Labeling also varies in the extent to which it is *transitory* or *permanent*. The label of "homicidal offender" is likely to persist throughout the individual's life. Imprinting through branding a symbol on the forehead of a deviant was in times past a highly tangible attempt to ensure lifelong permanence of the label. On the other hand, much labeling persists only for a short time. We call someone a nuisance because of a particular instance of annoying behavior yet there may be little long-range consequence. Sometimes, however, repeated instances of temporary labeling may take on a permanent quality. Someone labeled time and again as a fool because of small instances of foolish behavior may eventually take on the permanent label of fool.

Labeling may be *formal*, that is, carried out by such formal authorities as courts, prisons, boards of review, and so on. Or it may be highly *informal* as when children in the course of play label each other. Labels vary also in the extent to which they are or are not *engulfing*. That is, the label may apply to the total person or to but one behavioral aspect of a person. For example, the label of juvenile delinquent is far more engulfing that that of truant from school.

Labeling may or may not take place before an *audience*. If so, the size of the audience can of course vary greatly. Thus a person may be labeled a criminal in a small courtroom and with little public notice. Another may be so labeled with many members of the public and of the press in attendance and the labeling may then reach a vast audience through the mass media.

There may be greater or lesser degrees of *consensus* or *dissensus* about the efficacy of the label. Political opponents often engage in attempts to label each other negatively and themselves positively. The public reacts with varying degrees of agreement or disagreement. Finally, the *power* of the labeler and the one labeled will vary separately and in relation to each other. Generally speaking, the more power one possesses, the greater the likelihood of effectively labeling another negatively, of having oneself labeled positively, and of personally avoiding a negative label.

Some proponents of labeling hold that deviant behavior does not exist unless the individual who manifests it is labeled as a deviant.[47] (They are referring to negative deviance.) In other words, it is only when others react to behavior as negative deviance that it becomes such. We do not subscribe to this view. Behavior is deviant when it diverges from expectational or behavior norms. Negative deviance is behavior which departs from norms and which is socially disapproved. "Socially disapproved" refers to the definition of the behavior by the group as negative, unwanted, dangerous, and so on. There need be no reaction to the individual actor for negative deviant behavior to exist. The behavior or the "secret deviant," about which no others are aware, is as deviant as that of the sexual exhibitionist. The behavior is deviant but the actor is not defined by others as deviant. The actor may or may not define himself or herself as deviant.

Other advocates of labeling hold that there can be no career deviants, no taking on the role of the deviant without labeling. Again, they refer primarily to negative deviants. Here we are more in agreement. As we shall see in the following section, labeling by others is often the first step in taking on a deviant role. Acquiring a new role involves interaction with others. One does not learn a role in a social vacuum. Hence others must know that one is taking on a particular role if they are to react to that individual in ways that facilitate role learning and internalization. Labeling can be a key element in that; however, the impetus may come from the individual rather than others. The person may act in such a way as to motivate others to label him or her as a particular kind of deviant in order to expedite taking on of the role. Juvenile gang members may provoke the police into arresting them or closet homosexuals may "come out" and march in the streets.

Career or Secondary Deviance

Edwin Lemert,[48] Howard Becker,[49] and numerous others have written of the processes of societal reaction which move individuals to take on deviant careers in contrast to the sporadic manifestation of deviant behavior. Edwin Lemert in 1951 was the first analyst of deviance to distinguish explicitly between *primary* and *secondary* or *career deviance*. Later, he elaborated his ideas in an extended essay.[50] The distinction between primary and secondary deviance applies to negative deviance although it has implications for positive forms of deviance as well. *Primary deviance* refers to behavior designated as socially unacceptable by the society's members but which the individual actor construes as reasonable and acceptable given the circumstances. A primary deviant does not view himself or herself as carrying out a deviant role. Rather, the person sees the self as at times acting in ways which others define as deviant. *Secondary deviance* refers to behavior which both society's members and the actor view as negative deviance. The secondary deviant is one who has a self-image as a negative deviant, who internalizes and carries out a deviant role over months or years, usually the latter.

To illustrate, a man may write a check knowing he does not have the funds in his bank account to cover. He may write a check on an account that has been closed for some time. He knows this is technically not acceptable but he feels he has good reason for doing so. He will make the check good eventually, he tells himself. He does not consider himself to be a deviant, and he does not in fact have a deviant role. This is primary deviance, and he is a primary deviant. The professional forger, in contrast, passes bad checks regularly, agrees with society that this is socially unacceptable although advantageous to him, views himself as a forger, carries out the "professional" role of forger, tries to protect himself from arrest and conviction. This is secondary (career) deviance, and the individual is a secondary (career) deviant.

The distinction between primary and secondary deviance can be made in regard to positive deviance. When the innovative person behaves in ways that are positively evaluated by the members of society, and when over time they react to him or her as one who is a positive deviant (artistic or inventive person, say), and reward him or her for being so, then secondary deviance comes into play and the innovative person moves toward becoming a secondary deviant. The individual tends to internalize the role of artist or inventor, defines the self as such, and seeks not to protect himself or herself from societal punishment but rather to ensure continued social reward through innovative effort.

The process of moving from primary to secondary deviance and of assuming the role of secondary deviant, either positive or negative, is compounded by the individual's acceptance or refusal to accept the deviant label and role. Thus there are those who steadfastly maintain that they are, as it were, amateurs who engage in some behavior which, while technically deviant, is only occasional and that they in fact have no deviant role.

Gresham Sykes summarizes well the sequence which leads from primary to secondary deviance[51]: (1) primary deviance; (2) societal penalties (and labeling); (3) further deviation; (4) stronger penalties (and further labeling); (5) further deviation with hostility and resentment possibly beginning to be directed toward those doing the penalizing; (6) a crisis point where the community takes formal action and stigmatizes the deviant; (7) a strengthening of the deviant conduct as a reaction to the severe actions of society; and (8) finally, an acceptance (by the individual) of deviant social status and an attempt to adjust to the corresponding role.

Secondary deviance and the assumption of a deviant role can, however, occur without explicit societal reaction to primary deviance. Society's members may be unaware that the individual is behaving in a deviant way and yet the person labels himself or herself as a deviant, assumes a deviant role, and the deviant behavior becomes habitual, a way of life. "Closet" male homosexuals are illustrative. In such instances the individual is not, of course, functioning in a social vacuum. Usually, he *knows* that his behavior is deviant, that society's members would disapprove of it, would label him a deviant, and would attempt to thrust upon him a deviant role if they were aware of his deviance. This knowledge influences his self-conceptions.

Evaluation of the Societal Reaction Approach

We indicated earlier that a serious drawback of the societal reaction approach is that the concept of societal reaction and the more specific concept of labeling are often used in an overextended way. Many scholars who stress societal reaction believe that deviance does not occur unless society brings social controls to bear against the actor. As Gresham Sykes points out, this confuses the existence of behavior with the social characterization of behavior.[52] Simply put, the occurrence of deviant behavior depends on whether individuals act in ways that diverge from expectational or behavioral norms. If they do, deviance exists regardless of whether anyone, including the actor, is aware of it. How society reacts to deviant behavior—or conforming behavior—does, however, have much to do with how individuals will act in the future and whether they will take on deviant roles and careers (secondary deviance).

There is also a tendency for proponents of societal reaction and labeling to see the individual as a passive being on which society "works its will" despite Blumer's insistence on the active, coping nature of humans.[53] Certainly there will be times when the forces of the state, through its social-control apparatus, seem to overwhelm individuals. A person innocent of a crime may, for example, be apprehended by police, tried in a criminal court, convicted, spend many years in prison. More typically, however, an individual's life involves many "negotiated outcomes" during which the person and agents of social control reach some type of accommodation. Individuals accused of crimes "plea bargain," and individuals diagnosed as mentally ill agree to outpatient treatment as an alternative to confinement in a mental hospital. Such negotiations illustrate the force of societal reaction, but they also show the power of the individual to affect, at least to some extent, the outcome.

The societal reaction approach, then, makes a significant contribution to the understanding of how individuals become socialized into negative deviant roles and careers. It thus contributes to our comprehension of institutionalized deviance, for it is only through socialization into deviant roles that broad subcultures of negative deviance can be perpetuated. This valuable perspective should be extended to conformity and positive deviance. The ways society reacts to conforming and positive deviant behavior have much to do with socialization into conforming and positive deviant roles and careers, and with the institutionalization of conforming behavior and positive deviance. More particularly, labeling goes on in all realms of social life much of the time. It is a primary means of understanding the world, of controlling and socializing individuals, of providing social organization. As such, it deserves wider application than to negative deviance alone and requires sustained analysis of the social and individual conditions which lead to various consequences of labeling.

There is a further, important contribution of the societal reaction approach to deviance. It makes more understandable the social functions of deviance. We noted several such functions in Chapter 1: deviance contributes to social organization through defining what is not deviant, through helping to establish group boundaries, through the banding together of deviants and separately of nondeviants. Relatedly, through the creation of scapegoats, deviance provides escape value mechanisms for the aggressive tendencies of society's members; it provides jobs as agents of social control; and, very importantly, it makes social change possible.

As Kai Erickson and other pointed out,[54] societal reaction is the process by which deviants are created in order to fulfill their functions. Societal reaction is a core explanation of how society manufactures deviants and of how individuals are induced to engage in deviant behavior, to lead deviant roles, and to become careerists in deviance. Thus are the latent functions of deviance satisfied and institutionalized deviance perpetuated.

SUMMARY

There are four broad sociological explanations or theories of deviant behavior: social integration, cultural support, social disorganization and conflict, and societal reaction. Social integration theories focus on the extent to which individuals are or are not bound to and regulated by groups. Cultural support explanations stress the social learning of deviant behavior patterns. Social disorganization and conflict theories emphasize cultural and social conflicts of one form or another. Societal reaction theories focus on the way in which the society's members in their reaction to real or presumed deviance actually bring about the deviance they are ostensibly attempting to control.

Emile Durkheim laid the foundation for the social integration approach to the study of deviance. Persons are integrated into society to the extent that they share common life values. Durkheim theorized that suicide was a likely consequence of extremes of social integration. Central to Durkheim's formulation is anomie, a social condition marked by low integration and high social isolation. The concept of anomie was more specifically defined by Merton as the disparity between the institutionalized means and culturally approved goals of society. The less able individuals are to obtain the legitimate means to approved goals, the more likely that they will engage in deviant behavior. Merton linked combinations of acceptance and rejection of means and goals with various forms of deviant behavior.

Henry and Short and Straus and Straus took a social integration approach to deviance, focusing on two extreme forms of individual violence: murder and suicide. Henry and Short gave central attention to these variables: status, strength of the relational system (closeness of social relationships), and degree of external restraint (required conformity to the wishes of others). They predicted that as status or prestige increases, external restraints and strength of the relational system decrease, and suicide becomes more likely. Conversely, when prestige decreases and external restraint and the strength of the relational system increase, homicide becomes more probable.

Straus and Straus emphasized the closeness or looseness of the structuring of society as central to the explanation of homicide and suicide. A society is closely structured (high integration) when reciprocal rights and duties are stressed and enforced, and loosely structured (low integration) when they are not. Suicide results more from closely structured societies, homicide from loosely structured ones.

Sutherland's theory of differential association has had a major influence on cultural support theories. He emphasized the process of learning within a subcultural context to explain criminal behavior. Learning to commit crime essentially requires the same process as learning to conform. Burgess and Akers pointed out that inherent in Sutherland's theory is differential reinforcement, that is, the extent to which criminal or other behavior is consistently rewarding.

Cohen attempted to account for the development of delinquent subcultures. Lower-class boys, he argued, inevitably suffer frustration because of their inability to obtain middle-class status goals. As a result, a reaction formation occurs, that is, lower-class boys denigrate that which they want but cannot achieve. Delinquent subcultures arise to provide an alternate means for gaining status and respect from others.

Cloward and Ohlin outline three types of delinquent subcultures that may arise under various conditions. Access to illegitimate opportunity structures is the key to whether the subculture will be conflict, theft, or retreatist in nature. Subcultures of violence have been the central concern of Wolfgang and Ferracuti. Geographic areas are marked by varying degrees of patterned violence. Wolfgang and Ferracuti reasoned that in places where individuals learn that violence is acceptable, even expected, means of resolving conflicts, rates of homicide and assault will be high.

In the 1920s and 1930s, social disorganization and conflict explanation began to be formulated. Sellin linked culture conflict and criminal behavior. Miller analyzed subcultural patterns that conflict with those of the larger society. He outlined six focal concerns of lower-class life: trouble, toughness, smartness, excitement, fate, and autonomy. These values combine to generate behavior which is defined by the wider society as crime.

Quinney systematically related political and class power with criminal behavior. He argued that criminal law is used by the politically powerful segments of society to protect the capitalistic system, to create conceptions of crime, and to control dissident members of society. Similarly, Thio argued that differential power relations in society result in a wide variety of negative deviance. The powerful engage in highly profitable forms of low-consensus deviance while the less powerful commit acts of deviance available to them (high-consensus deviance). Such behavior results in oppressive retaliatory measures by the powerful.

Finally, much recent attention has focused on societal reaction and labeling perspectives on deviance. Societal reaction is the general process by which the group responds to actual or presumed deviant behavior of its members. Labeling is a more specific process within societal reaction by which attention is verbally focused on individuals because of their behavior or other attributes. Tannenbaum first analyzed the detrimental effects of dramatizing delinquent behavior by the court. The process of labeling an individual a deviant is often traumatic and may serve to exacerbate the very behavior official agents seek to control.

Careers in deviance are furthered by negative societal reaction and labeling. Lemert distinguished between primary and secondary deviance. Primary deviance refers to minor forms of norm violations. Individuals do not view themselves as deviant, nor are they playing the role of a deviant. Secondary deviance constitutes more serious forms of negative deviance. Individuals think of themselves as deviant; deviance constitutes a central role in their lives. A professional forger is an apt example.

All deviance does not, of course, depend on the awareness of others and their condemning reaction to it. Yet the processes of societal reaction and labeling are powerful influences behind the creation and perpetuation of deviant careers.

REFERENCES

1. For example, Ernest B. Hook, "Behavioral Implications of the Human XYY Genotype," *Science* 179(4069): 139–50, 1973.

2. One well known work is Franz Alexander and William Healy, *Roots of Crime* (New York: Knopf, 1935).
3. Emile Durkeim, *The Rule of Sociological Method*, 8th ed., trans. S. A. Solovay and J. H. Mueller, ed. G. E. G. Catlin (Chicago: University of Chicago Press, 1938), pp. 65–73.
4. Emile Durkeim, *Suicide*, trans. J. A. Spaulding and G. Simpson (Glencoe, IL: Free Press, 1951).
5. *Ibid.*
6. See Robert K. Merton, *Social Theory and Social Structure* (New York: Free Press, 1968).
7. Andrew F. Henry and James F. Short, Jr., *Suicide and Homicide* (New York: Free Press, 1954).
8. *Ibid.* p. 17
9. *Ibid.* p. 18.
10. Jacqueline Straus and Murray Straus, "Suicide, Homicide, and Social Structure in Ceylon," *American Journal of Sociology* 58(5): 461–69, 1953.
11. Durkheim, *Suicide.*
12. Travis Hirschi, *Causes of Delinquency* (Berkeley: University of California Press, 1969).
13. Emile Durkheim in *ibid.*
14. For full explication, see Edwin H. Sutherland, *Principles of Criminology* (Philadelphia: Lippincott, 1939).
15. Albert Cohen, *Delinquent Boys: The Culture of the Gang* (Glencoe, IL: Free Press, 1955).
16. Richard A. Cloward and Lloyd E. Ohlin, *Delinquency and Opportunity: A Theory of Delinquent Gangs* (Glencoe, IL: Free Press, 1960).
17. Edwin H. Sutherland and Donald R. Cressey, *Criminology*, 10th ed. (Philadelphia: Lippincott, 1978).
18. R. L. Burgess and R. L. Akers, "A Differential Association-Reinforcement Theory of Criminal Behavior," *Social Problems* 14(2): 128–47, 1966.
19. Cohen, *op. cit.*
20. Gwynn Nettler, *Explaining Crime* (New York: McGraw-Hill, 1978), pp. 97–107.
21. Federal Bureau of Investigation, *Crime in the United States* (Washington, D.C.: U.S. Government Printing Office, annual issues).
22. Cloward and Ohlin, *op. cit.*
23. Marvin E. Wolfgang and Franco Ferracuti, *The Subculture of Violence* (London: Tavistock, 1967).
24. Marvin E. Wolfgang, *Patterns of Criminal Homicide* (Philadelphia: University of Pennsylvania Press, 1959), pp. 188–89.
25. Wolfgang and Ferracuti, *op. cit.*, Chap. 5.
26. Robert E. L. Faris, *Social Disorganization* (New York: Ronald Press, 1948).
27. Joan K. Jackson and Ralph Connor, "The Skid Row Alcoholic," *Quarterly Journal of Studies on Alcohol* 14(3): 468–486, 1953.
28. Thorsten Sellin, *Culture Conflict and Crime* (New York: Social Science Research Council, Bulletin No. 41, 1938).
29. Walter B. Miller, "Lower Class Culture as a Generating Milieu of Gang Delinquency," *Journal of Social Issues* 14(3):5–19, 1958.
30. Richard Quinney, *Critique of the Legal Order* (Boston: Little, Brown, 1974), p. 16.
31. Richard Quinney, *The Social Reality of Crime* (Boston: Little, Brown, 1970), p. 154.
32. *Ibid.*
33. *Ibid.*
34. *Ibid.*
35. *Ibid.*
36. *Ibid.*
37. Alex Thio, *Deviant Behavior* (Boston: Houghton Mifflin, 1978).
38. *Ibid.*, p. 81.
39. *Ibid.*

40. *Ibid.*, p. 83.
41. *Ibid.*, p. 86.
42. Edwin M. Lemert, *Human Deviance, Social Problems, and Social Control* (Englewood Cliffs, NJ: Prentice-Hall, 1967), p. v.
43. Frank Tannenbaum, *Crime and the Community* (New York: Ginn, 1938).
44. *Ibid.*, pp. 19–20.
45. Herbert Blumer, *Symbolic Interactionism* (Englewood Cliffs, NJ: Prentice-Hall, 1969).
46. John Kitsuse, "Societal Reaction to Deviant Behavior: Problems of Theory and Method," *Social Problems* 9(3): 247–256, 1962; also Thomas Scheff, *Being Mentally Ill* (Chicago: Aldine, 1966); Edwin M. Schur, *Labeling Deviant Behavior* (New York: Harper and Row, 1971).
47. Schur, *op. cit.*
48. Lemert, *op. cit.*
49. Howard Becker, *Outsiders: Studies in the Sociology of Deviance* (New York: Free Press, 1963).
50. Lemert, *op. cit.*
51. Gresham M. Sykes, *Criminology* (New York: Harcourt Brace Jovanovich, 1978), p. 299.
52. *Ibid.*, p. 306
53. Blumer, *op. cit.*
54. Kai T. Erikson, *Wayward Puritans: A Study in the Sociology of Deviance* (New York: Wiley, 1966).

3

Criminal Homicide

THE MEANING OF HOMICIDE

Defining Crime

The mores of a society are those customs and values which its members believe must be followed to ensure the society's survival. Crimes are those deviant acts which violate the mores, which are believed to threaten the social fabric. All societies, literate and nonliterate, recognize crimes in this way. In the large, literate societies, criminal law is a codification of the given society's mores combined with specific punishments for violations.

Most societies stipulate that the individual can be held accountable for criminal behavior only if the commission of the act was intentional and if the person had control over his or her behavior. Yet these criteria are usually vaguely defined. In any case, accidental acts which violate the mores are usually seen as without intent and so are not prosecuted. Certain groups notably young children and those designated as seriously mentally ill, are often viewed as not being responsible for, not having control over, behavior which violates the mores.

Criminal and Justifiable Homicide

All societies recognize certain forms of killing of one person by another as serious criminal transgressions. But what precisely constitutes such crimes varies from one society to another. It is usual to distinguish between justifiable, noncriminal homicide and unjustifiable, criminal homicide. The distinction is generally made on the basis of two criteria. One is whether the killing is in the culturally prescribed line of duty. A police officer who kills an escaping arrestee may be judged to have committed justifiable homicide and not to have acted criminally. The second criterion is self-defense. An individual who seeks to protect himself and his family by killing an armed attacker may be found to have committed justifiable noncriminal homicide. However, criminal laws usually proscribe narrowly what constitutes self-defense: those who kill others and claim self-defense must demonstrate that they had little alternative but to kill their attackers if they or their families were to survive.

Criminal homicide, then, is a negative deviant act which meets the following criteria: it is a violation of the mores; there is intent or premeditation; the lethal act is not accidental; the individual is responsible for his or her act; the act is not in the line of culturally sanctioned duty; and the act is not one of self-defense.

Murder and Manslaughter as Forms of Criminal Homicide

Jurisdictions within the United States and elsewhere vary as to how instances of criminal homicide are legally classified. Two forms of murder and two of manslaughter are common. First-degree murder is considered the most serious form of criminal homicide and second-degree murder the next most serious. First-degree manslaughter is seen as the third most serious form and second-degree manslaughter the least serious.

Two main criteria are likely to be used in determining how serious is the particular form of criminal homicide. *Malice* refers to the degree of violence or sadism involved in the act of killing another. *Premeditation* concerns the extent to which the act was intentionally planned and carried out. The greater the malice and premeditation, the more serious the homicidal offense. In first-degree murder, malice and premeditation are considered to be especially great. They are of less magnitude in second-degree murder, of still less in first-degree manslaughter, and lowest in second-degree manslaughter. Severity of punishment is usually greatest in cases of first-degree murder and least in second-degree manslaughter cases.

Criminologists often combine under the heading of murder the two degrees of murder and first-degree manslaughter. These three forms of criminal homicide are functionally similar. There are substantial malice and intent in the legal senses just described and little likelihood of accident in the act of killing. Second-degree manslaughter is, in contrast, likely to involve a substantial degree of negligence. A considerable proportion of second-degree manslaughter in the United States is of the type where an intoxicated driver of a motor vehicle kills a pedestrian. This is quite a different form of homicide than, say, the armed robber who kills the bank teller or the person who, in the course of an altercation, grabs a rifle and kills a friend or relative. Most of the statistics which follow pertain to first- and second-degree murder and first-degree manslaughter combined and not to second-degree manslaughter.

INCIDENCE

Rates Defined

Statistics about the incidence of criminal homicide in a society are seldom if ever fully accurate. The reported, officially known incidence is likely to be somewhat below the actual incidence. Homicide stirs so much concern in most societies, however, that instances of it are very likely to be reported to and recorded by law enforcement agencies. Certainly statistics about criminal homicide are much more complete than those for most other crimes.

Rates of criminal homicide are usually expressed as the known number of first- and second-degree murders and first-degree manslaughters per 100,000 of the given population per year. (Some societies, of course, use other terms than degrees of murder and manslaughter to indicate what constitutes criminal homicide.) The main value of using such a rate is that the volume of homicide can be meaningfully compared across populations of varying sizes. Thus if a city has a population of 100,000 and one criminal homicide in a given year, the homicide rate for that society is 1.0. If another city has a population of 1 million and 10 criminal homicides in that year, the rate is also 1.0. Further illustration: In society A the population is 100 million and there are 10,000 homicides per year. The rate is 10.0 because there are 10 homicides for every 100,000 persons in the population. In society B the population is 50 million and 1000 homicides occur annually. Here the rate is 2.0, that is for every 100,000 persons, there are two homicides. Rates can be computed for various groups in a society; age, sex, race, and regional groupings are examples.

Looked at another way, the criminal homicide rate of a society or a group within it indicates the average risk to an individual of becoming a homicide victim within that year. If your city has a population of 100,000 and 10 homicides per year, on the average, a person's chance of being a victim of homicide is 10 in 100,000.

Rates around the World

For the world as a whole, the known annual rate of criminal homicide is about 1.5. The world's total population is approximately 5 billion and 60,000 of those are known to be the victims of criminal homicide each year. Rates for different societies vary greatly.[1] Some Latin and South American countries have rates approaching 20 or even 30, notably Nicaragua, Colombia, Mexico, and Guatemala. The United States rate of 8.3, while lower than those, is decidedly high. At the opposite extreme, Western European countries often have low rates, 1.0 or less.

This is especially true of the Scandinavian countries, England and Wales, and France.

Generally, those countries experiencing fast change and much turmoil, either because they are in the throes of becoming industrialized or for other reasons, have high rates of criminal homicide. Those long industrialized and with little turmoil tend to have low rates. The United States, with a high rate, is an exception in that we have been highly industrialized for a relatively long period. On the other hand, we are a young country with a great diversification of cultural backgrounds among our people, much social change, and a history of intermittent turmoil.

Research on small, nonliterate, and nonindustrialized societies around the globe is of much value. These societies, of course, do not calculate rates of criminal homicide; rates are arrived at by researchers on the basis of anthropologists' reports. An analysis by one of the present authors of 40 such societies found that those which stress unreciprocating interpersonal relationships, severe competition, individuality, and conflict in everyday life tend to have high rates of criminal homicide.[2] Those which emphasize highly reciprocating relationships, cooperation, and the group over the individual, and which devalue conflict are likely to have low rates. Reciprocity refers to the extent to which cultural customs of the society are such that individuals tend to facilitate the satisfaction of each other's needs and role demands. Unreciprocity refers to patterns of mutual blockage of those needs and demands. Of the 20 societies characterized by higher levels of reciprocity, 14 had homicide rates below the median level. And of the 20 societies characterized by low reciprocity and by unreciprocity, 13 had homicide rates above the median.

Thus everything considered, the findings for literate and nonliterate societies point to common themes: conflict, turmoil, and unreciprocity are conditions associated with higher incidences of homicide, while cooperation, absence of turmoil, and reciprocity are associated with lower incidences. The question of why these associations exist is discussed later in this chapter.

Rates in the United States

For many decades the rate of criminal homicide in the United States has been high in relation to the average world rate. During the latter half of the 1960s and first half of the 1970s, there was an especially sharp rise in homicides in the United States.[3] In 1964 the rate was 4.8; by 1974 it had more than doubled and was at a very high level, 9.8. It remained relatively steady until 1980, when a decrease occurred. In 1987 the homicide rate was 8.3.

New England has long been the region of the United States with the lowest rate of criminal homicide and remains so. In 1987, the rate for the six New England states combined was 3.4. The lowest of these were Maine and Vermont with rates of 2.5 and 2.7, respectively. However, a rate of 1.5 made North Dakota the lowest state in the entire United States. The southern states have consistently shown high rates. The west south central states of Arkansas, Louisiana, Oklahoma, and Texas composed the region with the highest rate in 1987. Their combined rate was 10.7, over three times that of New England. Michigan has the highest rate of 12.2 in the United States. The standard metropolitan areas with the highest homicide rates are typically in the South. Again, one sees the close relationship between social conflict and homicide. New England has been relatively free of conflict while the South has long experienced it, especially in the form of deep-seated racial antagonisms.

Rates for criminal homicide are highest in our largest cities and fall quite regularly as city size decreases. The average rate for cities with over 250,000 population was 20.4 in 1987. The smaller cities, those under 10,000 population, showed the lowest rates; their rates averaged 3.3. Thus rates for the largest cities were over six times as great as rates for the smallest cities. Suburban areas tend to have rates higher than those of the smallest cities yet relatively low in relation to the country as a whole; in 1987 the average rate for the suburbs was 6.0. Distinctly rural areas were somewhat lower, with an average of 5.7. Overall, one can conclude that our highest homicide rates tend to be found in those places, the largest cities, which are likely to have experienced the most intense racial, class, and political conflicts in recent times.

Austin Porterfield and other researchers conducted an interesting analysis of homicide in relation to the degree to which states and cities in the United States were characterized by "social well-being."[4] They devised an index of social well-being which was based on the extents to which health, educational, and other social services were provided by the government. Their findings showed a clear tendency for criminal homicide and social well-being to vary inversely, that is, the lower the social well-being (the less the social services) of a state or city, the higher the rate of criminal homicide was likely to be.

AGE, SEX, AND RACE

Age and Sex of Offenders

Age and sex of offenders are critical factors in the analysis of criminal homicide. Two highly significant findings are true for almost all societies: (1) homicide is committed primarily by young adults who are males; (2) regarding age, generally speaking, rates are very low for children, rise steadily over the teenage years, reach a high in the late twenties, and then decline steadily as age increases.[5]

As for sex of offenders, typically about 80 percent of criminal homicide is committed by males.[6] There are, of course, variations from one society to another. In some societies, homicides among females are exceedingly rare. In others, females commit a third or more of all criminal homicides. Seldom, if ever, do female rates exceed male rates.

These generalizations apply to nonliterate as well as literate societies, and they are applicable in the United States where four-fifths of the murders and first-degree manslaughters are committed by males and where rates by age group are highest in the 18- to 24-year range.[7]

Offenders' Race, Age, and Sex Combined

Many data are available concerning differences in criminal homicide arrest rates for blacks and whites in the United States. In recent decades, rates for each race have been quite stable. Those for blacks are approximately 12 times those for whites. About 52 percent of those arrested for criminal homicide in the United States are black, while blacks make up 12 percent of our total population. Forty-six percent of those arrested are whites; they constitute 85 percent of the population.[8]

Because homicide is an intensely intraracial crime, there is disproportionate involvement of blacks as both offenders and victims. Homicide ranks as the fifth leading cause of death among black Americans overall and the leading cause among blacks 15–34.[9] Black males between 20 and 24 are the single most likely group to commit murder or to be murdered in the United States.[10]

In many ways it is young adults who are most likely to experience awareness of failure to succeed in competition for success goals. Even if the given society prescribes that only later in life will success goals actually be obtained, it is usually apparent to the individual by age 35 whether this will come to pass. And it is likely to be the young adult males rather than females who are most affected in this way. Moreover, in the United States, it is young adult blacks, especially males, far more often than whites, who find themselves staring at personal failure to achieve in the competitive race for success goals of money, materials goods, prestige, and power. To a lesser yet significant extent, this is also true of young adult black females who often find themselves with one or more children to rear and no husband to provide for them. Like their black male counterparts, these young women have great difficulty in achieving sufficient income to support their children and themselves.[11]

Thus the highest criminal homicide rates are found among those who are located at points of greatest strain in the social system, who most often lose out in competition both for basic necessities and for success goals, and who therefore experience the greatest sense of relative deprivation.

Age, Sex, and Race of Victims

Age, sex, and race patterns of victims of criminal homicide are similar to those of offenders, although there are certain exceptions. Victims are typically a few years older than offenders. Infants under 1 year of age have a fairly high rate of victimization. Rates then drop off sharply for older children, begin to rise, reach a peak in the mid-twenties and early thirties, and then steadily decline. For example, most recently in the United States, the victimization rate for all ages combined was 8.8. For infants under 1 year the rate was 5.2. The group with the lowest rate was those aged 5–9 years, where the rate was 0.8. Rates then increased to a high of 19.5 among those aged 25–29 and then gradually declines to 5.8 for those aged 60 and over.[12]

In most societies male victimization rates exceed female rates by several times, as do offender rates. In the united States, for example, the probability of a male being murdered in his lifetime is 1 in 100, while the probability of a female being victimized is 1 in 323.

Being nonwhite in the United States markedly increases an individual's vulnerability to murder. Overall nonwhites are more than five times more prone to homicidal death than are whites. Nonwhite males have the highest risk of victimization: 1 in 28 nonwhite males will be murdered. That is, nonwhite males are almost six times more likely to be murdered than white males and 16 times more so than white females, the lowest risk for homicide (Table 1).

THE FAMILY BACKGROUNDS OF OFFENDERS

Frustrations

Homicide offenders show a strong tendency to have developed in family settings that were exceedingly frustrating to them and, to a lesser degree, to other family members. Numerous studies have focused on early physical and psychological frustrations of offenders and found them to be severe.[13]

One of the authors conducted an intensive analysis of the childhood and adolescent experiences of 51 homicidal offenders in New England.[14] their experiences were compared with those of their nearest-age brothers, who served as a control group. During infancy,

TABLE 1. Probability of Lifetime Murder
Victimization in the United States[a]

Classification	Probability of lifetime murder victimization
U.S. total	1 out of 153
Male	1 out of 100
Female	1 out of 323
White total	1 out of 240
Male	1 out of 164
Female	1 out of 450
Nonwhite total	1 out of 47
Male	1 out of 28
Female	1 out of 117

[a] Federal Bureau of Investigation, Uniform Crime Report, U.S. Government Printing Office, 1982, p. 339.

childhood, and adolescence, offenders experienced 9.2 severely traumatic incidents of physical or psychological frustration as compared to 4.2 for their nonhomicidal control brothers. These incidents ranged from birth traumas to physical illnesses and accidents to extremely severe beatings to rejection by others. Most took place within the home and were a consequence of the actions of other family members toward the offender-to-be. The most pertinent results were summarized as follows:

Interaction between the New England offenders as children and their mothers was characterized by continual exchanges of implicit or explicit aggression. Difficulties and antagonisms between them were greater in number and intensity than they were between mothers and control brothers. As noted, the offenders' births were often traumatic; they were traumatic for the mother as well as the infant. In the early months of the offenders' lives, mothers and children were both often ill. The infants did not eat properly. The mothers were not strong enough to care for the newborn and yet there was no one else to do so. The children's illnesses irritated the mothers and the mothers' illnesses resulted in irritation for the children. A spiraling interplay of unreciprocity was set in motion between mother and child. The mother tended to blame the child. She would withdraw emotionally as a means of punishment. Crying, she would lock herself in her room and remain there for hours or in some cases days. The child would retaliate at a later point with unruly behavior. The mother would tend to ignore the child when danger threatened. Many of the aforementioned accidents that befell the children were in part the result of "negligence" by the mother. Mothers put the children's carriages at the tops of stairs where they would topple down. Mothers left the children unattended with knives and matches.[15]

Socialization

Criminal offenders in general have histories of inadequate early socialization within the family, that is, they have neither been taught nor learned the socially acceptable customs and values of their society. Family socialization of homicidal offenders tends to have been more adequate than that of criminal offenders generally in the sense that homicidal offenders have been exposed to and learned acceptable behavior to a considerable degree. However, the socialization process has often been unduly harsh. Beatings for failure to comply are common. Mothers of homicidal offenders tend to use extreme emotional deprivation to force conformity from their children. A fairly common example is refusal by the mother to communicate with the offender-to-be for a day or more at a time because of minor infractions. Results of the New England study mentioned earlier showed a strong tendency for the early toilet and sexual training of the homicidal offenders by their mothers to be excessively severe and abrupt, more so than for the control subjects, the offenders' nearest-age brothers.[16]

The evidence is especially conclusive on one important dimension of early socialization in the family, that concerning physical aggression. Individuals who commit murder and often violent crimes are decidedly more likely than other persons to have witnessed physical aggression in childhood.[17] Frequently, that aggression has been directed at them; in any case, they have learned to view it as customary. The aggression that potential homicidal offenders witness in their early years may be a result of the institutionalization of violence in their neighborhoods, that is, of customs and values for committing violence expressed outside the family as well as within. In other instances, community customs and values which advocate violence may be relatively absent and yet the immediate family environment is one where physically violent behavior patterns are common.

Of considerable importance is a related finding that homicidal offenders are themselves likely to have histories of sporadic outbursts of violent behavior in childhood and adolescence.[18] Cutting up a cat at age 7, banging another child's head on the pavement at 10, dropping rocks on passersby below at age 14 are examples of such outbursts. Between these periodic outbursts of aggression, homicidal offenders are likely as children to be quiet and somewhat withdrawn and to conform more or less closely to acceptable standards. This alternation between conformity and aggressive deviance is a cardinal signal which, together with other early life characteristics, can be used as an indicator of future homicidal behavior.

Individuals who become homicidal offenders are likely to have had few if any socially adequate sex role models in childhood. Fathers of male homicidal offenders are frequently absent from the home entirely or for prolonged periods.[19] The fathers of the male offenders in the New England study, however, were more often than not regularly present in the home when the offenders were children. But the fathers tended to be very passive figures, whereas the mothers were extremely dominant. A cross-cultural study of nonliterate societies by Bacon, Child, and Barry found that aggressive crime was positively associated with young boys' lack of opportunities to identify with father figures.[20] Evidence regarding female homicidal offenders is less clear. It does tend to indicate that socially acceptable female role models in the family were lacking. And both mothers and fathers of female offenders appear likely to have been harsh, aggressive persons.

There is therefore considerable evidence to suggest that homicidal offenders experienced much frustration and inadequate socialization to socially acceptable norms at an early age, especially in regard to the manifestation of aggression and to sex roles.

EDUCATION, OCCUPATION, AND SOCIAL CLASS OF OFFENDERS

Schooling and Work

Educational levels of criminal homicidal offenders are on the average low. In the New England study of 51 offenders, 57 percent had not gone beyond the eighth grade.[21] Six percent had graduated from high school, and none had attended college. In general, males of a comparable age in New England had significantly more education, having completed 10 years of school on the average. Most of the evidence points to homicidal offenders as being of average intelligence. Generally their grades in school were satisfactory. They are likely, however, to have suffered a good deal of rejection by classmates and teachers. They have often been seen by others in the school setting as withdrawn, overly quiet, and occasionally, but not as a rule, disruptive.[22]

Study after study shows that homicidal offenders, whether white or black or male or female, tend to be unemployed or have records of unemployment and frequent job changing.[23] The occupational positions they have held are likely to be ones of low prestige: unskilled and semiskilled jobs that pay poorly. A study by Swigert and Farrell of 444 homicide defendants showed that only 3.6 percent were professionals, managers, proprietors, or administrative personnel; 4.8 percent were clerical workers; 27.1 percent were skilled or semiskilled laborers; 29.9 percent were unskilled laborers; and 34.7 percent were public assistance recipients.[24] Almost two-thirds of the homicide defendants were, then, unskilled workers or on welfare.

Social Class Standing

Most analyses of social class or prestige standing employ a five-class system: upper, upper middle, lower middle, upper lower, and lower lower. An individual's standing in the social class hierarchy is based on his or her level of education, on occupational prestige, and also on income and the prestige of his or her area within the community. Here, again, research findings are consistent; homicidal offenders show a strong tendency to come from the social classes of low prestige. In the New England study, offenders were more than twice as likely as other persons to come from the lowest class in a five-class system. They were about one-fourth as likely as others to come from one of the highest three classes. In a study of homicide in Fort Worth, Texas, Porterfield found that the average annual homicide rates were four times greater for those in the lower class than for those in the upper class.[25] At the same time, offenders and the families in which they grew up are likely to have had strong motivations to rise in the social class system. These upward mobility strivings have in most instances been totally blocked.

Homicidal offenders, then, have had little success in gaining education, occupational prestige, money, or social class standing. In the United States, they are among the most extreme losers in a social system which placed great emphasis on the attainment of these goals.

Studies of middle- and upper-class homicide are rarely carried out. However, Green and Wakefield analyzed 119 such cases reported in the *New York Times* over a 20-year period. Premeditated killing, often for financial gain, is far more common in murders committed by middle- and upper-class offenders than those in the lower classes. Green and Wakefield summarize their study in eight points[26]:

1. The upper-class killer is a white male over 30 years old. In the lower class, he is a black male under 30.
2. There are no ascertainable cases of victim-precipitated upper-class homicide compared to the one-fifth to one-third such cases in lower-class homicides.
3. Intrafamilial homicides predominate in the upper-class cases, occurring three times as often as in the lower-class cases (73%: 22.9–24.7%).
4. Homicide followed by suicide accounts for 27% of upper-class cases but only 0.8%–9% of lower-class cases.
5. The upper-class method of killing is seldom stabbing. It often involves shooting, though not proportionately more frequently than the lower-class offenders in studies with southern locales.
6. Alcoholic consumption is rarely related to upper-class homicide. Over one-half of the lower-class homicides are alcohol-related.

7. Upper-class homicides, like lower-class homicides, take place during the evening hours, 8 P.M. to 1:59 A.M.; however, unlike lower-class homicides, upper-class cases follow no diurnal pattern.
8. Upper-class killings are significantly more likely to occur at the victim's home than those in the lower-class cases.

PERSONALITY FACTORS

Identity

Personal identity is in some ways an ambiguous concept. What it connotes in one cultural setting can be far different in another. Yet the concept is useful as an important psychological factor when described adequately. Erik Erikson speaks of identity as "a subjective sense of an invigorating sameness and continuity" and as "an active tension . . . which furthermore must create a challenge 'without guarantee' rather than one dissipated by a clamor for certainty."[27] Identity is a sense of the self as a unique, recognizable creature who is nonetheless forever changing. Identity is knowing who you are.

It is understandable that homicidal offenders are likely to suffer from a weak, uncertain, fragmented personal identity. Physically and psychologically frustrated in the extreme as children, and with poor sex-role models, potential offenders become failures in adolescence and early adulthood in their strivings for prestige, material goods, and power. They are likely to see themselves as socially impotent outsiders and to have little self-esteem and sense of security. They often tend to see others as the source of their frustrations. When the actions of others seem to be destructive of whatever fragile identity they possess, they may use the violently aggressive behavior which they witnessed as children. The homicidal act is not infrequently one of protecting the self, even if from a self-exaggerated sense of danger. The violent act does give the offender a momentary sense of great power, of controlling rather than being controlled by the environment, and it does provide a sense of self which is both transitory and enduring. For the homicidal offender is always a homicidal offender and will very likely be seen as such by others because of adjudication and imprisonment. Even if these are escaped, the offender is likely to see himself or herself in this way throughout life. Thus is an identity, albeit a negative identity, forged and perpetuated.

Psychological Disorders

Evidence regarding the relationships between psychological disorders and criminal homicide is unclear. There is some tendency for homicide to be associated with two forms of psychosis: manic-depression and paranoia. However, the vast majority of persons with these disorders are not homicidal or otherwise physically violent. Statistics on the proportions of homicidal offenders who are judged legally insane are, of course, available. But legal insanity is a much narrower concept than psychosis. In any case, the percentage of homicidal offenders who have been found to be legally insane varies considerably from one society to another. In the United States, the figure is about 3 percent whereas in England it is 40 percent.[28] Differences in legal definitions of insanity account for some of the variation.

McGurk's[29] study of ostensibly normal homicidal offenders in England shows two broad types of personality disorders: the undercontrolled and the overcontrolled. The undercontrolled person tends to respond to frustration in an aggressive, unrestrained manner. The overcontrolled person inhibits the expression of aggression and develops alternative ways of dealing with frustration. Evidence of mental illness is less common among the overcontrolled than undercontrolled offenders. The aggressiveness of the undercontrolled is associated with an underlying psychiatric disorder, e.g., paranoia or psychopathic personality.

SITUATIONAL VARIABLES

Victim–Offender Relationships

Victims tend to be several years older than their killers. Males are the victims about three-quarters of the time in the United States and in many other countries. Offenders are very likely to kill those who are members of their own castes and social class groups. In the United States, about 88 percent of white victims are murdered by whites and 95 percent of black victims are murdered by blacks. Universally, victims and offenders are likely to be relatives, friends, or acquaintances rather than strangers. In 16.5 percent of the criminal homicides in the United States during 1987, victims and offenders were known to be relatives; in 40.4 percent they were friends, neighbors, or acquaintances; and in only 13.2 percent were they strangers. In the remaining 29.6 percent, the relationship was unknown. In about half of the cases where victim and offender were related—that is, in 7.9 percent of the homicides—offenders killed their spouses.[30] In some societies, the proportions of homicides that involve offenders and victims who are members of the same family are considerably higher than in the United States. For England and Wales, as an example, the percentage is about 40.[31] Females are much more likely to be killed by their husbands than males by their wives. In a five-year study in Philadelphia, Wolfgang found that 41 percent of all murdered women were killed by their husbands, while only 11 percent of the men killed were murdered by their wives.[32]

Black victims are more likely to know their assailants than are white victims. Two-thirds of black female victims and 58 percent of black male victims are at least acquainted with their killers compared to 56 percent of white females and 46 percent of white male victims. Females, either black or white, are twice as likely to be victimized by a family member as their male counterparts.[33]

Victim precipitation refers to the extent to which the potential victim in a criminal homicide contributes to his or her own death. The Wolfgang study of homicide in Philadelphia found that in 26 percent of 588 cases the victim made a physical attack on the offender just prior to the killing.[34] One of the present authors analyzed homicidal data concerning 29 nonliterate societies.[35] Victim precipitation was defined as the victim making the first aggressive move during the final encounter with the offender of a physical, gestural, or oral nature. This definition was broader than that used in the Wolfgang study. The central finding was that victim precipitation occurred in more than half the murders 15 of the 29 societies.

In any event, the evidence regarding victims and offenders makes it abundantly clear that homicide is seldom an impersonal act. Far more often than not, homicide is the end result of a period of altercation between victim and offender, frequently a longstanding period of upwardly spiraling aggression. The frustrations of two lifetimes are acted out aggressively in the interpersonal relationship. Eventually arguing and fighting escalate to lethal action.

Whether homicide is to a greater or lesser degree culturally patterned or individualistic deviance varies greatly with the setting. In a few countries, such as Colombia, homicide is decidedly culturally patterned and therefore quite highly institutionalized. This is also the case in some locales in the United States, most notably some of the black urban ghettos of the North and some states in the deep South. More generally, however, homicide is a somewhat individualistic act carried out by more or less ordinary people who find themselves under severe stress with which they cannot cope. At the same time, homicide can rarely be said to be innovative. In the vast majority of cases it is mundane, notwithstanding its lethality.

Places and Times

The places and times at which criminal homicide occur are in good measure socioculturally determined. Criminal homicide occurs most frequently in a private residence and next most frequently on the street. As expected, homicide within the family takes place at home, whereas stranger killings typically occur on the street. Acquaintances are more likely to victimize one another in public places, and strangers are the most likely to do so.

Murder is a phenomenon of darkness to a considerable extent. In most societies it predominates during the night and predawn morning hours. Fifty percent of homicide in the United States is committed between 8:00 P.M. and 2:00 A.M. In Western countries, rates tend to be highest on weekends, particularly the first hours of Sunday. Pokorny found in Houston that 61 percent of the homicides occurred during three days of the week: Friday, Saturday, and Sunday. Wolfgang indicated that 66 percent of Philadelphia homicides took place during those days.[36] Interpersonal conflicts, arguments, and brawls, which often immediately precede homicide, are especially prevalent during late Friday and Saturday. A further interesting finding regarding time, but one for which there is no compelling explanation, is that in societies with distinct seasonal variations in climate, homicide rates tend, by a slight margin, to be highest in summer and, also by a slight margin, lowest in winter.

Weapons and Alcohol

Many criminologists hold, and with considerable evidence, that criminal homicide offenders use whatever weapons are at hand and familiar to them.[37] In Western, industrialized societies, firearms tend to be the usual weapons for males whereas household knives are the usual weapons for females. In 1987 in the United States, 59 percent of criminal homicides were committed using firearms. Cutting and stabbing accounted for 20.3 percent of the homicides; hands, fists, feet for 6.5 percent; and clubs, poison, and other means for the remaining 6.0 percent.[38] Black victims (77 percent) are more likely to be shot than are white victims (60 percent).[39] In nonliterate societies, hunting weapons—knives, clubs, bows and arrows, spears—are commonly used, although sticks, bare hands, or feet are not unusual.[40]

Advocates of gun control often argue that reducing access to firearms will reduce the homicide rate in the United States.[41] This is certainly problematic. We have high rates for violent crimes of various kinds, whether or not firearms are employed, and firearms are so widely available that extraordinarily powerful legal controls would have to be instituted if the supply were to be significantly reduced. It seems fair to conclude that in a society characterized by physical violence, lethal weapons of one kind or another are likely to be available unless basic social change which leads to a reduction of violent tendencies comes about. In any event, if stricter gun control laws were instituted, it would be of much interest to see what the effect would be, if any, on homicide rates.

It has been commonly found that alcohol was present in both homicidal offenders and victims shortly after the crime occurred. Wolfgang's findings in the Philadelphia study are fairly representative of others: his results showed that alcohol was present in offenders in 54 percent of the cases; in victims in 53 percent of the cases; and in both offenders and victims 44 percent of the time.[42] Victims of homicide in southern cities are more likely to have been drinking than victims in cities elsewhere in the United States. [43] In a recent study in Los Angeles, 50.3 percent of all homicide victims were drinking at the time of their death. Drinking is twice as common among male than female victims. However, the percentage of victims under the age of 15 (13.6 percent) and over 64 (22.3 percent) who were drinking when murdered is markedly less.[44]

It is difficult to make comparisons with the general population. One would need to know whether individuals in other types of situations had been drinking. In any case, a statement by the anthropologist Bohannan about alcohol and homicide perhaps best summarizes the matter: "It would seem . . . to be a catalytic agent rather than as a cause that alcohol appears in situations of homicide."[45]

A Situational Profile

In summary, the following tendencies are common:

- Both offenders and victims are likely to be males, and offenders are somewhat younger than victims.
- Each is likely to be a friend, acquaintance, or relative of the other.
- More often than not, offender or victim was drinking alcohol just prior to the homicide.
- The victim may well have precipitated the lethal incident either physically or psychologically; in any case, an altercation of one kind or another is the most likely motive from an official point of view in the United States.
- The most usual places of occurrence are homes and public thoroughfares.
- In Western societies, homicide is most common during hours of darkness on weekends.
- Firearms are the most usual homicidal weapons in the United States and knives the second most usual.

CULTURAL SUPPORT EXPLANATIONS

Differential Association and Reaction Formation

The various major bodies of theory concerning deviance which were set forth in detail in Chapter 2 will be recapitulated and their relevance to criminal homicide assessed. Cultural support theories stress the degree to which customs and values conducive to deviance are learned and socially transmitted from one individual to another. Sutherland's differential association theory emphasized the extent to which a person's association with those who set forth the law- and rule-violating criminal subculture outweigh associations with those who set forth the law- and rule-following acceptable culture.[46] Cohen employed the concept of reaction formation to explain how the criminal subculture postulated by Sutherland arose.[47] Lower-class males, Cohen held, who are blocked from achieving upper-middle-class success goals behave in ways diametrically opposed to the values of that class. Thus they develop criminal customs and values.

The Sutherland and Cohen approaches are meant to apply to crime and delinquency in general, although they are also intended to embrace such particular forms as homicide. Sutherland's differential association theory is not especially applicable to homicide for a very fundamental reason: most homicidal offenders have not had extensive contact with those who act out the general criminal subculture. Cohen's reaction formation theory has relevance to homicide in a limited sense: those who commit homicide are likely to have aspired to upper-middle-class success goals at some previous time and to have been severely frustrated in their attempts to achieve them. They may have had a reaction formation to that which they were denied. But there is little evidence that they have gone on to develop and act out the customs and values of a generalized criminal or delinquent subculture.

Illegitimate Opportunity and Subcultures of Violence

The Cloward and Ohlin and the Wolfgang and Ferracuti approaches, also basically cultural support theories, have greater applicability to criminal homicide. The core of the Cloward and Ohlin illegitimate opportunity structure thesis is that individuals who cannot gain access to legitimate opportunity structures for success seek entrance to illegitimate structures for theft, conflict or violence, or retreat, the latter being largely drug usage.[48] In order actually to achieve entrance to such structures, they must meet recruitment criteria and properly learn the requisite roles. Both teenage gang violence in which homicide occurs and professional killings can often be explained on the basis of participation in a conflict or violent opportunity structure. Yet in the United States and many other countries, the proportion of homicides which fits these categories is low. Most homicides is neither a group nor a professional act. Rather it is individualistic deviance which is a result of accelerating hostility between two persons, offender and victim.

The Wolfgang and Ferracuti formulation, while possessing a certain explanatory power, is also of limited utility.[49] Those authors hold that especially where relative deprivation for economic goals is great, subcultures of violence develop. These are bodies of customs and values which advocate violence as a response to frustrating conditions. They are learned and socially transmitted as are ordinary, acceptable customs and values. In the United States, such subcultures are thought to be especially well formed in the black ghettos of our urban core areas. Put simply, this approach is valid to the extent that in residential areas where homicide rates are particularly high, subcultures of violence are likely to come about, be learned, and be perpetuated. The reasoning behind the formulation is circular in the sense that much individual violence is required to generate a subculture of violence and a subculture of violence can lead through learning to individual violence. Also, why some subcultures of violence give rise to homicide, as opposed to lesser forms of violence, and others do not is unclear. In any case homicide in this and other countries is not necessarily committed by individuals immersed in, and with deep commitments to, a subculture of violence. Rather, much homicide is carried out by persons who have little exposure either to a subculture of violence or to a more general subculture of crime. That is, many offenders, while they have typically experienced severe relative deprivation regarding success goals, have not necessarily interacted in their lifetimes with others who manifest violent behavior with one significant exception: during their early lives, other members of their families often tended to be physically aggressive. But that does not at all necessarily imply a well-rooted, pervasive subculture of violence in the surrounding community. It does suggest in many instances, however, an at least partially formed, *familial* subculture of violence.

The subculture of violence thesis has been advanced to account for the disproportionately high rates of homicide in the southern states. The tradition of violence in the South lead Hackney[50] to view the 11 original confederate states as a distinct region of the country. This region is marked by a sense of powerlessness in the face of persecution from the outside. A siege mentality develops which gives rise to the willingness to react violently to threats to one's family, property, or honor.

Gastil[51] also contends that the South comprises a "regional culture of violence." In the South there is a tradition of tolerance for lethal aggression. These norms and values related to violence, Gastil agrees, are transmitted from one generation to the next in the South. Gastil also proposed that these patterns of violence were disseminated to other parts of the country with southern emigration.

Loftin and Hill[52] argue that homicide rates are not explained by the presence of a violent subculture but by the condition of structural poverty. They constructed a structural poverty index from the following variables: infant mortality rates, percentage of persons 25 and over with less than five years of school, percentage of the population who are illiterate, percentage of families with an income of under $1000, Armed Forces Mental Test failures, and percentage of children living with one parent. The structural poverty index is found to successfully predict homicide rates across the United States.

More recently, Blau and Blau[53] reported that economic inequality or a situation of relative deprivation rather than absolute poverty provides a better explanation for differences in homicide rates. Messner,[54] however, found that in 204 Standard Metropolitan Statistical Areas the racial composition of the population and regional location influence homicide rates more so than economic indicators.

Corzine and colleagues[55] consider both measures of structural poverty and a subculture of violence in assessing variations in statewide homicide rates. They found that for states as a whole and for the white population overall homicide rates are affected by both poverty and subcultural considerations. Black homicide rates are not directly influenced by poverty.

The poverty/inequality subculture of violence debate is far from resolved. Most recent evidence suggests that a synthesis of these theoretical approaches may better explain variations in homicide rates in the United States.[56]

CONFLICT EXPLANATIONS

Culture Conflict

Culture conflict theorists such as Thorsten Sellin have argued that when individuals are exposed to severe conflicts between the customs and values of two cultures, subcultures, or roles, crime may result.[57] On the one hand, such conflict can cause confusion for individuals as to which of their acts constitutes crime since crime may be defined differently in different settings. On the other hand, the frustration that results from such ambiguity, if sufficiently severe, may generate aggressive crime. This approach may be applicable to homicide when in fact individuals move from one culture to another where certain forms of killing are seen as justifiable, noncriminal homicide in the original culture and as criminal homicide in the new culture. As an example, infidelity by a wife might be grounds for justifiable homicide by her husband against her or her lover in one culture and not in another. Certainly such cultural conflicts explain little criminal homicide in the United States at present although they may have been of greater relevance during the waves of migration from Europe to this country in earlier times.

Class Conflict

In a different vein, Lewis Coser suggested that it is the relative deprivation often brought about by social conflict that can lead to violent outbursts, homicidal and otherwise.[58] For example, social class conflict tends to result in some class groups being deprived of the prevailing cultural success goals (of money, prestige, power, etc.) at the expense of other class groups. It is the sense of relative deprivation, of injustice, rather than of absolute deprivation that kindles hostility and violence. If all are poor, there is less probability of violence than if some are poor and some are not and if there is a perception by the poor that others are not deprived because they are. As has been demonstrated, there is much evidence that in the United States, social class conflict and relative deprivation are powerful forces behind criminal homicide.

Walter Miller's formulation of lower-class culture in the United States as one where criminal and noncriminal customs are intertwined is fundamentally a conflict theory.[59] The higher classes are dominant in the society and so determine the overall cultural value system which stipulates acceptable, noncriminal behavior and criminal behavior. Lower- and higher-class behavior patterns are likely to vary from one another because of differentials in money, prestige, and power. Miller contends that the higher classes codify into law or criminal acts certain behaviors common to lower-class life, particularly physical violence and theft.

This approach is less applicable to criminal homicide than to other crimes of violence such as assault and rape and to theft crimes such as larceny and burglary. It is true that criminal homicide is more prevalent among lower than higher classes. Only a few would argue, however, that the higher classes have conspired to label most homicide as criminal for that reason. In most societies, there is agreement across social classes that criminal homicide is one of the most destructive and outlawed of human acts. Further, there is in Western countries little evidence that members of the higher classes who commit criminal homicide escape prosecution. There is some evidence, however, that because of greater resources, especially access to legal expertise, punishment may be less severe for those offenders in the higher classes than for others.

Political Conflict

Richard Quinney's approach stressed the social reality of crime.[60] While Quinney was not at odds with Miller's formulation, he emphasized the political aspect of social control as the basic explanation of crime. According to Quinney, the ruling classes wield their power to ensure that the criminal law is used to maintain domestic order, which means punishing the lower classes for violence or theft which might undermine the capitalist system. On the one hand, the powerful do oppress the unpowerful and this increases relative deprivation, which is in fact a force behind criminal homicide. In that sense, Quinney's "social reality" theory helps to explain homicide. On the other hand, far from using murder as a means of undermining the capitalist system, the poor tend to kill each other.

However, a further aspect of Quinney's social reality theory is that the powerful punish such crimes as murder by the powerless in order to distract attention from their own forms of deviance such as corrupt business practices. These can include polluting workplaces and the environment generally and producing defective products, such as automobiles—practices which may result in "murder" of innocent workers and other citizens and which go unpunished. It could be argued, then, that those who hold power commit a sophisticated form of lethal killing with impunity while those without power are punished for the more mundane transgressions of the laws regarding criminal homicide.

Power Theory

Alex Thio made a useful distinction between higher- and lower-consensus deviance.[61] Higher-consensus deviance is committed by the powerless. The powerful define it as negative, arrange to have it broadly recognized as negative through the mass media and to have it punished through the police, courts, and prisons. Lower-consensus deviance refers to the behaviors of the powerful which are exploitative of, and harmful to, others. Thus, Thio contends, the powerful arrange to keep their transgressions largely invisible, to have little social consensus about their negative quality, and to escape prosecution and punishment for carrying them out.

Thio's distinction between higher- and lower-consensus deviance is useful in regard to understanding homicide in much the same way as Quinney's formulation. It points to a category of behaviors sometimes perpetrated on society by those with prestige, influence, and money, that is, those with power, which forms what can be termed "hidden homicide." Deaths due to faulty and corrupt business and political practices constitute hidden homicide: the lung cancer deaths of those workers in highly polluted textile mills and asbestos plants, the deaths of children due to lethal toys, the deaths of drivers and passengers in ill-designed automobiles. This phenomenon is qualitatively somewhat different from criminal homicide, not necessarily less harmful to society but different. Hidden homicide is impersonal, tending to be institutionalized deviance, whereas criminal homicide is intensely personal, tending to be individualistic deviance. The latter, committed largely by the poor, is explained in part by oppression of them by the powerful. But it is also explained by a variety of other factors which lead to relative deprivation. Hidden homicide appears to be a result of "affluent relative deprivation" among the powerful, that is, it may be a response of individuals in business and political life to the competitive race for greater and greater money and power. Shortcuts to business profits and political success can breed lethal working conditions, the manufacture of lethal products, and the condoning of these by political aspirants who fear defeat.

SOCIAL INTEGRATION EXPLANATIONS

Anomie

Social integration and conflict theory are closely related. The social integration approach stresses the extent to which individuals share basic life values. The more they share values, the more they are integral components of the group. The less they share values, the more they are individualistic outsiders, unintegrated with the group. Durkheim termed this latter condition *anomie*.[62]

Social conflict often, although not always, contributes to a low level of shared values and thus to a low degree of social integration and a high level of anomie. An absence of shared values, that is, little social integration, and anomie are likely to lead to social conflict.

Robert Merton posited that anomie and low social integration would result to the extent that there was a disparity between the cultural goals of a society and the institutionalized means for achieving those goals.[63] When individuals learn to need and pursue cultural goals while being blocked from suitable institutionalized means, they become anomic and turn to other means, to various forms of deviance, including crime in general and criminal homicide. Here again the idea of relative deprivation can be seen as crucial. Socially structured thwarting of individuals' attempts to legitimately gain success goals leads to anomie, conflict, deviance, and in some instances homicide.

External Restraints

Andrew Henry and James Short emphasized three variables in their theory of homicide: external restraints, strength of the relational system, and status or prestige.[64] They predicted that homicide increases as (1) there is an increase in the strength of external restraints, that is, the extent to which individuals are required to conform to the demands and expectations of others; (2) there is an increase in the strength of the relational system or the degree to which individuals are involved in social, cathectic relations with others; and (3) the status (prestige) of individuals diminishes. The evidence supports the first and last of these. Those who commit homicide are likely to be so located in the social structure that external restraints on them are strong, where others of greater prestige and power make demands that they conform to expectations that they be lower-class persons who achieve few success goals. On the other hand, the evidence does not seem to support the Henry and Short contentions that homicidal offenders tend to be found at points in the social structure where relational systems are strong. Quite the opposite, they are likely to have histories of anomic separation from others and, as outsiders, they are seldom involved in ongoing close, cathectic social relationships with others. Their often close if contentious relationships with their victims are significant exceptions.

Reciprocity

Jacqueline and Murray Straus conducted research on homicide and suicide in Ceylon in the 1950s.[65] They placed particular emphasis on the extent to which a society or group within it is loosely or closely structured. They defined structuring in terms of reciprocal rights and duties: the more those rights and duties are stressed and enforced, the more closely structured is the group. In a closely structured group, the emphasis on reciprocity tends to preclude violence toward others. The more loosely structured a group is, the less such restraints operate, however, and the greater the likelihood of homicide as a response to frustration. This formulation fits the facts about criminal homicide quite well, for homicidal offenders tend not to come from points in the social structure where *reciprocal* rights and duties are common, but rather where unreciprocal, one-way restraints on them are stressed and attempts at enforcement made by others.

SOCIETAL REACTION THEORY

Societal reactionists hold that society, through its agents of social control, responds to problems of deviance in ways that beget the very deviant acts it is ostensibly trying to reduce.[66] One important process here is labeling. When agents of social control or others label a person a deviant, often because of a minor transgression, a self-fulfilling prophecy may be set in motion. Others then expect the individual to be deviant. They tend to process him or her through agencies of control—the criminal justice system, for example—*as a deviant*. They tend to provide reward for compliance with the new label and punishment for resisting it. The individual must admit waywardness and seek corrective treatment. Thus he or she is induced to take on the role of deviant, to become a career or secondary deviant.

Societal reaction theory has been shown to have much relevance to a number of forms of deviance, including some juvenile delinquency and such crimes as shoplifting and forgery.[67] Regarding homicide, offenders are rarely recidivists, that is, they seldom kill again.[68] Thus there is seldom the issue of societal reaction to one homicidal transgression begetting another by the same person. The case can be made, however, that highly frustrated and socially rejected children and youths are labeled negatively as "peculiar" and the like, and that this causes them to be embittered. The case can also be made, and somewhat persuasively, that through the notoriety and fame accorded some homicidal offenders by the mass media (and this is a form of societal reaction), others are motivated to kill in order to achieve such publicity. There is no doubt, then, that societal reaction can play a part in inducing homicide through negative labeling of individuals in early life and the lure of attention by the mass media. Yet in general it is probably safe to say that societal reaction theory is less applicable to homicide than most of the other theoretical formulations which have been discussed.

MAJOR EXPLANATORY THEMES

Three related major themes regarding the causes of criminal homicide are (1) sociocultural conflicts, including competition for success goals; (2) severe deprivation both in the absolute and relative sense; and (3) anomie. Societal reaction in the forms of negative labeling of individuals in early life and of the compelling nature of mass media attention to homicide are lesser factors.

Anomie, that is, low integration of individuals into groups, and deprivation, especially as a result of failure in the competitive race for success goals, reinforce each other: Resentment over the frustration of relative deprivation drives individuals away from the group and anomie reduces the probability of success in competition. Anomic, deprived individuals, being relatively powerless social outsiders, are especially susceptible to the long-range effects of negative labeling and to the lure of notoriety afforded by the mass media.

The more extreme are conditions of conflict, deprivation, and anomie in the experience of given individuals, the greater is the probability of homicide by those individuals. The more widespread are those conditions in the residential area of a group, the more they generate subcultures of violence as a response to frustration.

SUMMARY

Criminal homicide is the intentional killing of another human being that is neither in the line of culturally sanctioned duty nor in self-defense. Criminal homicide is usually classified as either murder in the first or second degree or manslaughter in the first or second degree. The first three of those usually involve malice and premeditation. Malice refers to the degree of violence or sadism involved in the killing; premeditation concerns the extent to which the act was deliberately planned and carried out. Typically, the more malice or premeditation present, the higher the degree of criminal homicide.

About 1.5 of every 100,000 persons in the world are murdered each year. Rapid sociopolitical and technological changes have been linked to high rates of violent crime; static societies tend to produce low levels of violence. Despite some decline in recent years, the criminal homicide rate in the United States remains high. Within the United States, murder rates are high in the South and West and low in New England. Murder rates are also highest in the largest urban centers and lowest in affluent suburbs.

In the United States, black homicide rates are several times greater than white rates. The typical homicide offender is a black male in his late twenties. His victim is a somewhat older black male. It is the young black who experiences the greatest strain in the social system, who most often loses out in competition both for basic necessities and for success goals, and who therefore suffers the greatest sense of relative deprivation.

Studies of the early socialization of homicidal offenders show that they tend to experience significantly more physical, psychological, and social frustration than individuals in general. A traumatic birth is typically followed by negligence and rejection by the mother. Physical and psychological abuse are common. Fathers, either absent from the home or withdrawn from the child, serve as poor sex-role models. Homicidal offenders tend to have done poorly in school and occupy low-paying jobs or are unemployed. Early frustrations are followed by repeated socioeconomic deprivations.

Murder usually occurs between persons of the same sex, race, and social class. Victims tend to be older than their assailants. Offenders and victims are most often relatives, friends, or at least acquaintances; only infrequently are they strangers. Slightly over one-quarter of the time victims precipitated their own deaths by first using physical force against their eventual murderers. Murders tend to occur at home, usually in the bedroom or kitchen, at night, and on the weekend. A handgun is the usual weapon, and commonly both offender and victim were drinking just prior to the murder.

Explanations of criminal homicide involve three related themes: (1) sociocultural conflicts, including competition for success goals; (2) severe deprivation both in the absolute and relative sense; and (3) anomie, or low social integration. Societal reaction in the forms of negative labeling of individuals in early life and of mass media attention to homicide are lesser factors. There is a greater probability of homicide by those individuals who experience extreme conditions of conflict, deprivation, and anomie. Subcultures of violence are generated to the extent that such conditions are widespread in the residential area of a group. Those subcultures then facilitate the expression of lethal violence as a response to frustration.

Criminal homicide is the felony most often reported to the police, cleared by arrest, and for which the accused is found guilty by the court and sentenced. Execution as a method of punishment for murder has declined sharply in the United States. There is considerable evidence that the death penalty and long prison sentences do not deter others from committing homicide. Murderers are significantly less likely than other types of offenders to repeat their crime.

Murder typically results from severe frustration experienced early in life compounded by relative social and economic deprivations in adulthood. Prevention of homicide depends in part on the lessening of the disparity between those who compete successfully in society and those who do not. Provisions must be made for individuals who do not succeed to try again. Also, children and adolescents who have suffered severe frustrations and show a pattern of violent outbursts should be helped to learn alternative responses to frustration.

References

1. *Demographic Yearbook* (New York: United Nations, 1984).
2. Stuart Palmer, *The Violent Society* (New Haven, CT: College and University Press, 1972), p. 30.

3. Data in this and the following paragraph are from Federal Bureau of Investigation, *Crime in the United States* (Washington, D.C.: U.S. Government Printing Office, 1984; and 1988).
4. Austin L. Porterfield and Robert H. Talbert, with the assistance of Herbert R. Mundhenke, *Crime, Suicide, and Social Well-Being* (Fort Worth, TX: Leo Potishman Foundation, 1948).
5. Marvin E. Wolfgang and Franco Ferracuti, *The Subculture of Violence* (London: Tavistock, 1967); also, Federal Bureau of Investigation, *op. cit.*; also, Palmer, *op. cit.*
6. Palmer, *op. cit.*; also, Wolfgang and Ferracuti, *op. cit.*; also, Federal Bureau of Investigation, *op. cit.*; also, Marc Reidel, Margaret A. Zahn, and Lois F. Mock, *The Nature and Patterns of American Homicide* (Washington, D.C.: Government Printing Office, 1985).
7. Federal Bureau of Investigation, *op. cit.*
8. *Ibid.*, 1988, p. 12.
9. Centers for Disease Control, "Homicide Among Young Black Males: United States, 1970–1982," *Morbidity Mortality Weekly Report* 34(41):629–633, 1985.
10. M. F. X. Jeff, "Why Black-on-Black Homicide," *Urban League Review* 6:25–34, 1981.
11. William B. Harvey, "Homicide Among Young Black Adults: Life in the Subculture of Exasperation," in *Homicide Among Black Americans*, ed. Darnell F. Hawkins (Lanham, MD: University Press of America, 1986).
12. U.S. Public Health Service, *Vital Statistics of the U.S., 1980*, Vol. 2, Mortality, Part A. Washington, D.C.: U.S. Government Printing Office, 1985.
13. As examples, John L. Gillin, *The Wisconsin Prisoner* (Madison, WI: University of Wisconsin Press, 1946); also, Stuart Palmer, *A Study of Murder* (New York: Crowell, 1960).
14. Palmer, *The Violent Society*, p. 54.
15. Palmer, *A Study of Murder*, *op. cit.*
16. *Ibid.*
17. *Ibid.*
18. Wolfgang and Ferracuti, *op. cit.* For a closely related analysis, see Albert Bandura and Richard H. Walters, *Adolescent Aggression* (New York: Ronald Press, 1959).
19. Palmer, *A Study of Murder*.
20. Margaret K. Bacon, Irvin L. Child, and Herbert Barry III, "A Cross-Cultural Study of Correlates of Crime," *Journal of Abnormal and Social Psychology* 66(4):291–300, 1963.
21. Palmer, *A Study of Murder*.
22. *Ibid.*
23. Marvin E. Wolfgang and Margaret A. Zahn, "Homicide: Behavioral Aspects," in *Encyclopedia of Crime and Justice*, ed. S. H. Kadish (New York: Free Press, 1983).
24. Victoria L. Swigert and Ronald A. Farrell, "Patterns in Criminal Homicide: Theory and Research," in *Murder, Inequality, and the Law*, ed. Victoria L. Swigert and Ronald A. Farrell (Lexington, MA: Heath, 1975), p. 193.
25. Austin L. Porterfield, "Suicide and Crime in the Social Structure of an Urban Setting," *American Sociological Review* 17(3):341–349, 1952.
26. Edward Green and Russell P. Wakefield, "Patterns of Middle and Upper Class Homicide," *Journal of Criminal Law and Criminology* 70(2):172–181, 1979.
27. Erik Erikson, *Identity: Youth and Crisis* (New York: Norton, 1968), pp. 19–20.
28. Wolfgang and Ferracuti, *op. cit.*; also, Donald E. West, *Murder Followed by Suicide* (Cambridge, MA: Harvard University Press, 1965).
29. Barry J. McGurk, "Personality Types Among 'Normal' Homicides," *British Journal of Criminology*, 18(1):146–161, 1978.
30. Federal Bureau of Investigation, *Crime in the United States*, 1988.
31. British Home Office, *Criminal Statistics, England and Wales, 1975* (London: Her Majesty's Stationary Office, 1976).
32. Marvin E. Wolfgang, *Patterns in Criminal Homicide* (Philadelphia: University of Pennsylvania Press, 1958).
33. Patrick W. O. Carroll and James A. Mercy, "Patterns and Recent Trends in Black

Homicide," in *Homicide and Black America*, ed. Darnell F. Hawkins (Lanham, MD: University Press of America, 1986).

34. Marvin E. Wolfgang, *Patterns in Criminal Homicide*.
35. Stuart Palmer, "Characteristics of Homicide and Suicide Victims in Forty Non-Literate Societies," in *Victimology: A New Focus*, Vol. 4, ed. Israel Drappin and Emilio Viano (Lexington, MA: Heath, 1975), pp. 43–53.
36. Alex D. Pokorny, "Human Violence: A Comparison of Homicide, Aggravated Assault, Suicide, and Attempted Suicide," *Journal of Criminal Law, Criminology, and Police Science* 56(4):488–497, 1965; also, Wolfgang, *Patterns in Criminal Homicide*.
37. Wolfgang and Zahn, in S. H. Kadish (ed.), *Encyclopedia of Crime and Justice*.
38. Federal Bureau of Investigation, *Crime in the United States*, 1988.
39. Patrick W. O. Carroll and James A. Mercy, "Patterns and Recent Trends in Black Homicide," in Darnell F. Hawkins, ed. *Homicide in Black America*.
40. Palmer, "Characteristics of Homicide and Suicide Victims in Forty Non-Literate Societies."
41. Reidel, Zahn, and Mock, *op. cit.*; and J. H. Wright, P. H. Rossi, and K. Daly, *Under the Gun: Weapons, Crime and Violence in America* (New York: Aldine, 1983).
42. Wolfgang, *Patterns in Criminal Homicide*.
43. Reidel, Zahn, and Mock, *op. cit.*
44. University of California at Los Angeles, Centers for Disease Control: The Epidemiology of Homicide in the City of Los Angeles, 1970–1979, Department of Health and Human Services, Public Health Services, Centers for Disease Control, August 1985; also P. W. Haberman and M. M. Baden, *Alcohol, Other Drugs and Violent Death* (New York: Oxford University Press, 1978); also, Centers for Disease Control, "Alcohol and Violent Death: Erie County, New York, 1973–1983," *Morbidity Mortality Weekly Report* 33(17):226–227, 1984.
45. Paul Bohannan, ed., *African Homicide and Suicide* (Princeton, NJ: Princeton University Press, 1960), p. 249.
46. Edwin H. Sutherland and Donald R. Cressey, *Criminology*, 10th ed. (Philadelphia: Lippincott, 1978).
47. Albert Cohen, *Delinquent Boys* (Glencoe, IL: Free Press, 1954).
48. Richard A. Cloward and Lloyd E. Ohlin, *Delinquency and Opportunity* (Glencoe, IL: Free Press, 1960).
49. Wolfgang and Ferracuti, *op. cit.*
50. Sheldon Hackney, "Southern Violence," in *The History of Violence in America*, eds. Hugh Davis Graham and Ted Robert Gurr (New York: Bantam, 1969), pp. 505–527.
51. Raymond H. Gastil, "Homicide and a Regional Culture of Violence," *American Sociological Review* 36(3):412–427, 1971.
52. Colin Loftin and Robert H. Hill, "Regional Subculture and Homicide: An Examination of the Gastel-Hackney Thesis," *American Sociological Review* 39(5):714–724, 1974.
53. Judith H. Blau and Peter Blau, "The Costs of Inequality: Metropolitan Structure and Violent Crime," *American Sociological Review* 47(1):114–129, 1982.
54. Steven F. Messner, "Poverty, Inequality, and the Urban Homicide Rate," *Criminology* 20(1):103–114, 1982; also, Steven S. Messner, "Regional Differences in the Economic Correlates of the Urban Homicide Rate," *Criminology* 21(4):477–488, 1983.
55. L. Huff-Corzine, Jay Corzine, and D. Moore, "Southern Exposure: Deciphering the South's Influence on Homicide Rates," *Social Forces* 64(4):906–924, 1986.
56. For a reexamination of Blau and Blau and Messner, see Kirk Williams, "Economic Sources of Homicide: Re-estimating the Effects of Poverty and Inequality," *American Sociological Review* 49(2):283–289, 1984.
57. Thorsten Sellin, *Culture Conflict and Crime* (New York: Social Science Research Council, 1938).

58. Lewis Coser, *Continuities in the Study of Social Conflict* (New York: Free Press, 1967).
59. Walter B. Miller, "Lower Class Culture as a Generating Milieu of Gang Delinquency," *Journal of Social Issues* 14(3):5–19, 1958.
60. Richard Quinney, *The Social Reality of Crime* (Boston: Little, Brown, 1970).
61. Alex Thio, *Deviant Behavior* (Boston: Houghton Mifflin, 1978).
62. Emile Durkheim, *Suicide*, Trans. John A. Spaulding and George Simpson (Glencoe, IL: Free Press, 1951).
63. For an expanded statement of the original article, see Robert K. Merton, *Social Theory and Social Structure* (Glencoe, IL: Free Press, 1957).
64. Andrew F. Henry and James F. Short, Jr., *Suicide and Homicide* (New York: Free Press, 1954).
65. Jacqueline Straus and Murray Straus, "Suicide, Homicide, and Social Structure in Ceylon," *American Journal of Sociology* 58(5):461–469, 1953.
66. Edwin M. Lemert, *Human Deviance, Social Problems, and Social Control* (Englewood Cliffs, NJ: Prentice-Hall, 1967).
67. *Ibid.*; also, Edwin M. Schur, *Labeling Deviant Behavior* (New York: Harper and Row, 1971).
68. Palmer, *The Violent Society*.

4

Violent Crime: Assault, Rape, Robbery

Major Forms

In addition to criminal homicide, the main forms of serious violent crime are aggravated assault, forcible rape, and robbery. Technically, assault refers to placing another in fear of bodily harm. Battery designates the actual process of bringing about injury of another person. Thus the phrase, *Assault and battery.* Aggravated assault is the common term for serious, felonious assault and battery. Minor assaults are misdemeanors and are not emphasized here. Generally speaking, aggravated assault is said to occur when at least one of the following criteria is met: the assailant intended to commit a more serious crime such as murder or rape, a deadly weapon was used, or severe bodily injury resulted. Attacks on police officers are usually designated as aggravated assault even if none of these criteria is met.

Two main types of rape are usually distinguished: statutory and forcible. Statutory rape refers to sexual intercourse without force between an adult male and a minor female who are not married to each other. The sheer fact of intercourse between a man and a female minor constitutes the crime of statutory rape in most jurisdictions in the United States and in some other countries. While the effects on the victim can be extremely harmful, violence in the physical sense is not present. Consequently, statutory rape is not a focal concern of this chapter. Forcible rape involves sexual intercourse between a male and a female which is against the female's will and in which actual or threatened force, fraud, or deceit is used. Whether forcible rape can in a legal sense occur between marital partners is presently at issue in the courts. Courts in some states (Oregon and Massachusetts, for example) have taken the position that it can. And in Massachusetts in 1979, for the first time in the United States, a man was found guilty of committing rape against his wife.

Robbery is a combination of violent crime and theft or property crime. Most official systems of recording crime include robbery as a crime of violence. Robbery is the taking of, or attempted taking of, money or goods from an individual through the use or threat of force. A deadly weapon may be used or the assailant may be unarmed and employ only "strong-arm" methods.

Incidence in the United States

The Federal Bureau of Investigation (FBI) publishes annual reports on the incidence of officially recorded crime in the United States. Included within the crimes of violence category are criminal homicide (first- and second-degree murder and first-degree manslaughter), aggravated assault, forcible rape, and robbery. In recent years, the U.S. National Crime Survey had provided data on the incidence of violent and other crime regardless of whether those crimes found their way into the official records. This has been done by interviewing samples of households and businesses across the country. In effect, individuals in everyday life report whether they have been the victims of violent or other crime, how often, and provide details of the crime situation and, where possible, of the offenders. These data will be discussed shortly.

Approximately 1.5 million serious crimes of violence were officially recorded and reported to the FBI by police departments in the United States during 1987. (About 12 million serious property crimes were reported by police during the same period.) Of the crimes of violence, about 20,100, or 1.4 percent, were criminal homicides; 91,110, or 6.1 percent, were forcible rapes; 517,700, or 35 percent, were robberies; and 855,090, or 57.6 percent, were aggravated assaults. The latter, serious assault, is then the most frequent violent crime, at least from the point of view of official records on crime.

Over the ten-year period 1978–1987, the annual rate of recorded violent crime per 100,000 population rose by 22.5 percent. Criminal homicide decreased by 7.8 percent over the ten years; forcible rape increased by 20.6 percent; robbery by 8.6 percent; and aggravated assault by 34.0 percent.

These figures refer to officially recorded violent crimes only. The U.S. National Crime Survey sheds light on the extent to which the *true* crime rate varies from the recorded rate. For 1985 the results of that survey indicate that an estimated 5,822,000 forcible rapes, aggravated assaults, and robberies actually occurred.[1] The officially recorded *Uniform Crime Report* (FBI) figure was 1,327,770. Thus the true volume of violent crime may have exceeded the recorded volume by 4.4 times. For the three main types of violent crime, the estimated total figures exceeded the official figures: for forcible rape, 1.5 times; aggravated assault, 1.9 times; and robbery, 1.8 times.

In the World at Large

Rates for criminal homicide for countries around the world show a wide variation (see Chapter 3), and homicide rates are good indicators of rates for violent crime in general. But the fact remains that *comparable* rates for violent crime in most countries are unavailable. The classification of crimes and recording procedures vary greatly. We do know in an approximate way that some countries are low in violent crime—Iceland, Sweden, England, and Wales are examples; and that others are high—Colombia, the United States, Mexico.[2]

One comparison that can be made is between England and Wales and the United States. Classification of crimes and recording procedures are reasonably similar in the two countries. In 1974, for example, the annual rate per 100,000 population in England and Wales for officially recorded serious violent crime was 144.[3] The comparable rate for the United States for the same year was 459.[4] This means that allowing for population differences (the United States population is four times that of England and Wales), the United States officially records three times as much violent crime as England and Wales, a rate of 459 compared to 144. While these figures are for 1974, they typify the differences between the two countries in the years preceding and following that.

There is no simple explanation for this significant disparity between the two countries. The United States has had a history of violent crime from the time of the Revolutionary War onward.[5] As we discussed in regard to homicide in Chapter 3, competition for success goals of prestige, power, and money is and has been very great in this country. Violent crime is one result because of the alienation and aggression which are consequences of failure to achieve success in the competitive race. In recent centuries, England and Wales have had a history of peaceful, nonviolent relationships among people in everyday life. While social class lines have been strong, direct competition for success goals has been relatively low. There have been proportionately fewer failures in the race for success in England and Wales than in the United States. Violent subcultures have had little basis on which to develop. Class and racial struggle and competition for money, prestige, and power appear to have intensified considerably in England and Wales in recent years. This may very well result in a pronounced increase in the violent crime rate in the decades ahead.

Variations within the United States

Officially recorded violent crime rates are much higher in urban than in rural areas of the United States. In 1987, the FBI reported the following annual rates per 100,000 population for violent crime in general: 720 in the large Standard Metropolitan Statistical Areas (SMSAs), 351 in cities not included in metropolitan areas, and 178 in rural areas. Robbery especially is a big-city crime. The rate for SMSAs was 269. For other cities it was 50, one-fifth of that for the metropolitan areas. The robbery rate for rural places was 15, only one-eighteenth that of the metropolitan areas. The pattern is the same, although not quite as pronounced, for the other two crimes of violence—forcible rape and aggravated assault—which are of concern in this chapter. The rate for each was highest in metropolitan areas and lowest in rural areas. (Criminal homicide was highest in metropolitan areas and lowest in other cities.)

These rates allow for differences in population concentration. They mean, for example, that any one person's chances, on the average, of being victimized by a robber were 269 out of 100,000 in metropolitan areas of the United States in 1987. In rural areas, any one person's chances, on the average, were 15 out of 100,000.

Concentration of violent crime in the large urban areas is true year in and year out in the United States. It is true, generally speaking, for the various states and regions. And it is true for most countries around the world where data are available. The frustrations born of failure to achieve in the competitive race for success goals, and born of many other factors as well, seem to increase as population density increases.

Officially recorded rates of violent crime vary considerably from one geographic region of the United States to another. In 1987 the midwestern states showed the lowest rate for violent crime in general—504 per 100,000 population. The western states had the highest rate—714. The Northeast ranked second highest with 635, and the South was third highest with 607. Closer analysis shows some of the western states to have especially high rates of violent crime. In 1987 the only western states with rates close to or over 714 (the rate for the total western region) were California with a rate of 918 and Nevada with 696. The state with the largest population, California, accounts then for much of the high violent crime rate in the western states. California is known as a place of migrants. Much has been written of the alienated nature of many who leave other states for California. The struggle for success goals is on balance fierce in big, heterogeneous California. The "dropout" communes of San Francisco and other parts of the state attest to this. These factors provide clues to understanding the high rate of violent crime here.

Characteristics of Offenders and Victims

Age, Sex, and Race of Offenders

In general, assaultive offenders are under 25 years of age. This is true in the United States and many Western countries.[6] Data on persons arrested for violent crimes in the United States in 1987 show that 46.5 percent of the arrestees were under age 25, while 38 percent of the country's total population were below that age. Homicidal and assaultive offenders tended to be somewhat older than rape and robbery offenders. Typically, robbery offenders were in their late teens, rape offenders in their early twenties, and homicide and assault offenders in their late twenties.

Those who commit violent crimes are from five to 10 times more likely to be male than female. Again, this is the case in many Western countries as well as the United States.[7] Figures from 1987 show that in the United States, about 89 percent of arrestees for serious violent crimes were male and 11 percent female. Apart from the fact that forcible rape is almost solely a male offense, percentages of arrest by sex vary considerably. In 1987 in the United States, females composed 12.5 percent of all persons arrested for criminal homicide and 13.3 percent for aggravated assault. They were least represented in arrests for robbery, only 8.1 percent of the time.

Female involvement in crime generally in the United States, vis-à-vis male involvement, appears to be rising. As will be clear in the next chapter, this is mainly in regard to property crime. The percentages of arrests for serious violent crimes which were male and female were the same for 1976 as for 1987: 89 percent of those arrested were male and 11 percent were female.[8]

Robbery—holding someone up, usually on the street—is a form of behavior quite alien to the female role. Homicide and assault may not be especially compatible with that role. Nevertheless, cultural values as to sex roles are such that when a woman commits murder or assault, it can be explained as due to anger, exasperation, and the like. The woman's status as a female is not questioned. When a woman commits robbery, however, others may question her femininity. While the form that crime takes may not necessarily be compatible with the dominant roles in the individual's life, it is unlikely to be highly incompatible with those roles.

Blacks in the United States are, proportionate to their numbers in the population, far more often arrested for violent crimes than are whites or other races. In 1987, blacks represented 12 percent of the United States population but made up 47.3 percent of arrestees for serious crimes of violence. Whites made up 85 percent of the population and 51.2 percent of the arrestees; for other races, the percentage was 1.4 for serious crimes of violence. Blacks were overrepresented among arrestees by about four times while whites were underrepresented by almost half. The single violent crime on which blacks were most overrepresented was robbery; they composed 63.3 percent of arrestees.

The question, of course, arises as to what extent blacks are more frequently arrested than whites because of possible prejudice against them. Using National Crime Survey data, Hindeling compared victims' perceptions of their assailants with police reports of arrestees which are included in the FBI *Uniform Crime Reports,* issued annually as *Crime in the United States.*[9] He found that for robbery the figures were identical: victims reported that blacks were their attackers 62 percent of the time and blacks constituted 62 percent of arrestees. For forcible rape and aggravated assault, however, there were differences. Victims perceived rape offenders as black 39 percent of the time compared to 48 percent of arrestees designated as black. And in cases of assault, victims reported that offenders were black in 30 percent of the cases as contrasted to an arrest percentage of 41. Thus it may be that a somewhat sizable proportion of the racial discrepancy is due to selective bias in arrests for forcible rape and aggravated assault but not for robbery. (Criminal homicide was not included in the study.)

Age, Sex, and Race of Victims

The best United States national data on age, sex, and racial characteristics of victims of violent crimes are also from the National Crime Survey. These provide *rates* of victimization per *1000* population annually. Statistics show that the age group 16–19 years had the highest victimization rate for serious violent crime in general in 1985: the rate was 33.0. This means that among persons aged 16–19 in the United States, data from the national survey showed that for every 1000 of those persons, 33.0 were the victims of forcible rape, robbery, or aggravated assault. The second highest victimization rate was for those aged 20–24; the third highest rate was for the age group 12–15 years. There were differences by type of crime, however. The forcible rape and aggravated assault victimization rate was greatest for those aged 16–19; robbery was highest for the 20–24 group. After age 24, rates for each of these crimes decreased as the population at risk grew older.

Sex of victims of violent crimes varies markedly in the United States. The *rate* of victimization (per 1000 population annually) for victims of violent crime was 19 for males and 9.5 for females. Thus males were twice as often victimized as females. This contrasts sharply with the figures for offenders: males are arrested in the United States for violent crimes between eight and nine times more frequently than females. While forcible rape victims are necessarily almost always females, robbery victims are over twice as likely to be males as females; and aggravated assault victims are two-and-a-half times as likely to be males as females.

Regarding race, data show a black victimization rate of 23.5 (per 1000 population) for violent crime in general as compared to a white rate of 12.7. This means that, based on the National Crime Survey sample, the chance of a black being the victim of violent crime is about twice that of a white. The racial discrepancy was greatest in the specific violent crime of robbery where the black rate was two-and-a-half times the white rate. It was least in forcible rape: the black victimization rate was a third higher than the white rate.

Background and Social Characteristics

Violent criminal offenders, whether the offense be homicide, assault, rape, or robbery, tend to have grown up in disorganized and conflicted families. The early lives of assaultists are often characterized by severe physical and psychological frustrations as are those of homicidal offenders.[10] Those who commit forcible rape tend to have sexual identity problems generated at least in part by weak fathers and mothers who repeatedly rejected them.[11] Robbery offenders have often been subjected as children to especially severe economic deprivation rather than physical frustration or sexual identity problems.[12] They grew up with a political attitude that for them economic conditions would never improve.

Typically, violent offenders, and victims as well, are drawn from destitute minority residents of urban slums. The National Commission on the Causes and Prevention of Violence reiterated what other such commissions found: that the connection between violent crime and urban ghetto life is "one of the most fully documented facts about crime."[13] Persons who are socialized under the usual conditions of urban slums are especially prone to commit violent offenses and to be the victims of violence. The Commission finds that these areas are characterized by:

Low income
Physical deterioration
Dependency
Racial and ethnic concentrations
Broken homes

Working mothers
Low levels of education and vocational skills
High unemployment
High proportions of single males
Overcrowded and substandard housing
Low rates of home ownership or single-family dwellings
Mixed land use
High population density[13]

Taken together, these factors of inner-city life create a desperate "underclass" of persons. Children are forced to live in dilapidated, unsanitary, and overcrowded housing. The demoralizing nature of their physical surroundings is exacerbated by widespread family disruptions. Parents are often more concerned with their own lives than the welfare of their children, who are considered a liability. Intrafamilial conflicts are rampant and abandonment by fathers common. Women must take low-paying jobs to attempt to support their families. Little time, energy, or inclination is left for the supervision of children. Chaotic romantic entanglements mark the lives of the mothers. Children witness a rapid succession of their mothers' paramours, who are commonly referred to as "uncles." Physical and emotional survival in the ghetto is dependent on acceptance of "premature autonomy." Unstable and inconsistent family relations, lack of adequate sex-role models, socioeconomic deprivations, and an oppressive physical environment combine to obviate effective socialization of children. As adults, those who commit homicide, assault, rape, and robbery share patterns of low levels of education, low-prestige jobs, and high levels of unemployment.[14] In short, violent crime is predominantly a lower social class phenomenon.

This extends to victims of violent crime. The National Crime Survey provides data on rates of victimization by level of family income. Serious violent crime victimization rates per 1000 of the population aged 12 years and over are twice as high for the poor as the well-to-do. This pattern holds for each of the specific major forms of victimization, that is, assault, forcible rape, and robbery.

The unemployed are especially prone to be victims of violent crime. The unemployed are over two-and-a-half times more likely to be the victims of serious violent crime than were the employed. They are twice as likely to be assaulted, two-and-a-half times as likely to be robbed, and four-and-a-half times as likely to be raped. The unemployed tend to live in or near very high-crime areas; very often they are poor; and in disproportionately great numbers, they are black.[15]

Social Psychological Characteristics of Offenders

Assault

Typologies of assaultive behavior have not been as systematically developed as those of robbery or rape. Gibbons has, however, offered two broad categories of assaultists: situational and psychopathic.[16] Situational assault offenders are commonly found in urban ghetto areas where there prevails a readiness to resort to violence in order to resolve conflicts. These subcultures of violence emerge in places characterized by marked social and economic deprivations and their resultant tensions.[17] It is expected that males will respond immediately and aggressively to affronts by others. The stresses and tensions of their increasingly debilitating circumstances often explode in physical attacks on those closest at hand. Wives, children, and longstanding friends often are victims of such violence.

Psychological imbalances may also generate assaultive behavior. Psychopathic, sociopathic,* or "unsocialized aggressive" personalities are often the result of some defect in the early socialization process. McCord and McCord defined the psychopath as "an asocial, aggressive, highly impulsive person, who feels little or no guilt and is unable to form lasting bonds of affection with other human beings."[18] Such individuals have not internalized the usual restraints on behavior. They suffer little guilt or remorse for their aggressive actions. They are highly impulsive and driven by uncontrolled desires. They lack empathy for their victims and think only of avoiding "getting caught."

Research has shown that children whose early socialization involves secondary or impersonal perfunctory relations with those who care for them are more likely to develop sociopathic personality traits. Such children do not learn to associate affect or feeling with their behavior. They respond to others as they have been treated. Impervious to the feelings of others, their behavior is cold, calculated, and self-serving. Yet, lacking insight into the usual "give-and-take" of human relations, they often exhibit self-defeating aggression.

Rape

Several typologies of rape offenders have been formulated. Cohen and his coinvestigators offered the following threefold categorization of rapists: (1) aggressive aim rapists, (2) sexual aim rapists, and (3)

*In recent years there has been a tendency to use the term *sociopathic* instead of psychopathic.

sexual-aggression defusion rapists.[19] To the aggressive aim rapists, sexual relations with the victim are secondary to the desire to vent their destructive rage. The rape victim is a vicarious target for their longstanding hostility toward women, particularly those who stand in some role relationship to them, such as their mother, wife, or a girlfriend. They consider women to be "hostile, demanding, ungiving, and unfaithful." And frequently women who are important to the rapist are domineering, licentious, and impervious to the feelings of the offender. As a consequence, the rapist commonly manifests pronounced difficulties with heterosexual relationships.

In other spheres of life, however, these offenders seem to fare quite well. They are above average in intelligence and occupationally successful. The rape, which tends to occur either in the victim's home or in the offender's car, is usually an "isolated instance(s) in an otherwise relatively normal social and psychiatric history." The clinical prognosis for such rapists is much better than other sexual offenders.

The sexual aim rapist, on the other hand, uses aggression to ensure the sexual conquest of his victim. Since adolescence, this offender has had a confused sexual identity. His erotic feelings extend to both males and females, and he exhibits "voyeuristic, fetishistic, and exhibitionistic" tendencies. Despite distorted sexual proclivities, this rapist is not usually openly antisocial. He most often is employed, but in a job that is far below his capabilities. Overall he manifests low self-esteem. The sexual aim rape is the offender's response to fears of impotence and homosexuality. These fears appear to be strongest when the offender is in his late teens or early twenties. Finally, he strikes at a random victim, who typically is walking alone in a dark park or other nonpublic place. Typically, he attacks the woman from behind; if she resists, he will often flee. As a consequence, many such offenders are charged with attempted rather than actual rape. Excessive violence is rarely used. Because of the offender's deep-seated sexual conflicts and lack of self-esteem, therapy, while often effective, may continue for several years.

The sexual-aggression defusion rapist is extremely sadistic and relies on violence to become sexually aroused. However, aggression is rarely used after intercourse. This offender is typically "assertive, overpowering, and hostile." His total disregard for the welfare of others is fueled by his distinctly paranoid views of the world. The sexual-aggression defusion rapist is characteristically resistant to psychiatric treatment.

Rada formulated a second typology of rapists.[20] Offenders are characterized according to (1) situational stress, (2) masculine identity conflict, (3) sadistic tendencies, (4) sociopathic or (5) psychotic personalities. The situational stress rapist seems to be responding to severe disruption in his personal life. His job may be in jeopardy, his wife may have left him or threatened to do so, or he may be facing financial ruin. In a climate of personal turmoil, the person may lash out against a vulnerable target. Usually these offenders do not have a history of sexual deviation or violent behavior. They usually suffer considerable guilt and remorse following their sexual assault and are less likely than other rape offenders to be recidivists.

Masculine identity conflict offenders, unlike the situational stress offenders, seriously question their sexual adequacy and masculine self-image. Most are heterosexual but can also exhibit a propensity toward homosexuality. These men consciously and deliberately plan the rape and carry it out with excessive violence. Sadistic rapists, like the masculine identity conflict offenders, commit extremely violent sexual assaults. The venting of aggression appears to be as important to them as sexual relations with their victims. Such men, however, constitute a distinct minority of offenders. The sociopathic offenders, who probably account for the largest proportion of sexual offenders, tend to be primarily motivated to rape by sexual desires. While they are exceedingly antisocial and have lengthy records of criminal violations, their acts of rape do not ordinarily involve unnecessary aggression.

Rada concludes that "rape is a crime of control, power, and dominance. The primary motive in the rapist is the desire to control the victim in the specific instance of rape and, by extension, all women."[21] The rapist's need to dominate springs from his inability "to establish a satisfying love relationship with a woman, . . . and [he] reponds in rage and frustration with a vain attempt to control by force what he feels inadequate or unable to obtain on a voluntary basis."[22]

Robbery

There is little evidence that robbery offenders are motivated by underlying psychological disturbance. They seldom suffer psychotic or highly neurotic disorders. Robbery is distinctly a predatory crime directed toward pecuniary gain. This offense involves a minimum investment, considerable but calculated risk, and the return may be substantial. For the "underclass" whose economic future is limited at best, robbery affords an opportunity to reverse a dire situation.

Conklin offers a fourfold categorization of robbery offenders.[23] On the basis of interviews with 67 men convicted of robbery and incarcerated in Massachusetts prisons, he suggested that they may be classified as (1) professionals, (2) opportunists, (3) addicts, and (4) alcoholics. The professional robbers were defined as "those who manifest a long-term commitment to crime as a source of livelihood, who plan and organize their crimes prior to committing them, and who seek money to support a particular lifestyle that may be called hedonistic." There are two types of professional robbers: those who concentrate on robbery as their primary criminal activity and those who commit robbery along with various other kinds of crimes. Both types plan their robberies carefully. There is a serious professional commitment to the "art" of robbery. Occupational hazards, such as the unexpected arrival of the police, or some "nosey jerk," security devices, and the possibility of attack by the victim, must be anticipated and strategies planned. The escape route and alternates must be mapped out.

Professional robbers usually work in small groups. These groups are formed to carry out a particular "job" and are quickly disbanded thereafter. Distinct roles are evident within the group. One drives the getaway car, another holds the victim and others at bay, and a third is responsible for taking the money. Professional robbers are usually armed and are more apt to use their weapons to ensure escape than other types. Commercial establishments are common targets for such robbery and typically the "score" exceeds $500 and may be more than $10,000. The rewards allow the professional robber to leave the state where the robbery was committed, often to spend the money on personal luxury, and to begin to plan the next job.

Opportunists, or "muggers," unlike the professionals, are not committed to a career of robbery. They prey on readily available and defenseless targets, "elderly ladies with purses, drunks, cab drivers, and people who walk alone at night." Typically, they gain less than $20 in each such robbery. The motivations of offenders are simply to get "a little extra spending money," "some nice clothes," or "some cash in the pocket." In contrast to their professional counterparts who tend to be white males, about 25 years old, and from working or middle-class families, opportunists are apt to be black teenagers from destitute backgrounds. Little if any planning precedes a mugging. No escape routes are devised, and cars or weapons are rarely used. In brief, an opportunist robber is frequently a "street kid" who is apt to strike when a promising situation presents itself. Conklin points out that the robbery usually "just happens."

To Conklin, there are two types of addict robbers. Opiate and heroin addicts make up the first group while the second comprises those who commit robbery to support an amphetamine or other habit, or who were under the influence of LSD or other hallucinogens at the time of the crime. Generally speaking, addicts do not intend to pursue robbery as a lifelong means of income but steal to support their daily need for drugs. Robbery is considered by addicts to be a higher risk offense than burglary, shoplifting, or theft from a car. Yet drug habits are extremely expensive and large sums of cash must be had day after day. When safer means of illicit funds are not available, robbery remains a common alternative.

Although the addict robber does not plan his crime as carefully as the professional, he does attempt to minimize his chances of apprehension. Addicts are less interested in the "big score" than in getting whatever funds are immediately needed. Interestingly, addicts tend to fear hurting or killing their victims and, as a consequence, being charged with a more serious felony. Often they do not carry guns, or if a gun is used to intimidate the victim, it may not be loaded. Simply put, low-risk, nonviolent, and impersonal acts of theft tend to be preferred by addicts. Robbery is resorted to only when the addict's financial situation becomes desperate.

Lastly, there is the alcoholic robber. Typically this offender is unemployed yet he rarely depends on robbery as a primary means of financial support. His robberies are not planned. Rather, the offense tends to evolve from an unrelated assault, usually precipitated by excessive drinking. Or, the victim is chosen by happenstance, with little or no thought to the risk involved or the amount of money to be gained. As a consequence, such offenders are often apprehended.

Assault within the Family

In recent years, assault and other forms of violence within the family have received much attention. The results are startling to many observers of family life. Straus and his associates conducted a national study of violence between husbands and wives and parents and their children.[24] A sample of 2143 United States couples was interviewed. Rates of various forms of family violence were compiled. These are rates per 100 couples, parents, or children per year, for the year 1975.

Those researchers found that over the year, severe violence, equivalent to aggravated assault, occurred between husband and wife at least once in 6.1 percent of the couples. That included couples where the husband assaulted the wife, or the wife the husband, or each the other. Wives seriously assaulted husbands in 4.6 percent of the couples and husbands seriously assaulted wives in 3.8 percent of the couples, that is, slightly more wives beat husbands than husbands wives. However, the wives' assaults on the husbands, while serious, were less severe than the husbands' attacks on the wives.

Using 4.0 as a rough average of the annual rate of spouse beating per 100 husbands or wives, that means a rate of 40 per 1000 and of 4000 per 100,000. The FBI gives officially recorded figures of about 351 aggravated assaults per 100,000 population (all persons in the United States).

The data of the national study of family violence also show that the annual rate of a parent seriously assaulting a particular offspring aged 3–17 years was 14.2 per 100 parents. This means that the parent did one or several of the following: kicked, punched, bit, hit with an object, beat up the child, or used a knife or gun. Hitting with an object such as a belt or hair brush is sometimes considered "normal" physical punishment of a child by a parent. When hitting with an object is excluded from the list, the rate is about 4 per 100 parents. Assume for the moment that about half of those cases where the parent hit the child with an object were serious assault and the others were not. This would mean a rate of serious assault of parents on children of about 9 per 100 parents or 1 out of 11.

The national study also found that mothers are more likely to assault their children (aged 3–17) seriously than are fathers.[25] The annual rate per 100 is 75 percent greater for mothers than fathers, the respective rates begin 17.1 and 10.1. (Data are not available for rates when "hitting with an object" is excluded.) As the researchers point out, among other things, mothers are likely to be with their children more hours of the day than fathers; "opportunities" are greater. As with the findings on homicide in Chapter 3, a general conclusion of much importance is this: While females are in general less often physically violent than males, much of this violence occurs within the family and in that setting often exceeds that of males.

Children seriously assault their parents much more than is generally realized. The national study's findings show that the annual rate of children aged 3–17 years victimizing a parent in that way was 9.4 per 100 children or, again, about 1 in 11. Moreover, children who are siblings frequently assault each other. Over half, 53 percent, of the children in the national survey sample who had siblings seriously assaulted a brother or sister during the one-year period.

The same study found these interesting variations in family violence[26]: Rates of assault of husbands by wives, wives by husbands, and children by parents varied inversely with family income—the lower the income, the higher the assault rate. This was not true for children assaulting their siblings, however, where there was little or no association with family income. Spousal violence and child abuse by parents were more prevalent when the husband or father was a blue-collar worker than when he was a white-collar worker. Again, there was no difference in regard to children assaulting their siblings. There was also a clear tendency for spousal violence and child abuse rates to be lower when the husband or father was employed full time than when he was employed part time or unemployed.

Blacks definitely had higher rates of spousal abuse than whites. Their rate of child abuse was higher, but only very slightly, than that of white parents. Residents of large cities were more prone to engage in spouse or child abuse than small-city, suburban, or rural residents. In general, spouse and child abuse were higher in Catholic than in Protestant families while rates in Jewish families were distinctly lower than in the Protestant families. Race, residence, and religion were not related to rates of children victimizing their siblings.

EXPLANATIONS OF ASSAULT

Major Sources of Assaultive Behavior

Serious assault is from a behavioral standpoint similar to homicide. It occurs largely between individuals who know each other and who have been in contention for some time. Circumstance often determines whether assault leads to homicidal death. The extent and speed with which effective medical services are provided are often major considerations. The basic health of the victim is another. Consequently, explanations of homicide and assault are similar. Those explanations, discussed in the previous chapter, will be briefly summarized below. Forcible rape and robbery, however, are sufficiently distinct from homicide and assault, and from each other as well, that they require somewhat different explanations.

Sociocultural conflicts including competition for success goals are major forces behind homicide and aggravated assault. Anomie and severe absolute and relative deprivation are closely related factors. Societal reaction in the form of negative labeling of individuals early in life and later as well plays a part; so does the compelling nature of mass media attention to physical violence. The more these reverse conditions are widespread in an industrial area, the more subcultures of violence are generated. Those subcultures then facilitate homicide and assault as responses to the frustrations of conflict, anomie, and relative deprivation.

Put simply, physically assaultive and homicidal persons are generally the products of alienation, social and psychological deprivation, negative labeling, the suggestive power of the mass media, and participation in the customs and values of subcultures of violence. In some settings, black urban ghettoes for example, physical violence is stongly institutionalized, that is, subcultural customs and values are learned and that learning is often heavily rewarded, especially among young males. At the same time, much serious assault and homicide is individualistic deviance; therefore, individuals with little contact with a subculture of violence may react to severely frustrating circumstances with violent aggression toward others, and particularly those close to them.

An Explanation of Family Violence

Straus developed a special theory of family violence.[27] He stresses various aspects of family organization: the association of violence with love through the use of punishment to correct a loved child; the observation of parental and sibling violence by children; training children, especially males, in physical aggression in order to "hold their own" in a violent adult world. Straus also emphasized the following: marriage as a legitimate relationship for violence; conflict and antagonism among roles in the family (parent–child and husband–wife); the value on privacy of the family in United States society which allows for hidden violence and cuts off support and the possibility of social control by kin and community; the disparity in resources, physical power, status, etc., of husband and wife; the frequent inability of members to escape from violent families; the economic frustration experienced by many United States families.

This adds up to a general explanation of family violence which emphasizes the institutionalized use of violence as social control in the family, which reflects the customs and values of the wider society and culture; role conflict and consequent antagonisms in the family; and status frustration due to relative economic deprivation of family members and whole families.

EXPLANATIONS OF FORCIBLE RAPE

Social Integration

Social integration theories of defiance have some relevance to rape. Those who commit rape are likely to have had life histories of failure to achieve cultural success goals. They are likely to be alienated, anomic individuals. But there is an additional factor usually present. Rape offenders tend to have had difficult, contentious relationships with adult females, mothers or otherwise, in their early years. They cannot relate successfully to women and in fact see women as at least in part to blame for their lack of achievement.[28] This may be a purely psychological abnormality on the part of rape offenders. More accurately, it is a sex-role problem which developed under generally anomic conditions in earlier years. The offender's rage at the social system which has blocked him from achievement is directed toward those whom he perceives as more responsible. Why rape rather than, say, assault? One explanation is that the offender's concomitant sense of sexual insecurity is reduced by the act of overpowering females sexually.[29] Rape, then, can serve the dual purpose of providing a target for aggressive tendencies and a "validation" of masculinity. This is not to say that all rape is explained in this way. Other theoretical perspectives are equally useful.

Cultural Supports

Cultural support explanations stress the transmission through imitation and training of deviant behavior patterns and values. To the degree that subcultural customs and values are socially transmitted and shared among individuals, deviance is institutionalized. To what extent does forcible rape take the form of institutionalized as opposed to individualistic deviance? While a precise answer is impossible, there are some clues. Amir found that almost half of the rape episodes in his study involved two or more offenders and one victim.[30] To be sure, group rape does not necessarily mean that the deviant behavior involved is institutionalized. Two or more individuals without previously learned common behavior patterns for deviance can spontaneously engage together in deviant acts. That is individualistic deviance even though two or more persons are acting in conjunction with each other. However, group rape does appear often to be institutionalized, that is, to involve commonly shared, learned behaviors and values.

Amir posited a lower-class, black male, urban subculture (the group rape offenders were usually poor, black youths) with the following characteristics: idealization of violence and sexual prowess; the seeking of excitement through aggression and sex; and the defense of masculine identity and the gaining of status through promiscuous sex with females.[31] This is no doubt an explanation that has some validity in regard to rape, especially group rape, by lower-class, young black males in urban ghettos. However, much rape, very likely most rape, is committed on an individualistic basis by others such as rural whites, urban loners of any race, affluent men in prestigious occupations, and so on.

Social Disorganization and Conflict

Socially disorganized areas probably spawn forcible rape by single or multiple offenders to some extent because of the consequent alienation and development of the type of subculture Amir delineated. Cultural and subcultural conflicts, as emphasized by Thorsten Sellin,[32] can lead to rape because of a confusion in definition of what constitutes that deviant act: what is prosecutable rape in one cultural setting may be permissible if quite violent conduct in another. Miller's formulation

of lower-class focal concerns may have some relevance in that the upper class may designate as serious crime physically coercive sexual behavior that is not considered especially deviant in the lower class.[33]
Quinney's political conflict theory has a similar relevance.[34]

But these theoretical approaches do not explain one important dimension of rape as well as does the power theory of Thio.[35] That dimension has to do with what Thio terms officially unrecognized rape:
that which is especially likely to be carried out by higher-status males
who use non-life-threatening but coercive methods against females such
as threat of layoff from a job. The powerful condemn the lower-class
offenders, who use physically coercive methods, as heinous rapists while
deflecting public attention away from their own psychologically coercive sexual exploitations. This has been a hidden area of deviant behavior only recently illuminated by such writers as Susan Brownmiller.[36] The question remains, however: where does the ordinary
negotiating for sexual intercourse that is part and parcel of everyday
life end and where does distinctly coercive, if not physically forcible,
rape begin? Thio's formulation helps to explain the negotiation process
but does not distinguish between those forms of sexual intercourse that
involve rape as opposed to pragmatic persuasion.

Societal Reaction

Attempts at social control do not appear to play a large part in
rape. As far as we know, there are few career or "professional" rapists.
It may be, however, that the notoriety given to repeating rapists, those
who presumably commit a series of rapes in a given residential area,
may motivate others to commit the crime. While the latter may carry
out one or two rapes and never gain public attention, the aura of notoriety given to the "serial" rape cases by the mass media may be a
compelling factor. (Often the mass media writers do not actually know
whether the repeating rapist is in fact a single individual: he may be
an "imaginary composite" of, say, 12 men who have committed 12
rapes, perhaps some imitating others because of publicity about the
modus operandi of the earlier offenders.)

Considering these various explanations, it seems fair to say that
rape is in good measure a result of anomic conditions and relative deprivation coupled with early life experiences of contention with dominating females. Some degree of support from subcultures of violence
may be present to the extent that those subcultures advocated aggressive sexual prowess, and the unequal distribution of power in a society
may serve to explain rape, to the extent it actually is rape, in higher
status settings where the force used involves threat of economic
sanctions.

Explanations of Robbery

Social Integration

Conklin, one of the major researchers on robbery, stresses relative deprivation as an explanation of this form of violent (and property) crime.[37] He posits that the increase in economic level of blacks during the 1960s in the United States led them to have heightened expectations of achieving cultural success goals which went unfulfilled. Economic conditions for whites improved even more than those for blacks. This further increased the sense of relative deprivation and frustration of blacks. The burgeoning robbery rate, especially by young, lower-status, black males, during the 1960s was one response to that. This is closely related to Merton's anomic theory.[38] However, since much robbery is also committed by whites, it can only be considered a highly selective explanation.

Gould combines the idea of relative deprivation with that of opportunity in an effort to explain the lower rates of robbery in the United States prior to World War II and the rising rates since then.[39] An increase in ownership of property of all kinds after World War II caused those who did not share in that increase to suffer greater relative deprivation than non-property owners of the 1930s, when most individual were in more or less poor economic straits. Moreover, the proliferation of property after 1945 simply made it easier to steal.

This form of explanation can, of course, be readily applied to sheer property crimes such as burglary and larceny as well as to robbery. In any event, robbery does appear in part to be a dual-pronged response to relative frustrations that may well be especially psychologically rewarding from the offender's standpoint. Needs for aggression and money can be simultaneously met in an activity that also provides a temporary sense of power over others.

Cultural Supports

Roebuck and Cadwallader found that black armed robbers tended to have grown up in disorganized family settings where the criminal subculture often flourished.[40] Robbery was a common phenomenon of everyday life. Einstadter found that professional robbers interact in loosely knit temporary groups in order to pull off particular jobs.[41] They do not have hierarchical organizations as professional thieves sometimes do. On balance, these and other sources of evidence indicate that robbery offenders, especially armed professionals, have learned law-violating behaviors and values early in life in much the same way as that set forth by Sutherland and Cressey.[42] But robbery offenders do not tend to be *intensively* involved in delinquent or criminal organized opportunity structures of the type emphasized by Cloward and Ohlin.[43]

Social Disorganization and Conflict

As has been said, robbery offenders are likely to have grown up in socially disorganized families and neighborhoods. Thio tends to accept relative deprivation, cultural supports, and conflict as partial explanations of lower-class robbery.[44] However, he attempts to define another form of robbery and to explain it in terms of power theory. Thio refers to economic exploitation of lower-status persons by higher-status persons through the use of subtle (or not so subtle) coercion. He cites these examples: physicians who threaten nontreatment, and therefore bodily harm, to patients unless patients pay high fees; landlords who use the threat of eviction, and therefore of bodily harm also, to collect exorbitant rents from the poor; and governments which threaten imprisonment in order to collect taxes.[45]

Certain specific instances of these forms of coercion might conceivably involve negative deviance, such as illegal threats by the government, for example. For the most part, however, such conduct is either part of everyday economic negotiation or of ordinary, agreed on political process. It may at times be exploitative, but it hardly qualifies as robbery. Shakedowns of workers by unions, management, or political officials to obtain financial kickbacks where threat of job loss is involved might possibly qualify as a form of robbery. This is often illegal and seldom part of the agreed-on economic and political processes. However, Thio does not consider shakedowns in this context. Here, and frequently in regard to other forms of behavior, Thio's power formulation is more relevant to the issue of why some in a society obtain more rewards than others than it is to explaining negative, or for that matter, positive deviance. Put another way, power theory helps to explain why absolute and relative deprivation exists. It then labels these processes as negatively deviant in themselves. It neglects at many points to distinguish the deviant from the conforming aspects of those processes.

Societal Reaction

Societal reaction may play a somewhat larger role in inducing robbery than rape. However, it is not likely that that role is especially great. The glamorous image of the professional bank robbers first developed in the mass media in the 1930s may continue to have a crime-generating effect on some alienated male youths. More important, society's official reaction to an attempt at robbery by a boy in his early teens may have significant consequence later. The youth who is sent to a state reformatory because of a spur-of-the-moment, bungled attempt to rob someone may thereby be set on a course of learning crime and the criminal role. This example reflects the dilemma of present day criminal justice: if one is robbed, one is likely to be perturbed at the very least and feel that official action should be taken though the offender may be a youthful amateur; if the youth is "processed" by the criminal justice system, the outcome may well be inducement toward a criminal career.

Robbery, then, very likely to a greater degree than rape, involves relative deprivation and anomie due to a disjuncture between cultural goods and institutionalized means for achieving those goals. Cultural supports in the forms of criminal and violent subcultures probably contribute more to professional than amateur robbery. Social and family disorganization and conflict may be important factors. When these five factors—relative deprivation, anomie, criminal subcultures, disorganization, and conflict—occur together in the lives of developing individuals, then the probability of violent crime in general and robbery in particular is considerable.

SUMMARY

This chapter considers serious, nonfatal forms of violent behavior: aggravated assault, forcible rape, and robbery. Aggravated assault is the common term for serious, felonious assault and battery. Aggravated assault occurs when the assailant intended to commit a more serious crime such as murder or rape, or a deadly weapon was used, or severe bodily injury resulted. Also, in the absence of these criteria, aggravated assault is said to occur when a police officer is the victim. Rape is usually divided into two categories: statutory and forcible. Statutory rape refers to sexual intercourse without force between an adult male and a minor female who are not married to each other. Forcible rape involves sexual intercourse between a male and female which is against her will and in which actual or threatened force, fraud, or deceit is used. Robbery may be either "strong-arm" or armed, and involves elements of both violent and property crime.

About 1.5 million crimes of violence are officially recorded in the United States each year. Of these, 58 percent are aggravated assaults, 35 percent robberies, and 6 percent forcible rapes. National victimization surveys show that three to four times more violent crime actually occurs than is reported to the police. Rates of violent crime in the United States are high, approximately four times that of England and Wales, for example. Within the United States, violence predominates in metropolitan areas and in the southern and western states.

Violent offenders in the United States tend to be young, male, and disproportionately black. Persons arrested for violent crime are most often under the age of 25, between five and 10 times more likely to be male than female, and are black about half the time. National Crime Survey data, however, suggest that blacks may be more susceptible than whites to arrest for forcible rape and aggravated assault but not for robbery.

Victims of violent crime also tend to be young, male, and black. Teenage and young adults are considerably more likely to be victimized violently than are older persons, males twice as likely as females, and blacks twice as likely as whites. Both victims and offenders are drawn from similar backgrounds. Considerable evidence links urban ghetto life with violent crime. Trapped in cycles of poverty, residents of the inner city constitute a desperate "underclass" of persons who characteristically vent their aggression on those closest to them.

Violent crime is distinctly male; in the United States, males are both victims and offenders in 85 percent of armed robberies, 60 percent of unarmed robberies, and 57 percent of aggravated assaults. When female offenders are involved, they most often victimize a male. Aggravated assaultists and their victims are somewhat older than offenders and victims of rape. And victims of robbery are decidedly older than their assailants.

Robbery is the only distinctly interracial violent offense and the one most likely to occur between strangers. Rape is second most apt to involve strangers, while aggravated assault usually involves persons who are at least acquainted with one another.

Recent data show that these acts of violence do not tend to be victim-precipitated. That is, in the vast majority of cases, the victim did not use physical force against the offender first, or renege on a promise to engage in sexual relations, or fail to take reasonable precautions when handling money in public.

Both aggravated assault and forcible rape tend to occur on weekends and during the evening hours. Robbery, however, occurs somewhat earlier in the week, usually from Thursday through Saturday. Aggravated assault is usually carried out with a knife or other sharp instrument or with the assailant's hands, fists, or feet. Guns are used in the majority of robberies; and when violence is employed in rape, it is usually in the form of beating or choking. Alcohol is associated with aggravated assault and rape, but less so with robbery.

A national survey of family violence concluded that husbands and wives are over four times more likely than others to be the victims of aggravated assault at the hands of their spouses as are all persons aged

12 or over to be seriously assaulted by anyone. Mothers are more apt to seriously assault their children than fathers, and about one in 11 children seriously assaults their parents each year.

Theoretical explanations of assault focus on the offender's alienation, social and psychological deprivation, negative labeling, the suggestive power of the mass media, and participation in subcultures of violence. Family violence has been attributed to particular aspects of family organization: the institutionalized use of violence as social control in the family, familial role conflicts, and the wider sociocultural climate of violence and deprivations.

Rape may be generated by low social integration and the inability to achieve the usual success goals in our society. Typically, rapists have been unable to establish adequate sex-role relationships with adult females. Rape is a means of venting aggression against women and establishing masculine identity. Gang rape may be subculturally influenced. Such rape is more usual in socially disorganized and destitute areas than in others. Robbery, too, is common in economically disadvantaged places. Subcultures arise that transmit motives, techniques, and rationalization for violent crime. Severe negative societal reaction may further induce economically exploited persons to adopt criminal careers.

Conditions that generate violent behavior are an inherent part of our social fabric. Fundamental changes are needed in the distribution of socioeconomic rewards, in family organization and role relationships, and in general reliance on violence as an acceptable means of social control and conflict resolution.

REFERENCES

1. U.S. Department of Justice, *Criminal Victimization in the United States, 1985* (Washington, D.C.: U.S. Government Printing Office, 1987), p. 12.
2. Stuart Palmer, *The Violent Society* (New Haven, CT: College and University Press, 1972).
3. British Home Office, *Criminal Statistics, England and Wales, 1974* (London: Her Majesty's Stationary Office, 1975).
4. Federal Bureau of Investigation, *Crime in the United States, 1987* (Washington, D.C.: U.S. Government Printing Office, 1988).
5. Hugh Davis Graham and Ted Robert Gurr, *Violence in America: Historical and Comparative Perspectives* (New York: Bantam Books, 1969). An official report to the National Commission on the Causes and Prevention of Violence.
6. Palmer, *op. cit.*
7. *Ibid.*
8. Federal Bureau of Investigation, *op. cit.*
9. Michael Hindelang, "Race and Involvement in Common Law Personal Crimes," *American Sociological Review* 43(1) (February 1978):93–109.
10. Palmer, *op.cit.*

11. Murray L. Cohen, Ralph Garofalo, Richard B. Boucher, and Theoharis Seghorn, "The Psychology of Rapists," in *Forcible Rape: The Crime, The Victim and The Offender* ed. Duncan Chappell, Robley Geis, and Gilbert Geis, (New York: Columbia University Press, 1977).
12. John E. Conklin, *Robbery and the Criminal Justice System* (Philadelphia: Lippincott, 1972).
13. National Commission on the Causes and Prevention of Violence, *To Establish Justice, To Insure Domestic Tranquility* (Washington, D.C.: U.S. Government Printing Office, 1969), pp. 17–37.
14. Cohen *et al.*, *The Psychology of Rapists;* also Conklin, *Robbery and the Criminal Justice System;* Palmer, *op. cit.*
15. U.S. Department of Justice, *Criminal Victimization in the United States, 1983* (Washington, D.C.: U.S. Government Printing Office, 1985), p. 28.
16. Don C. Gibbons, *Society, Crime and Criminal Careers* (Englewood Cliffs, NJ: Prentice-Hall, 1968), pp. 362–366.
17. Marvin E. Wolfgang and Franco Ferracuti, *The Subculture of Violence* (London: Tavistock, 1967); and Gibbons, *op. cit.*, p. 362.
18. William McCord and Joan McCord, *The Psychopath* (Princeton, NJ: Van Nostrand, 1964), p. 3.
19. Cohen *et al.*, *op. cit.*
20. Richard T. Rada, ed., *Clinical Aspects of the Rapist* (New York: Grune and Stratton, 1978), pp. 121–131.
21. Rada, *op. cit.*, p. 24.
22. *Ibid.*, p. 25.
23. Conklin, *op. cit.*, pp. 59–78. See also U.S. Department of Justice, *Patterns of Robbery, Characteristics* (Washington, D.C.: U.S. Government Printing Office, 1976).
24. Murray A. Straus, Richard J. Gelles, and Suzanne K. Steinmetz, *Behind Closed Doors: Violence in the American Family* (Garden City, NY: Anchor Press, 1980). See also Richard J. Gelles, "Family Violence," in Ralph H. Turner and James F. Short, Jr., eds., *Annual Review of Sociology*, Vol. 11, pp. 347–367, 1985; and Richard J. Gelles and Claire P. Cornell, *Intimate Violence in Families* (Beverly Hills, CA: Sage, 1985).
25. *Ibid.*
26. *Ibid.*
27. Murray A. Straus, "A Sociological Perspective on the Causes of Family Violence" (Paper presented at the American Association for the Advance of Science, Houston, January 6, 1979). See also Murray A. Straus, "Ordinary Violence, Child Abuse, and Wife-Beating: What Do They Have in Common?" *The Dark Side of Families*, eds. David Finkelhor *et al.* (Beverly Hills, CA: Sage, 1983).
28. A. Nicholas Groth, "Rape: Behavioral Aspects," in *Encyclopedia of Crime and Justice*, Vol. 4, ed. Sanford H. Kadish (New York: Free Press, 1983).
29. *Ibid.*
30. Menachem Amir, *Patterns in Forcible Rape* (Chicago: University of Chicago Press, 1971).
31. *Ibid.*
32. Thorsten Selling, *Culture Conflict and Crime* (New York: Social Science Research Council Bulletin No. 41, 1938).
33. Walter B. Miller, "Lower Class Culture as a Generating Milieu of Gang Delinquency," *Journal of Social Issues* 14(3):5–19, 1958.
34. Richard Quinney, *The Social Reality of Crime* (Boston: Little, Brown, 1970).
35. Alex Thio, *Deviant Behavior* (Boston: Houghton Mifflin, 1978).
36. Susan Brownmiller, *Against Our Will* (New York: Simon and Schuster, 1975).
37. Conklin, *Robbery and the Criminal Justice System.*
38. Robert K. Merton, "Social Structure and Anomie," *American Sociological Review* 3(5):672–682, 1938.

39. Leroy C. Gould, "The Changing Structure of Property Crime in an Affluent Society," *Social Forces* 48(1):50–59, 1960.
40. Julian B. Roebuck and Mervyn L. Cadwallader, "The Negro Armed Robber as a Criminal Type: The Construction and Application of a Typology," *Pacific Sociological Review* 4(1):21–26, 1961.
41. Werner J. Einstadter, "The Social Organization of Armed Robbery," *Social Problems* 17(1):64–83, 1969.
42. Edwin H. Sutherland and Donald R. Cressey, *Principles of Criminology* (Glencoe, IL: Free Press, 1978).
43. Richard A. Cloward and Lloyd E. Ohlin, *Delinquency and Opportunity* (Glencoe, IL: Free Press, 1960).
44. Thio, *op. cit.*
45. *Ibid.*, p. 165.

5

Property, Corporate, and Government Crime

Major Forms of Property Crime

The various forms of stealing constitute property crime. The most prevalent are burglary and larceny. *Burglary* refers to unlawful entry into a residence or place of business in order to commit a theft. Usually doors or windows or other points of access are forced in some way. *Larceny* is theft without force or fraud. Shoplifting, purse snatching, pickpocketing, and theft of vehicles are major forms. *Grand larceny* refers to theft of items of higher value, often $100 or more, while *petit larceny* involves theft of items of lesser value. In most jurisdictions, burglary and grand larceny are considered felonies and petit larceny a misdemeanor. *Robbery*, it will be recalled, is both a property and a violent crime: force or the threat of force is used against an individual in order to steal money or goods from that person. In other words, force is used against a structure in burglary, against a person in robbery, and not at all in larceny.

Still other forms of property crime involve *fraud*. Confidence games, forgery, and embezzlement are examples. When fraud occurs in higher-status business settings, it is termed *"white-collar"* crime; embezzling of funds is a common form. When fraud occurs outside of business settings, it is usually designated as *"blue-collar"* crime. Confidence games are the most common forms. In this chapter, burglary, grand larceny, and auto theft are first analyzed. Auto theft is actually a subtype of grand larceny, but official statistics on it are usually maintained separately from larceny. These are the "big three" of property crimes. White-collar crime and crime in government are discussed in a separate section later in this chapter.

Incidence

Data were gathered by the International Criminal Police Organization (Interpol) for 22 countries around the world.[1] The results provide annual rates of crime in general per 100,000 population. Included are murder, other violent offenses, sex offenses, major (grand) and minor (petit) larceny, fraud, counterfeiting of currency, other theft offenses, and drug violations. Those are officially recorded rates for each country. Since legal definitions and recording procedures vary, they are not strictly comparable; however, they are the best cross-national data on crime in general which are available. Since most, over 90 percent, of these "crimes in general" are thefts of one kind or another, although dated, these data give a fairly good indication of the officially recorded incidence of property crime across societies.

The mean annual rate varies from a high of 14,218 (per 100,000 population) for the West Indies to a low of 476 for Cyprus. The highest rate, then, is about 30 times as great as the lowest rate. The higher-ranking countries are on balance more technologically advanced than the lower-ranking ones. However, the country with the highest rate, the West Indies, is more similar in its level of technology to the lower-ranking countries. For the bast majority of countries, 20 of the 22, rates increased between 1976 and 1980.

In the United States, about 12 million serious property crimes were officially recorded in 1987. About 7.5 million of these were larcenies, 3.2 million were burglaries, and 1.3 million were auto thefts. These property crimes constitute about 89 percent of the country's serious recorded crimes. One and one-half million violent crimes make up the other 11 percent. Thus, as officially recorded, the number of property crimes is nine times that of violent crimes. Over the 1978–1987 period, the annual rate of recorded serious property crime per 100,000 of the population increased by 6.4 percent. The highest increase was in auto theft and was 15 percent, followed by larceny, 12.2 percent. Burglary, however, decreased by 7.3 percent. Violent crime rose more rapidly than property crime: 22.5 percent increase as compared to 6.4 percent.[2]

National Crime Survey data are available for comparable categories of property crime for 1985.[3] For that year the *officially recorded* number of serious property crimes, as calculated by the FBI, was about 11,102,600.[4] The National Crime Survey estimated 29 million or 2-½ times as many actual as recorded property crimes. For burglaries, the ratio was 1.7:1; for larcenies, 3:1; and for auto thefts, 1.1:1.

As is true for violent crime, official rates of property crime are much higher in urban than rural areas of the United States. For 1987, the rate for officially recorded serious property crimes per 100,000 population was 5575 in large metropolitan areas, 4548 in smaller cities, and 1723 in rural areas.[5] Thus, per unit of population, the large metropolitan areas have over three times as much property crime as the rural areas. The same is roughly true for violent crime. There is, of course, less of it than property crime. But like property crime, per unit of population, violent crime is over three times greater in the large urban concentrations than in rural places. Crime is much more a big-city than a small-city or rural phenomenon. The one major exception is criminal homicide where rural rates approach metropolitan rates.

The same general patterns hold for the three specific major forms of serious property crime as for property crime in total. The official rate for each is greater in the metropolitan areas, least in the rural areas, and middle range in the other cities. The disparity is greatest for auto theft: per unit of population, over five times as much is recorded in metropolitan as rural areas. The larceny rate is almost four times as great in metropolitan as rural areas.

Property crime rates vary considerably by region of the country as do rates of violent crimes. The rate for total serious property crime is highest in the West. It is next highest in the South and lowest in the Northeast and Midwest. As to specific property crimes, burglary follows this pattern: highest rates are in the South, next highest in the West, and lowest in the Midwest and Northeast. The rates for larceny and auto theft are also greatest in the West.[6]

Characteristics of Offenders and Victims

Age, Sex, and Race of Offenders

Property crime offenders in the United States tend to be even younger than violent crime offenders. Of persons arrested for serious property crimes in the United States in 1987, 62.1 percent were under the age of 25 years. For violent crimes, the figure was 46.5 percent and for all serious known crime, 58.8 percent. Among burglary offenders, 69.5 percent were under 25 and 35.2 percent were less than 18. Roughly the same was true for those arrested for auto theft: 73.2 percent were under the age of 25 and 39.9 percent under 18. Larceny offenders were on balance not as youthful: 58.6 percent were less than 25 years old and 30.9 percent less than 18.

The variation by sex in arrest figures for property crime is great although not as great as for violent crimes. Of persons arrested for property crimes in the United States in 1987, 24.4 percent were females and 75.6 percent males. Females were less involved in violent crimes: they made up 11.1 percent of arrestees and males 88.9 percent. Regarding specific property crimes, females were most represented in larceny:

they accounted for 31.1 percent of all arrests. Females accounted for only 7.9 percent of burglary arrests and 9.7 percent of auto theft arrests. Shoplifting, a form of larceny, is one of the few crimes in which females in the United States are involved rather heavily.

There is a tendency in various societies for females to avoid the commission of crimes which are especially at odds with the female role. On the one hand, it would be difficult to argue that larceny fits well with the female role in the United States. On the other hand, it is reasonable to argue that larceny in the form of shoplifting is decidedly less at odds with the female role than breaking into and stealing from, that is, burglarizing, a home or office or place of business or driving off in a stolen car.

Much discussion has taken place in very recent years as to whether female involvement in serious crime has been on the rise. The greater freedom of women, the movement of women outside the home and into jobs, has provided more opportunities to commit serious crime. Sex roles are probably becoming more similar. This might well reduce disparities between the sexes in terms of involvement in crime. In an analysis of arrests for serious crimes by sex for 1972 as compared to 1987, females were only slightly more involved in 1987 than 15 years earlier. The percentage of all arrests for serious property crimes rose for females from 20.2 in 1972 to 24.4 in 1987.

In interpreting these small changes, it is prudent to ask whether they are due to an actual increase in female criminality *vis-à-vis* males or to a greater tendency for police to arrest females as the years of the 1970s went by. Traditionally, police have been somewhat reluctant to arrest females for all but the most serious crimes such as murder. There has been a feeling among police and males in general that females are too "good" to be criminal and that if they do commit crimes, it is because of special and possibly mitigating circumstances. If the sex roles are in fact growing more similar, then perhaps this perception of females by males is changing. Males may be becoming less reluctant to arrest females. That may account for the modest increase in the proportions of females arrested as compared to males.

Whether the true participation of females in serious crime is increasing is simply not known at this time. The National Crime Survey's research should eventually throw light on whether female participation in *violent* crime is increasing. Victims of violent crime can often report the sex, race, and approximate age of offenders.

Regarding race of offenders, there is a marked disparity between blacks and whites in regard to property crime, yet the disparity is less than is true for violent crime. In 1987, 32.4 percent of arrests for serious property crimes were of blacks; 65.6 percent of whites; and 2.2 percent of other races. For serious violent crime the percentages were 47.3 black, 51.2 white, and 1.5 other races. In the total United States population,

12.0 percent were black; 85.0 percent white; and 3.0 percent other. Thus, blacks were more than two and a half times overrepresented in arrests for serious property crimes as compared to about four times for serious violent crime.[7]

As to specific property crimes, blacks were most overrepresented in motor vehicle theft. Of all arrests for that crime in the United States in 1987, 38.6 percent were of blacks and 59.5 percent of whites. For larceny, the figure for blacks was 32 percent and for whites 65.8 percent. Blacks were least overrepresented in arson cases: 25.5 percent of all arrests were of blacks and 72.9 percent were of whites.[8]

How much of a high representation of blacks in property arrest figures is due to prejudice and a greater readiness to arrest them than whites is unknown. In the previous chapter we noted that the National Crime Survey found that about the same proportion of black robbery offenders were reported by victims as were reported in the FBI's arrest data: 62 and 63 percent, respectively. Since robbery is a property or theft crime as well as a violent crime, those figures may provide some basis for concluding that blacks are not necessarily arrested for serious property crime, because of prejudice, more often than whites. In any case, National Crime Survey data are not available for race of property crime offenders, as they are not for other characteristics of offenders. Victims are unlikely to actually observe offenders when property crimes are concerned.

Age, Race, and Income of Victims

The best United States data on victims of property crime come from the National Crime Survey's[9] analysis of characteristics of the heads of households which did and did not suffer burglary, larceny, or the theft of motor vehicles. (Property crime against business establishments is reported separately by the Survey.) Age and race of head of household and household or family income are among those characteristics for which information is available. Sex of head of household is not available. Rates for each form of major property crime—burglary, larceny, auto theft—are highest where heads of households are youths and decrease with age of household head. The rate of burglary was 213 per 1000 households where heads of household were but 12–19 years of age. This means that over one-fifth of all such households were estimated, on the basis of the sample surveyed, to have been burglarized during that year. In contrast, where head of household was age 65 or greater, the rate of burglary was 33 per 1000 households, one-seventh that of the rate where household heads were youths. The rates for larceny are quite similar. The rates for auto theft follow the same pattern but are much lower: where heads of households were aged 12–19 years, the auto theft rate was 18 per 1000 households; where the age of heads was 65 and over, the rate was 5.

A limited comparison can be made between these rates of property crime victimization by age of head of household and the age of victims of violent crime. The two are not, of course, fully comparable. In the case of property crime, the head of household may not even be on the scene when the theft occurs; in the case of violent crime, the victim, whether head of household or otherwise, is directly physically harmed or threatened with harm. In any case, violent crime victimization is greatest for persons aged 16–19 years and after that decreases steadily with age. This is the same basic pattern as for age of heads of household and property crime victimization. The young are the most heavily involved in both property and violent crime as victims and as offenders as well. The older individuals are, the less likely they are to be victims or offenders of either property or violent crime.

Black households are more likely to suffer property crime victimization than white or "other race" households. The most recent National Crime Survey found the overall rate of property crime victimization to be 226 per 1000 households where heads of households were black; 169 where they were white; and 150 where they were of other races.

It is clear that in general black households are victimized more than white in regard to property crime, and black persons are more likely to be the victims of violent crime than whites (see Chapter 4). Further, both property and violent crime offenders are likely to be black to a much greater extent than their representation in the overall United States population. In general, property crime victimization rates rise as family income of households increases. For households with annual incomes under $7500, the property crime rate was 195 (per 1000 households). The burglary rate per 1000 households was highest, 86, for families with annual incomes under $7500 and next highest, 67, for families in the $10,000–$14,999 level reported. The lowest burglary rate, 54, was for families with incomes of $25,000–$30,000. In contrast, data in the previous chapter indicated that violent crime rates tended to be highest for low-income families. While there were small exceptions, generally speaking rates for overall violent crime and for specific violent crimes decreased as family income grew.

SITUATIONAL FACTORS AND COSTS

Reliable data on characteristics of the situation in which property crime occurred and of offenders at the time of the crime are difficult to obtain. Often there were no witnesses, and offenders were often apprehended quite some time after the crime, if at all. However, the National Crime Survey does provide useful data on the estimated time of occurrence of property crimes against households. (Those against business establishments are excluded.) Overall, household property crimes occurred 28 percent of the time during the daytime, that is, between 6:00 AM and 6:00 PM, and 44 percent of the time at night, between 6:00 PM and 6:00 AM. The time was unknown in 28 percent of the cases. Burglary was more likely than larceny or auto theft to occur during the daytime: 36 percent of burglaries occcurred then. On the other hand, auto theft was the most likely property crime against households to occur during the night, 63 percent of the time.

The FBI reports that property crime rates tend to be lower during the first half of the year (January to June) than the second half. August is the peak month for each major property crime.[10]

The FBI also reports that two-thirds of burglaries were against household residences and the other third involved businesses and other nonresidential buildings. Almost three-fourths (70 percent) entailed actual forcible entry, while 9 percent entailed attempted forcible entry, and 21 percent unlawful entry without physical force.[11]

Regarding larceny, theft of motor vehicle accessories (17 percent) and theft from motor vehicles (21 percent) were the most common forms. Shoplifting accounted for 15 percent and theft of bicycles 6 percent. Purse snatching, pickpocketing, and thefts from coin machines each accounted for 1 percent of the total officially recorded larcenies.

The FBI estimates the value of property stolen in thefts which were officially recorded to have been in 1987 as follows: burglaries, $3.2 billion; larcenies, $3 billion; and auto thefts, $6.0 billion. These total $12.2 billion.[12] The results of the National Crime Survey indicate that the volume of actual property crime probably exceeds that which is officially recorded by four times.[13] If so, then possibly $48 billion worth of property was stolen annually in the United States. This does not include, of course, white-collar crimes such as embezzlement and corporate crime.

Types of Offenders[14]

Property offenders can sometimes be distinguished on the basis of the specific types of crime they commit: burglary when no one is on the premises ("regular" burglaries); burglary by stealth when others are on the premises ("cat" burglaries); check forging (professional and "naive"); automobile theft, including that by "joyriders" who simply steal cars to cruise around; larcenist shoplifting (by amateur "snitches" and professional "boosters"); robbery, at once a property and violent crime, engaged in by armed "robbers" or unarmed "muggers." Yet many property offenders turn from one form of theft to another and so cannot be classified solely along these lines. Gibbons suggested a useful typology of property offenders which ranges from the most professionalized to the unprofessional: *"professional heavies," professionals, semiprofessionals, amateurs.*

Professional Heavies

These are men who are experts at big-time burglary or robbery. They make large "hauls"; they operate in groups or mobs; they plan carefully. They are specialists in safecracking, driving the getaway car, and so on. Heavies seldom find it necessary to use force on others although they are prepared to do so in emergencies. They see themselves as successful professionals, the cream of the criminal crop. They are contemptuous of police and of establishment persons generally. They are scornful of conventional work roles.

Heavies tend to have grown up in lower-class families in criminally saturated urban areas. Often their parents neglected them in the sense of being absent, of not providing socially approved forms of guidance. In some instances parents were themselves professional criminals. However, families and parents were not especially conflicted. These men learned the customs and values of the criminal subculture early in life. They joined delinquent gangs in childhood or early adolescence. They were arrested early in life and brought to juvenile court. Later they were likely to be imprisoned. As adults they are likely to lead stable, married, family lives, but tend to be close only to other heavies and members of their own families. They are psychologically "normal," highly professional, successful men in their chosen occupation—theft crime.

Professionals

These men, although thoroughly professional, are one step down from the top, from the heavies, in the status hierarchy of criminal offenders. While successful, they are seldom really in the "big money." Some specialize in one crime; others commit a range of offenses. They are experts at shoplifting, picking pockets, burglary, "con" games. Very seldom do these professionals use violence, since they are able technicians, craftsmen, who do not need to do so. They, like heavies, frequently operate in groups with various generic names, "whiz mobs" in the case of some pickpocket rings. They have high self-esteem and see themselves as successful professionals. They are exceedingly skillful at avoiding arrest and accept the police as an inevitable part of the society machinery to be circumvented.

Professionals are seldom born into poverty, but are lower-middle or upper-lower class. They grow up, however, in families beset by marital strife and other conflicts, and there is a tendency for them to learn to exploit the differences between their parents and others, "to play off one against another," in ways beneficial to themselves. They carry these characteristics of manipulativeness and deviousness into their adult criminal careers.[15] They begin their lives of crime in early adolescence, but are not immersed in a criminal subculture and do not necessarily operate in juvenile gangs. Often they take jobs in late adolescence or early adulthood which are sometimes considered on the periphery of crime, especially in congested urban areas; jobs as taxi drivers, bartenders, bellhops, as examples. Gradually, they move into property crime as a way of life. As adults, they become deeply involved in the criminal subculture, and their criminal behavior becomes as institutionalized as that of professional heavies. But while successful, they seldom pull off the big "heists" that are the mark of the heavy. These professionals are competent, successful men in a line of work which pursues the "profit motive." At some point there seems to be little distinction between the deviant means they employ to reach cultural success goals and the conforming means of the legitimate professional.

Semiprofessionals

Burglary, shoplifting for a living, and strong-arm robbery are forms of crime commonly carried out by the semiprofessional. Often a given individual offender switches from one to another as circumstances dictate. Skills are not well developed. Planning is rudimentary or, more usually, nonexistent. The main hallmark of the semiprofessional is simply repetition of property crime. Offenders tend to operate as individuals, although two or three may team up on the spur of the moment to carry out a given "job." Semiprofessionals see themselves as professional criminals who had little choice but theft as a way of life. They are hostile toward police and the courts with whom earlier in life they had encounters. They scorn the "square" world: "only slobs work." Lacking skill, semiprofessionals are likely to have long records of arrest and incarceration.

The early social environment of the semiprofessional is more similar to that of the "heavy" than that of the professional: they are likely to have grown up in poor lower-class families. As children and adolescents they learned the criminal subculture in the urban neighborhood and were members of juvenile gangs at an early age. Unlike full professionals, as adults they are not especially immersed in the criminal subculture, but are loners. Their friends, if any, are unlikely to be other offenders. They are marginal men and, in a few cases, such as professional shoplifting, marginal women. They are marginal in the sense that they are not fully participating professionals in either the criminal world or the legitimate world.

Amateurs

Shoplifters

The amateur property offender may or may not commit crimes repeatedly. The central criteria are these: crime is peripheral to the main line of work, including housework; criminal skills are not highly developed and there is on the part of the offenders little or no sense of being a criminal. Amateurs may commit a variety of offenses or only one specific type. Amateur shoplifters, amateur auto thieves, naive check forgers, and one-time losers are four subtypes considered here.

Shoplifting in the United States is extremely widespread. Stores estimate that 1.5 percent of the inventories are stolen in this way. Most shoplifting is by amateurs. They may be youths or older adults, often the middle-aged. "Snitches," as they are called, may very well be female. They steal for personal use as opposed to professional shoplifters, "boosters," who sell their goods to middlemen "fences" or others. Adult snitches usually work alone while juveniles are likely to team up temporarily. The act of shoplifting is repeated more than once, often many times, by the snitch. While skills are not at a professional level, they may very well reach a moderate level of expertise after repeated thefts.[16]

Snitches see themselves as honest citizens. They have conventional values. They come from lower- or middle-class family backgrounds. While juvenile shoplifters may be from poverty families, adult offenders are usually middle class. They do not have histories of severe conflict in their early family environments. They have had little contact with the criminal subculture. Blacks are not overrepresented among amateur shoplifters although they are more likely than whites to be arrested for this crime. Adult amateurs are usually married and tend to lead fairly stable lives.

Many snitches are apprehended by store detectives or police. They seldom end up in court because storeowners and managers do not like to spend the time required in prosecution. Also, owners and managers want to avoid the supposed stigma of having a store where crimes occur. Interestingly, research shows that a severe warning by store detectives and managers or by police serves far better as a deterrent than formal arrest, prosecution, and punishment. The warnings brings home to the offender how much is to be lost in status if shoplifting continues. Prosecution and conviction mean loss of status and are likely to change the offender's self-image to one of thief. He or she may then go on to more professional levels of shoplifting.

Auto Thieves

Professional thieves steal automobiles for profit; they sell the car for parts or "deliver" certain wanted models on demand. Amateur car thieves are likely to be joyriders. They cruise around, having a good time, then abandon the stolen vehicle. Most are between 13 and 20 years of age, male, and middle class. They "joyride" time and again but with little expertise. Rarely do they carry out other offenses. They operate in shifting groups of two to five boys. They see themselves as nondelinquent. They have conventional middle-class values except for car theft. While not especially hostile toward police, they view them as stupid bunglers.[17]

Joyriders grow up in modestly affluent middle-class neighborhoods and have no contact with the criminal subculture. They have experienced close parental supervision and discipline but are not close to their fathers. These boys appear to have male identity problems and want to prove they are "macho." They are often arrested and brought to either juvenile or adult criminal court where they may be found delinquent or criminally guilty and placed on probation but seldom incarcerated. While they view this legal processing as confirming their self-image as macho, it does not create a self-fulfilling prophecy. They seldom continue as criminal offenders in adulthood, but rather marry, take conventional jobs, rear children, and become "solid citizens."

Check Forgers

Amateur check forgers, like professional forgers, are repeaters. Major distinctions are that the professional makes a living at passing bad checks whereas the amateur seeks to supplement income or get out of debt through forgery; and the professional is far more skilled than the amateur. The naive check forger, as the amateur is termed, passes a number of bad checks, often on his own checking account, within a short time. (There are very few female forgers.) If not caught, he may, after months of abstention, go on another check-passing binge. The naive forger seldom fabricates paychecks or alters the checks of others; these are methods of the professional. The amateur sees himself as a law-abiding citizen who is legitimately tiding himself over tight financial times. He has conventional values, was probably brought up in a stable middle-class family, and has had no appreciable contact with the criminal subculture before or after forgery began. He tends, however, to be bitter over his lack of outstanding success in conventional roles.

Often the initial round of forgery is preceded by occupational and marital instability, job loss, separation, and so on. As forgers, these people have few social ties; they are isolated. Naive check forgers are fairly readily apprehended. Unlike professionals, they remain in the district where they are known. Upon conviction, they are usually placed on probation. They are prone to violate the conditions of probation and may then be incarcerated. They later continue in their criminal activity. Both naive and professional check forgers seem to gain reward out of risk taking, out of taking their chances both of gaining quick money illegitimately and of being apprehended and punished. It may be that they seek to alleviate periods of psychological depression through the stimulation of high risk.[18]

One-Time Losers

These are the amateurs who suddenly commit, or attempt to commit, one large theft or embezzlement. They may hold up a bank or retail store. They may embezzle many thousands of dollars in one try. They may steal valuable jewelry. They have no history of crime or of early development problems in family or school, no record of participation in the criminal subculture, and no criminal skills. They are extremely law abiding, usually lower-middle class. Suddenly, they find themselves with serious financial problems or family problems or both. They risk all on one doomed attempt to pull off a big coup without any of the requisite skills. Inevitably, they fail, are quickly apprehended, and convicted. Although their crime is a first offense, they are incarcerated for several or more years in a state prison because of the magnitude of the theft. When released, they resume law-abiding lives.

Two Broad Types

These are all types of property offenders. They vary tremendously not only in degree of professionalization but in early social background, participation in the criminal subculture, and the kinds of values, family situation, and occupational conditions which characterize their adult lives. If apprehended, they also vary greatly as to whether they later commit further crimes. One constellation of factors is composed of a conflicted and economically impoverished family and neighborhood experience in early life, usually in an urban setting; a consequent lack of socially acceptable means for achieving culturally approved success goals; and early and later participation in the criminal subculture. A second constellation of factors is made up of early experience in middle-class unconflicted family and neighborhood; little if any early exposure to the criminal subculture; and unsuccessful use of conventional means to achieve money, status, and power. Psychological problems may or may not be found in relation to either constellation. (This may depend more, however, on whether particular research studies sought or were able to find psychological difficulties in offenders than on whether they actually exist.) Broadly, the first constellation tends to be characteristic of professional property offenders and the second of amateurs.

SOCIAL INTEGRATION AND CULTURAL SUPPORT EXPLANATIONS

A Summary of the Evidence

Property crime rates are high among adolescents, especially those who are black and male. Adolescent offenders may operate in gangs, very small groups, or alone. Many come from poverty-stricken, lower-class homes where conflict is high and from disorganized neighborhoods where the criminal subculture flourishes. Others are from middle- or upper-class families where conflict may or may not be great and from neighborhoods where the criminal subculture is absent.

Habitual adult offenders may be members of the lower or higher classes, more typically the former. They may be professionals or amateurs. Professionals usually have images of themselves as criminals and amateurs seldom do. Professionals are likely to be immersed in the criminal subculture and amateurs are not. Very often professionals developed in lower-class conflicted families and neighborhoods where as children they were exposed to the criminal subculture. There are, however, numerous exceptions to this.

Nonhabitual offenders are always amateurs (although some amateurs are habitual offenders). They are very likely to be middle-class persons with positive views of conventional roles who define themselves as law-abiding persons. As adults they may lead family lives characterized by either stability or conflict. They have had little if any participation in the criminal subculture either as adults or children. Their early lives were frequently spent in middle-class, relatively unconflicted settings.

While fragmentary, there is some evidence that if an offender is upon initial apprehension warned of the consequence of repetition of property crime and released, the likelihood of recidivism is low. When initial apprehension leads to processing through the criminal justice system, on the other hand, recidivism may well be induced.

Social Integration

Clearly, social integration explanations in the form of Merton's formulation of goals, means, and anomie is highly relevant to much property crime.[19] This is likely to be so whether offenders are classified according to the type of offense—burglary, larceny, or auto theft—or the type of professional or amateur status they hold.

Low social integration and anomie are endemic to lower-class, black neighborhoods in which so many youthful offenders live and develop. These young property offenders internalize culturally approved goals for success. They see others in the society making use of institutionalized means for achieving those goals while they are blocked from doing so. Relative deprivation is great. They become alienated, unintegrated outsiders. Many tend to engage in illegitimate behavior to gain the material success goals they cannot gain legitimately.

Low social integration and anomie are also characteristic of the early lives of professional heavies and of semiprofessional offenders. It is true in terms of the adult lives of naive check forgers and one-time losers. Low social integration does not, however, characterize the early or later lives of professional offenders, as distinct from professional heavies, or of amateur shoplifters, who are frequently middle-class adults. Neither does low integration characterize auto thieves who are adolescent joyriders. Seldom have any of these three developed under conditions of poverty. Generally speaking, then, low social integration, anomie, and alienation have loomed large in the lives of lower-class property offenders but not of middle-class offenders.

Cultural Supports

Sutherland and Cressey's theory of differential association has much importance for understanding property crime.[20] The overwhelming majority of known offenders have had in early life or adulthood strong, rewarding associations with individuals who act out the criminal subculture. Poor young black males often grow up in ghetto neighborhoods where it is difficult to avoid immersion in the criminal subculture. The childhoods of professional heavies and semiprofessionals are characterized by involvement in the criminal subculture. This is not the case with "nonheavy" professionals. However, they and heavies participate as adult offenders in the criminal subculture while semiprofessionals seldom do. Amateur adult shoplifters, often middle class, do not generally show histories of involvement in the criminal subculture either as adolescents or adults. The same is true of adolescent amateurs, joyriding auto thieves, and naive (amateur) check forgers. In sum, the various types of professional property offenders have considerable

or more contact with the criminal subculture in adulthood or preadult-
hood or both. Lower-class, amateur property offenders, epitomized by
black ghetto youths, are likely to have contact with the criminal subculture while for adult amateurs this is unlikely.

Cohen's reaction formation theory of delinquency is certainly applicable to many lower-class youth who persistently commit property
crimes.[21] They react to anomie, that is, to being blocked from access to
institutionalized means for achieving cultural success, by developing
or following delinquent (criminal) customs and values. Cohen's formulation attempts to explain property offenses by middle-class male
youths in terms of a reaction formation to their mothers rather than to
anomic conditions. He argues that middle-class mothers want their sons
to reflect strongly proper training in middle-class morality. This means
a conformity that can readily make their sons appear as boys who are
"too good." The masculine identity of the boys is threatened. They
react against their mothers and act out deviant behavior—theft and violence—dramatically opposed to middle-class morality. Doing so vali-
dates their masculinity. Being apprehended for criminal offenses and
thereby stigmatizing their families is an indirect form of retaliation against
the frustrating mothers.

Cohen's explanation may help to explain joyriding auto thefts by
middle-class boys and conceivably professional (but not heavy or semiprofessional) property theft. Perhaps these males are reacting to domineering, conformity-demanding mothers. This is a hypothesis worthy
of further research.

Cloward and Ohlin's opportunity structures approach stresses that
to become functioning members of the professional theft segment—
and also violent and retreatist segments—of the criminal subculture,
individuals must meet recruitment criteria and learn to carry out appropriate criminal roles effectively.[22] Put differently, the professional theft
opportunity structure is not open to anyone who desires to enter any
more than are, say, the legitimate professions. Professional property
offenders and professional heavies as well operate in groups which
demand expertise. Opportunity structure theory applies well to these.
Bunglers, undependables, and alcoholics are not wanted in, and are
often excluded from, professional crime. The application of opportunity structure theory to semiprofessional property offenders is more
limited. They usually operate on their own insofar as the commission
of crimes is concerned. Admission to a theft opportunity structure is
not a necessary condition for this as it is in fully professional theft.
However, most semiprofessionals have loose ties to other parts of the
illegitimate world, particularly fences or middlemen who buy the stolen goods from them and then either sell to retailers or retail the goods
themselves. Semiprofessionals must gain admission to such loose or

quasi forms of illegitimate opportunity structures if they are to have any chance of making a continuing livelihood from crime.

Conflict and Societal Reaction Explanations

Social Disorganization and Conflict

It is clear that much property crime occurs in socially disorganized, poor areas of the large urban concentrations of populations. But much also occurs in the less disorganized middle- and upper-income districts, that is, where the money is. Similarly, many property offenders have grown up in disorganized, poverty neighborhoods while others, probably far less in number, have developed in relatively affluent middle- and upper-class neighborhoods. The main point to be made is that social disorganization and the conflict of conduct norms which often accompanies it is an important generating source of much, but not all, property crime.

This parallels the situation in regard to low social integration and criminal subculture supports: those are critical forces behind property crime in many but by no means all instances. One major cross-cutting variable is social class. Offenders who were born into lower-class families are likely to have experienced low social integration, anomie, and alienation because of a dislocation of cultural success goals and institutionalized means for achieving them, because of exposure to the criminal subculture, and because of social disorganization. Offenders who were reared in middle- and upper-class families are not likely to have had appreciable experience with those.

However, both higher- and lower-status property offenders are prone to have experienced interpersonal conflict within the family, in either early or adult life or both. One reasonable hypothesis is that lower-status families, beset by failure to achieve success goals, may develop patterns of marital strife and parent–child contention as ways of working off the frustration and tensions that failure brings. Higher-status families may develop intrafamily patterns of conflict also but for different reasons. The stress of striving, albeit successfully, for cultural goals may also cause severe frustration and tensions that are vented through family members' aggression toward each other. Fear of losing cultural success goals that have been achieved may have similar consequences. In sum, family conflict often results from failure to achieve in the wider society, from the burdens of achieving success, or from the fear of losing the symbols of success.

Sellin's culture conflict thesis and Miller's lower-class subculture formulation are in a related way relevant to property crime.[23] Miller's view is that lower-class everyday patterns of theft (and violence) are part of lower-class subculture, not elements of a separate and distinct criminal subculture. The higher classes define certain lower-class behavior patterns—theft and physical violence—as criminal deviance and prosecute those who are apprehended for carrying them out. In Sellin's terms, the two subcultures—lower and higher class—have conflicting values and customs. The lower class, acting out what is natural, that is, subculturally prescribed, find themselves apprehended, tried, and punished.

Two main problems with the conception are that first, higher-status persons do steal. Shoplifting and embezzlement are forms of property crime for which higher-status persons are apprehended and prosecuted. They may receive greater leniency than lower-status persons at various stages in the criminal justice processing. Nevertheless, they commit property crimes in more than insignificant numbers and they are clearly not immune to prosecution. The second problem is that it is somewhat doubtful as to whether patterns of theft are part of lower-class everyday culture. Much theft *occurs* in lower-class neighborhoods. But that does not necessarily mean that it is woven through lower-class culture. More likely, theft patterns are part of the criminal subculture which coexists with lower-class culture in many urban settings. After all, lower-status individuals are just as outraged at being the victims of property offenses as higher-status persons. Often they are more outraged because what is stolen from them may well be a large part of what they possess.

Thio's power theory is meant to explain property as well as violent crime and other forms of negative deviance.[24] The core of Thio's approach is that the powerful induce higher-consensus deviance in the powerless while themselves committing lower-consensus deviance. Higher-consensus deviance is that about which there is broad agreement in the society that punishment should be meted out to those who commit it. In the case of lower-consensus deviance, there is not broad agreement about punishment. Consequently, those who commit lower-consensus deviance are very likely to escape punishment while higher-consensus deviants are likely to suffer punishment. This explanation is more relevant to property than to violent crime. As discussed later in the chapter, the powerful commit white-collar, corporate, and government crime, often with impunity. The powerless have almost no opportunities to commit such crimes. They do have opportunities to burglarize, shoplift, pick pockets, and the like. What power theory does not explain is why so many powerless individuals (and powerful also) are extremely law-abiding persons who almost never steal.

Societal Reaction

To what extent does the way society reacts to a deviant act or to the presumption that a deviant act has occurred impede or beget future acts of deviance? More specifically, how does the way the criminal justice system responds to acts of theft affect whether offenders do or do not commit further thefts? The findings in the previous section on "Types of Offenders" are mixed. Professional heavies frequently have been arrested early in life and brought to juvenile court. Later they are likely to have been imprisoned. This does little or nothing to impede their criminal careers. Professionals (nonheavies) are skillful at avoiding arrest from an early age and have little history of arrest or prosecution. Semiprofessionals continue to ply their trade although many have been arrested and incarcerated numerous times. Amateur shoplifters, many of whom are middle class, show a decided tendency to desist from further thefts if given a severe warning by store detectives or managers or police. Actual processing through the criminal justice system—formal arrest, trial, punishment—works less well as a deterrent. This process often serves, through the stigma of adjudication, to erode the individual's middle-class standing and to make taking the self-concept of criminal a seemingly necessary alternative. Youthful joyriding auto thieves, in contrast, are frequently arrested and brought to court, but seldom incarcerated. This processing and labeling by the criminal justice system may well validate their masculine self-image. Yet they are not thereby launched on a life of crime. Most become law-abiding adults. Naive check forgers are usually arrested and convicted. Seldom are they impeded from further passing of bad checks. Amateur one-time losers are in many instances severely punished. They seldom recidivate.

Some general principles emerge: Those property offenders who are or have been immersed in the criminal subculture are unlikely to be deterred from further crime by official labeling as criminals. They accept arrest, prosecution, and incarceration as occupational hazards. Amateur property offenders are likely to terminate their thefts regardless of whether they are processed through the criminal justice system. The exception is the amateur shoplifter, who is best deterred by a strong, informal warning rather than by formal processing.

It has become clear in recent years that processing first offenders through the criminal justice system should be done sparingly. Each step—arrest, prosecution, incarceration—may increase the individual's self-concept as a criminal rather than a law-abiding citizen. Also, incarceration tends to increase the person's repertoire of criminal skills and values as well. The system we have designed to deter crime frequently induces it. This is especially applicable to property offenders. Granting exceptions, most commit their first offense in early adolescence.

That is the time to provide constructive guidance rather than negative labeling.

WHITE-COLLAR, CORPORATE, AND GOVERNMENT CRIME

Major Types

White-collar crimes are those carried out by middle- and upper-class persons, "respectable" citizens, in the course of their occupations, usually in business settings. White-collar crime takes two main forms: that carried out for the individual's direct personal gain and that carried out in the interest of the company or corporation. Embezzlement is the most common form of *personal white-collar crime.* It often involves falsification of company financial records for gain. Accepting kickbacks, offering and receiving bribes, illegal use of company transportation, and theft through tampering with computers are other forms of personal white-collar crime. *Corporate white-collar crime* takes such forms as price rigging in violation of the Sherman Antitrust Act, false advertising, unfair labor practices, restraint of trade, and infringements of copyrights, trademarks, and patents.

The most notable series of corporate violations in recent years was the conspiracy of high-level employees in the electrical industry to fix prices. Criminal charges were brought against 29 corporations and 45 officials of those corporations by the United States government. Officials met more or less secretly in various parts of the country and conspired to rig bids on various electrical products and to fix prices across the industry in a number of other ways.

The biggest violator was the General Electric Company. Fines levied against that company totaled $437,500; 32 executives were known to have been involved. The Westinghouse Company was fined $372,000. In all, seven officials served jail sentences, most for 30 days. Twenty-four other officials received suspended jail sentences. Some officials were fired by their companies and others were retained in much the same capacities they had filled prior to conviction.

Competition was very great in the electrical field. At General Electric, top officials set sales quotas impossibly high. (Those officials had long issued directives pointing out that price rigging was illegal. Yet some knew the practice existed. None of these officials were convicted.) The market was extremely uncertain and unstable. Demand fluctuated greatly and prices shifted rapidly unless stabilized through conspiracy. Some senior employees had the choice of either being fired or entering into collusion with representatives of other companies to fix prices. All violators knew they were breaking the law. Many viewed their behavior as technically illegal but not criminal and not unethical. They considered their actions to be usual in the industry, which they were. They felt they should be excused because they were acting under orders. And they believed that their actions were ethical and necessary because they stabilized the market. Few were able to see that that which is usual, which is done because someone else orders it, and which contributes to stability can also be unequivocably criminal.[25]

Clinard and Yeager[26] provide the most extensive analyses of corporate illegal activity in recent years. Their study of the 620 largest publically owned corporations in the United States shows that (1) 60 percent of the corporations were charged with at least one violation; the average number of offenses was 2.7; (2) three industries—oil, pharmaceuticals, and automobiles—were disproportionately involved in corporate violations, accounting for half of all offenses; and (3) executives in about half of the 25 largest corporations in America either plead guilty to or were convicted of illegal business practices.

Yet, as was the case in the electrical anti-trust case, executives convicted of corporate crime continue to receive token sentences. Eighty percent of the fines levied against corporations were for $5,000 or less; the average was $1,000. Sixty-eight percent of the executives found criminally liable were granted probation. Incarcerated executives served an average of 37 days. No sentence exceeded six months imprisonment.[27]

Government crime overlaps to some degree with white-collar crime. Yet in other ways it is quite distinctive. Government crime is carried out by public officials and other government employees in the course of their jobs. Thio divides government crime into three categories: that which is done for money; to maintain power; and because of arrogance of government workers toward the public.[28] Government crime for money involves taking bribes in exchange for official favors, accepting illegal campaign contributions, embezzling the government. This, of course, is in many respects fundamentally the same form of deviance as white-collar personal crime in business settings. Government crime to maintain power, or to gain more power, often takes the form of abuse of power on a grand scale. The Watergate Scandal of the Nixon administration during the early 1970s epitomizes this form. Specific examples of crimes carried out then included harassment of enemies with income tax audits; illegal wiretapping; burglarizing the Democratic National Headquarters; printing false charges about opponents and mailing them under false pretenses; and many more.

Government crime because of arrogance of public officials is the third form. Thio cites as examples judges who abuse criminal defendants by illegally denying bail, shifting the burden of proof to the defendant (by law the burden of proof is on the prosecution), finding individuals guilty of crimes because they associated with others who were found guilty. Other examples are officials who reward themselves with such perquisites as free vacations for themselves, families, and friends; free trips abroad; and so on at the taxpayers' expense. These fall in the "crime for money" category, of course, but usually appear to contain large measures of arrogance and contempt.

Incidence

Very likely, white-collar and government crime are underreported and unknown to the public to a far greater extent than "ordinary" violent and property crime. "Respectable" white-collar and government offenders are probably far less apt to be prosecuted and convicted than "unrespectable, black-collar" offenders. On the one hand, it is clear that white-collar and government crime are widespread in this and many other countries. But how widespread is presently an unanswerable question and may well remain so. Businesses are reluctant to recognize, report, and prosecute white-collar crime. Owners and managers do not want their businesses stigmatized by having dishonest employees. In the case of corporate crime, owners or managers are usually indirect supporters of, if not directly involved in, the illegal actions that are designed to further the corporate interest.[29]

Where government crime is concerned, officials may well be able to exert control over the very agencies designated to enforce laws and dispense justice. Officials who violate the law are unlikely to sit idly by while the criminal justice apparatus is brought to bear against them. And when lower level employees of government commit criminal offenses in the course of their jobs, higher officials are frequently reluctant to see those offenses aired and prosecuted; this would imply mismanagement. In other words, criminal offenses in government, as the Watergate Scandal so clearly exemplified, are likely to be followed by cover-ups, by subversion of justice.

There are, however, estimates of the scope and cost of white-collar and government crime for money in the United States. They vary widely. Since they are all we have as indicators of these forms of higher-status negative deviance, they nevertheless have some value. Common forms of property crime, e.g., robbery, burglary, larceny, and auto theft, result in annual losses of $12.5 billion.[30] However, the financial costs of white collar crime are estimated to be over $200 billion.[31] And while there is no adequate way of measuring it, white-collar and government crimes of all types obviously cost the society dearly in terms of the erosion of moral values. Younger and older citizens alike see business and political leaders violating the law with impunity. This contributes substantially to the growing ethic, "Get what you can, while you can, any way you can."

Characteristics of Offenders

As we might anticipate, information on the characteristics of white-collar and government criminal offenders is sparse; studies of known offenders are few. It is clear that most violators are middle- or upper-class, middle aged, hold conventional social values, and have had little or no contact with the criminal subculture. Lower-class individuals rarely have access to situations in business or government where they would have opportunity to violate the law. Usually one must be in a position of trust. This requires middle- or upper-class status and very likely middle age since it takes time to acquire positions of trust. Moreover, if a person had any known past or present connections with the criminal subculture or possessed a criminal record, he or she would be unlikely to have been given a position of trust in the first place. Of course, there are exceptions, especially in goverment where criminal violators are sometimes elected to office; and offenders are also occasionally appointed to government positions.

Violators are very likely to be male since traditionally have been excluded from positions of trust in business and from higher-level positions in government. They may have held positions such as executive secretary which required trust in the sense of extreme discretion, but seldom did they hold positions of financial trust and of power. Obviously, this is changing. As women become integrated into the higher reaches of business, industry, and government, it can be expected that their involvement in white-collar and government crime will increase significantly.

In the main, research has discovered very little regarding personality characteristics which differentiate white-collar and government offenders from other persons. Donald Cressey conducted an extensive study of white-collar crime, specifically of embezzlement where offenders criminally violated financial trust vested in them by their employers.[32] Cressey found that the following conditions characterized the criminal violators: offenders saw themselves as having a financial problem they could not share with others, due to gambling, for example. They reasoned that the problem could be secretly resolved by violating financial trust, and they saw the opportunity within their company to do so. They were able to rationalize their violation *before* as well as during and after committing it: they were "borrowing" the money and would eventually pay it back; the company "owed" them money because of their unreasonably low salary over the past years; and so on.

Institutionalization of Corporate and Government Crime

In corporate and government crime, the customs and values of the business or government agency together with the opportunities for violations have much to do with whether crimes are actually carried out. In other words, corporate and government crime tend to occur to the extent that it is institutionalized and individuals are in a position to learn and carry out criminal customs and values.

As Clinard and Quinney point out, lawbreaking may become an internally acceptable pattern in some corporations.[33] Officials of corporations may themselves break the law regularly and expect their subordinates to do the same. Thus officials can become strong, influential role models for criminality. Corporations sometimes formally *draw up plans* for violating the law. Further, business people may be isolated during the working day from customs and values which support adherence to the law. And they may well be shielded from outside criticism by corporate policies about imparting information.

Regarding government crime, one unfortunate fact that in a general way lends support to violations and potential offenders is that many members of the public hold the view that it is acceptable for the government to break the law in order to get people to follow the law, in order for government officials to govern effectively. The assumptions are that extralegal methods must be used to stop "extremists" from activities that might threaten public order and the government itself and that, in any case, if government had to adhere to the letter of the law at every turn, it would be paralyzed.[34]

Further, some government agencies are in the business of violating laws of one type or another. While it is difficult to determine the precise legal or illegal nature of secret activities by the Central Intelligence Agency and the Federal Bureau of Investigation, there is no doubt that programs of domestic surveillance, the suppression of political dissent, and repeated burglarizing of citizens' homes have been illegally carried out. Those were not acts of negative deviance by particular individuals in these organizations violating orders of their superiors. Rather they were systematic, institutionalized activities of government agencies.

In addition, illegal physical violence is systematically employed by some police departments and prisons. Suspects are subjected to "third-degree methods" (torture) in order to extort confessions. Prison guards may use excessive force to induce conformity. These methods are usually rationalized by police and corrections personnel as being necessary to deal adequately with "the criminal element." The fact is, however, that there are legal restraints on the force to be used against suspects and inmates by those personnel in given types of situations. Again, violations tend not to be by single individuals acting purely alone. They tend to be systematic, institutionalized violations carried out in the name of protecting the public.[35]

Explanations of White-Collar, Corporate, and Government Crime

Social Integration and Cultural Supports

White-collar embezzlement and corporate crime and much government crime are in part explained by social integration theory. Merton's goals-means formulation is especially important. To be sure, middle- and upper-class offenders have been able, unlike lower-class violators, to gain access to the institutionalized means for achieving cultural success goals. Merton's ideas are relevant for these reasons: middle- and upper-class violators tend to be fearful of losing the means to insure continued success goals, or they are actually losing success goals attained earlier and need more effective means to counteract that, or they desire success goals beyond those already achieved and seek additional means to attain them.[36]

Embezzlers often face financial ruin, and their offenses are desperate means of attempting to shore up a crumbling world. Corporate offenders' violations in the interest of company profits may be designed to curry favor with those superiors in a position to reward them with salary increases and promotions. Government offenders may be attempting to stave off real or imagined threats from either dissidents or political opponents. They may seek to avoid political defeat through illegal means including abuse of power; again they may be attempting "to win big" in elections or otherwise in an attempt to increase their perhaps already considerable power and prestige.

Cultural support theories have much importance in explaining corporate and government crime, less in regard to embezzlement. Sutherland's differential association formulation has little bearing on embezzlement.[37] This crime tends to be quite individualistic rather than institutionalized. Offenders have seldom had significant contact with the criminal subculture either in or out of the business setting. A revision of Cloward and Ohlin's opportunity structure thesis is, however, germane to explaining the crime of embezzlement.[38] To embezzle, one usually must be located within a business or government organization as a legitimate employee or official. While having a position of trust in the organization is not always necessary, it is certainly usual in cases of embezzlement. Put differently, having been accepted into the legitimate opportunity structure of an organization and having learned the requisite social roles in the organization also provides illegitimate opportunities that would otherwise not exist.

To commit corporate crimes in the interests of the business organization, and to commit government crime as well, it is also usually necessary to have gained access to legitimate opportunity structures, corporate or governmental. One can seldom if ever engage in price fixing or abuse of official power without first having become a legitimate member of a business or governmental organization. Generally speaking, such criminal activities require planning, coordination, and cooperation among numerous employees and officials.

Price fixing, for example, must be an enterprise that involves a number of persons in a given company, and it must involve at least two companies, usually more. Abuse of power in the form of violations of citizens' civil rights by government officials could conceivably be carried out on a very limited scale by one or a few persons. Far more often, however, a considerable network of "public servants" is required. This all means that customs and values for cooperative illegitimate endeavors within corporate and governmental structures must exist and be learned and followed by individuals within those structures. In other words, these forms of crimes are institutionalized and require the existence of a special form of criminal subculture within the organizations.

Culture Conflict

Culture conflict formulations are somewhat useful in explaining crimes of a corporate nature and in government. Regarding embezzlement, their relevance is marginal. Those who embezzle are usually individuals facing financial difficulties. They may or may not have much power in the organization. They resort to illegitimate means that are a hybrid of business practices and larceny. As a rule, they steal by falsifying records. Conflict theories have little application.

With respect to corporate and government crime, the reverse is often true. Both Quinney's political conflict formulation of crime and Thio's power explanation of deviance in general are especially relevant.[39] Quinney's thesis is that the powerful in a capitalistic society create the idea of crime, define it in terms of behavior common to the powerless, cause the powerless to take on criminal roles, and then punish them for criminal transgressions. The powerful capitalists do this as a means of exerting social control over the powerless, thereby keeping them from usurping power. It also allows the powerful to carry out exploitative business and governmental practices. These tend to go undetected because they are not defined as crime while public attention is focused on the criminally defined behavior of those without power.

Thio's approach, being concerned with deviance in general, is broader but from the standpoint of corporate and government crime is similar to Quinney's explanation. The powerful, Thio contends, arrange to have behavior of the powerless officially defined as negatively deviant and to shape public opinion so that there is broad consensus in the society over that. At the same time, the powerful engage in negatively deviant expliotative acts in business and government in order to maintain and increase power. In focusing public opinion on the deviance of the powerless, they deflect attention away from their own deviance. Thus, the powerful carry out lower-consensus deviance with relative impunity while the powerless carry out higher-consensus deviance at considerable risk of punishment. Both Quinney and Thio hold, then, that the powerful engage in deviant behaviors which exploit the poor and the powerless in order to maintain power.

This explanation fits corporate and government crime well. Corporate managers engage in quasi-legal and illegal business practices, and in legal practices which exploit the public as well, in order to increase company profits. They do so, generally, not simply out of altruistic concern for the welfare of the company (whose stockholders are sometimes the same members of the public who are exploited) but in order to increase their own wealth, social standing, and power. Government officials carry out illegal activities which exploit the public, constitute abuses of power, and set destructive role models for the society, not simply in order "to get things done" or "to make government work." They frequently, if not always, do so with the aim of either maintaining or increasing social standing, authority, power, and sometimes wealth.

It is not necessary to conceive of negatively deviant corporate managers and governmental officials as individuals engaged in a gigantic conspiracy to exert social control over the poor. Individuals "cut corners," sometimes very large corners, for such specific reasons as gaining a promotion or getting reelected. The institutionalized illegitimate means and values for doing so are usually already there, means evolved over decades for protecting self-interests in powerful roles. Corporate and government offenders learn these means and values, they act them out, and in so doing they very often strengthen them.

Social Control and Societal Reaction

Crimes carried out to benefit the corporation and government crime are, then, institutionalized with corporate and government structures to a significant degree. That being so, social control mechanisms for preventing crime are weak in government and corporate settings. Moreover, because government agencies and corporations often work closely with each other and because the same individuals frequently move from positions in one to positions in the other, government controls over corporate crime are also weak. As for business and government employees who steal directly from their employers, usually embezzlement or pilfering, they are unlikely to be prosecuted for two reasons: the corporation or government department does not want to be characterized as having crime within it; and superiors are reluctant to have any publicity that employees are criminal since that could reflect negatively on their managerial abilities.

As a consequence, the statutes regarding white-collar and government crime tend to be loose and lenient and enforcement is lax. One study found that but 5 percent of those convicted of stealing from the company were incarcerated; most of the rest were placed on probation.[40] And those convicted form a very small proportion, probably but a few percentage points, of all such offenders. As for crimes carried out to benefit the corporation, these are even less often prosecuted. When they are, it is usually the corporation rather than an individual that is found to have violated the criminal law. Very moderate fines are the usual penalty. On those rare occasions when corporate officials are prosecuted and convicted, the sentence is as a rule extremely light and incarceration is very seldom the outcome. As for government offenders, if they are ever charged, charges are usually dropped before trial. If tried in criminal court, offenders tend to be found not guilty. Those few found guilty have usually plea-bargained such that punishment is very minimal, often no more than the mild stigma of having been convicted of a misdemeanor and fined a small sum.

How central is societal reaction theory to explaining the "respectable" deviance of personal and corporate white-collar crime and government crime? The business and political worlds in which higher-status persons who engage in these crimes operate provide a considerable degree of immunity against overt societal reaction. Moreover, higher-status offenders are often individuals adept at avoiding adverse societal reaction. At the same time, the evidence, while not conclusive, tends to indicate that white-collar and government offenders are unlikely to engage in further criminality if prosecuted and punished.

There exists, then, the anomalous situation that societal reaction to these crimes in the forms of stigmatization and punishment appears to prevent recidivism yet is only very infrequently brought into play. Generally speaking, societal reaction much less often prevents recidivism among those who commit the "ordinary" property crimes of burglary, larceny, and auto theft except where offenders are middle class. It may very well be that the more powerful members of the society design formal systems of social control which are most effective in regard to themselves. Yet those systems are most often brought to bear against the powerless with whom they are relatively ineffective. This in Quinney and Thio's terms can have the result of focusing attention on lower-status crime without preventing it, while higher-status crime continues relatively unnoticed and unabated.

SUMMARY

Property crimes have been traditonally viewed as burglary, larceny, and robbery, the last being a violent crime as well. More sophisticated yet commonly known forms of property offenses include fraud—confidence games and forgery are examples. These crimes of theft are usually thought to be carried out by persons from the lower classes, so-called "black-collar" crimes. Strikingly, however, more dollars are lost each year by property crimes committed by middle- and upper-status individuals—"white-collar" crimes. Such crimes may be committed for personal gain as in the case of embezzlement, accepting kickbacks, offering and receiving bribes, and so on; or for the benefit of a corporation, as in the case of price rigging, false advertising, and restraint of trade among others.

The main traditional forms of property crime, burglary and larceny, are found to be particularly high in technologically advanced countries and are on the rise around the world. About 12 million felonious property offenses are reported to the police each year in the United States. Sixty-two percent of these are larcenies, 27 percent burglaries, and 11 percent auto thefts. Property crime accounts for about nine of every 10 serious recorded crimes in this country. The National Crime Survey data show that four times more property crimes are said to have occurred than are reported to the police. Urban centers are victimized by property crime over three times more often than rural areas. And the western and southern regions of the United States have the highest rates of property crime.

Property offenders tend to be even younger than violent criminal offenders; almost six in 10 of those arrested for a property crime are under the age of 25. Females tend to be involved more in certain thefts, particularly shoplifting, than in violent offenses. Slightly more than 24.4 percent of persons arrested for all serious property crimes are females. The issue of whether females are actually engaging in more crime or have become more prone to arrest remains unresolved. Blacks are disproportionately overrepresented among persons arrested for serious property crimes, but less so than for violent crimes.

Little is known about the characteristics of white-collar criminals. Most are male, middle-aged, upper-middle class, and act independently of other criminal offenders. They occupy positions of trust within a corporation or governmental agency. Such offenders have typically encountered a financial problem they could not share with others but were in a position to embezzle or otherwise convert to personal use funds entrusted to them.

Types of property offenders include "professional heavies," professionals, semiprofessionals, and amateurs. Professional heavies specialize in the big score. They work in small, highly skilled groups. Such thieves are drawn from lower-class, crime-ridden urban areas. Their involvement with law violation began early in life and typically resulted in arrest and incarceration. As adults they carry on stable family lives supported, in the main, by large-scale theft.

Professionals rank below professional heavies in the theft hierarchy. They commit a range of property crimes, such as, shoplifting, "con" games, or burglary, but seldom are arrested. Their early family lives, marked by parental marital strife, are where they learned to manipulate situations, pit parent against parent, for their own advantage. Only as adults did they become involved in criminal subcultures and begin to realize financial profit from theft.

Semiprofessionals commonly engage in burglary, shoplifting, or strong-arm robbery. These crimes are likely to be unplanned and are carried out on the spur of the moment as opportunities arise. Offenders tend to work alone, or at times with one or two others. Their backgrounds resemble those of the "heavies"; but unlike heavies they continue to be arrested often, are loners, and are only marginally successful at crime.

Amateur thieves include shoplifters, auto thieves, check forgers, and one-time losers. For the amateur, crime is peripheral to the main line of work, including housework; criminal skills are not highly developed; and offenders have little or no sense of being a criminal. They usually come from relatively stable middle-class families and rarely have had contact with criminal subcultures.

Most major theories of deviance are applicable to property crime. Low integration and the condition of anomie, which indicate institutionalized blockage of success goals, characterize the lower-class lives of property offenders.

Criminal subcultures arise in urban slum areas to combat the effects of economic deprivation and blatant status deprivation. Opportunities for illegitimate enterprises are considerably more prevalent in such places. For example, the availability of fences makes theft immediately profitable. In addition, the rampant social disorganization and inevitable conflict of conduct norms that set such subcultures apart from the legitimate society further generate much lower-class property crime. Middle- and upper-class property crime, on the other hand, are explained by intrafamilial patterns of conflict that result not from failure to achieve success goals but from the stress involved in striving for such goals and the fear of losing them.

Negative societal reaction may or may not deter further property crime. Offenders who are integrated into a criminal subculture most likely will continue to steal; amateurs terminate their thefts regardless of contact with the criminal justice system. The adverse effects of negative labeling are felt most by youthful first offenders.

Corporations and certain governmental agencies themselves provide institutionalized means for the commission of theft or abuse of power. The goals of powerful corporations or governmental agencies often conflict with the general welfare of the public. Illegal behaviors that serve these ends are less apt to be consensually viewed as criminal than the less damaging acts of theft committed by lower-class individuals.

Corporate and governmental crime does not on the whole elicit intense societal reaction. Laws governing such transgressions are vaguely defined, and enforcement is less than zealous. Justice is often said to be served simply by bringing white-collar crime to the attention of the public. Further punishment of perpetrators may be considered unnecessary. In contrast, incarceration of traditional property offenders who are apprehended is far more certain. Also property offenders are less apt to be acquitted than violent criminal offenders. And recidivism is especially high among such offenders.

Our highly competitive, win-or-fail society tends to precipitate considerable property crime by persons from the various social classes. An easing of the emphasis on success at the expense of others and greater concern with reciprocating social relationships may serve to diminish rates of property crime.

REFERENCES

1. Rita James Simon, *Women and Crime* (Lexington, MA: Heath, 1975), pp. 111–20.
2. Federal Bureau of Investigation, *Crime in the United States, 1987* (Washington, D.C.: U.S. Government Printing Office, 1988), p. 41.
3. U.S. Department of Justice, *Criminal Victimization in the United States, 1985* (Washington, D.C.: U.S. Government Printing Office, 1987).
4. Federal Bureau of Investigation, *Crime in the United States, 1986* (Washington, D.C.: U.S. Government Printing Office, 1987), p. 43.
5. Federal Bureau of Investigation, *op. cit.*, p. 42.
6. *Ibid.*, pp. 44–51.
7. *Ibid.*
8. *Ibid.*, p. 182.
9. U.S. Department of Justice, *op. cit.*
10. *Ibid.*, pp. 24–34.
11. *Ibid.*

12. *Ibid.*
13. U.S. Department of Justice, *op. cit.*
14. This section draws heavily on the typologies developed by Don C. Gibbons, *Society, Crime, and Criminal Careers* (Englewood Cliffs, NJ: Prentice-Hall, 1987).
15. Richard L. Jenkins, *Breaking Patterns of Defeat* (Philadelphia: Lippincott, 1954), pp. 148–58.
16. Mary Owen Cameron, *The Booster and the Snitch* (New York: Free Press, 1964).
17. Don C. Gibbons, *Changing the Lawbreaker* (Englewood Cliffs, NJ: Prentice-Hall, 1968).
18. Edwin M. Lemert, "An Isolation and Closure Theory of Naive Check Forgery," *Journal of Criminal Law, Criminology, and Police Science* 44(3):296–307, 1953.
19. Robert K. Merton, "Social Structure and Anomie," *American Sociological Review* 3(5):672–682, 1938.
20. Edwin H. Sutherland and Donald R. Cressey, *Principles of Criminology* (Chicago: Lippincott, 1978).
21. Albert Cohen, *Delinquent Boys* (Glencoe, IL: Free Press, 1955).
22. Richard A. Cloward and Lloyd E. Ohlin, *Delinquency and Opportunity* (Glencoe, IL: Free Press, 1960).
23. Thorsten Sellin, *Culture Conflict and Crime* (New York: Social Science Research Council, Bulletin No. 41, 1938); also Walter B. Miller, "Lower Class Culture as a Generating Milieu of Gang Delinquency," *Journal of Social Issues* 14(3):5–19, 1958.
24. Alex Thio, *Deviant Behavior* (Boston: Houghton Mifflin, 1978).
25. From Stuart Palmer, *The Prevention of Crime* (New York: Behavioral Publications, 1973), pp. 51–52. See also Gilbert Geis, "The Heavy Electrical Equipment Anti-Trust Cases of 1961," in Gilbert Geis and Robert F. Meier, *White-Collar Crime* (New York: Free Press, 1977).
26. Marshall B. Clinard and Peter C. Yeager, *Corporate Crime* (New York: Free Press, 1980); and Marshall B. Clinard, Peter C. Yeager, Jeanne Brissette, Petra Shak, and Elizabeth Harries, *Illegal Corporate Behavior* (Washington, D.C.: U.S. Government Printing Office, 1979).
27. Clinard and Yeager, *op. cit.*
28. Thio, *op. cit.*, p. 358.
29. Marshall B. Clinard, *Corporate Ethics and Crime: The Role of Middle Management* (Beverly Hills, CA: Sage, 1983).
30. Federal Bureau of Investigation, *op. cit.*, 1988.
31. Raymond J. Michalowski, *Order, Law, and Crime* (New York: Random House, 1985); Ronald C. Kramer, "Corporate Criminality: The Development of an Idea," in Ellen Hochstedler (ed.), *Corporations as Criminals* (Beverly Hills, CA: Sage, 1984); and Clinard and Yeager, *op. cit.*
32. Donald R. Cressey, *Other People's Money* (New York: Free Press, 1953).
33. Marshall B. Clinard and Richard Quinney, *Criminal Behavior Systems* (New York: Holt, Rinehart and Winston, 1967), pp. 213–214.
34. Jethro K. Lieberman, *How the Government Breaks the Law* (New York: Stein and Day, 1972), pp. 22–23.
35. Jack Newfield, "The Law Is an Outlaw," *The Village Voice*, December 17, 1970, p. 1.
36. Merton, *op. cit.*
37. Sutherland and Cressey, *op. cit.*
38. Cloward and Ohlin, *op. cit.*
39. Richard Quinney, *The Social Reality of Crime* (Boston: Little, Brown, 1970); also Thio, *op. cit.*
40. Gerald D. Robin, "The Corporate and Judicial Disposition of Employee Thieves," *Wisconsin Law Review* (Summer 1967):685–702.

6

Prostitution

THE MEANING AND PREVALENCE OF PROSTITUTION

This and the next chapter are concerned with two major forms of sexual deviance: prostitution and homosexuality. While these have some factors in common, they are in many respects quite different forms of deviance. Both are divergences from the sexual norms. Both are usually, although by no means always, seen as forms of negative deviance. Both are fairly widespread in many societies. And a significant proportion of prostitution is homosexual rather than heterosexual. Nevertheless, as will be clear, the differences between the two forms of sexual deviance are many and great.

Defining Prostitution

It is a common saying that prostitution is the oldest profession. However, among historians it is often said that the priesthood is the oldest profession. In any case, prostitution is an ancient form of deviance; it exists at least to some degree in a very large majority of human societies, and it is quite widespread in many. Moreover, prostitution takes many and varied forms. Its very variety makes definition difficult.

While most prostitutes are young adults, many are youths and children. Some are male and some female. Male prostitutes who have other males as customers are fairly common. Prostitution between female prostitutes and other females is exceedingly rare, but it does occur. The same is true of prostitution between male sellers and female buyers.

Many prostitutes ply their trade as employees of a business organization such as a massage parlor or a whorehouse. Many others operate alone. Most are full time, which is to say they gain their livelihood largely through selling sex. Yet many are part-time prostitutes.

Prostitutes generally have low social status, but some hold high status. Most are paid in money; others are paid in rent, clothes, gifts, favors. The crux of prostitution is that there is a payment of money or goods in some form or other for sexual relations. Seldom do the individuals involved have a close, intimate, enduring, and affectionate relationship, although this is possible as in the case of the "mistress." Occasionally, it is argued that for some couples marriage may represent prostitution: the husband buys the wife's sexual services by providing a home, food, clothes, and so on. From a practical standpoint, however, it is well to exclude marriage from the realm of prostitution. *Prostitution, then, is an economic exchange of sexual relations for money or goods which seldom involves an enduring, close, stable relationship between the participants.*[1]

Who is a prostitute? It is anyone who makes a part-time or full-time paid occupation of engaging in sexual relationships. These may be males as well as females, of course, and they may be quite young. Thousands upon thousands of teenagers are engaged in prostitution as an occupation. Often much of their earned income goes to entrepreneurs of one type or another. That is often true of adult prostitutes as well.

Laws are widely variable as to what constitutes prostitution. *Soliciting* for prostitution—by prostitutes or pimps or other entrepreneurs—is in many jurisdictions in the United States the primary criterion. The sexual act of the prostitute may itself be a crime. So may the involvement of the customer in seeking out and entering into prostituted sex. Prostitution is usually a misdemeanor, that is, an offense of lesser severity. However, some forms of prostitution, such as the employment of minors as prostitutes, may be felonies. Some aspects of prostitution—soliciting, engaging in—are illegal everywhere in the United States except certain counties of Nevada.

Prevalence

The World at Large

Vern L. Bullough provided a wide-ranging legal history of prostitution from its prevalence in ancient Greece and Rome to the present.[2] Prostitutes held high status in India and Japan for many centuries. Prostitution was widespread in Europe during the Middle Ages. It was a part of the way of life in many colonial and frontier communities in the United States during the eighteenth and nineteenth centuries. Thomas Jefferson, who designed the University of Virginia, included in his plans a whorehouse for undergraduates there.[3] In modern Russia it was seen as an exceedingly serious problem and was apparently abolished during the 1930s. However, it appears today to flourish there.

As Kingsley Davis points out, prostitution seems to adapt, to take hold, in a wide range of institutional systems.[4] Unlike many forms of negative deviance, it always involves an economic transaction. It is a business, even when an independent one, and except in the smallest societies, business is universal the world over. At the same time, it is for the most part a business that carries a stigma for practitioners and sometimes for clients as well. This makes determination of its incidence and prevalence in various societies exceedingly difficult. In fact, it is usually impossible to estimate with any accuracy whatsoever how widespread prostitution is in most societies.

We can say with certainty that in some societies prostitution has been or is nonexistent or nearly so. The Polar Eskimos of northwest Greenland, for example, did not traditionally practice it. They had, however, institutionalized the practice of wife lending. The basic reason for this was economic. If a Polar Eskimo were to go on a long hunt, he needed his wife along to share the work. Only she knew how to properly carry out certain practices such as mending the sled. Thus, if a wife were ill or pregnant beyond a certain time, the hunter borrowed a wife primarily for economic purposes. Not to hunt meant starvation. A second example is the Icelanders, among whom, today as in the past, prostitution is rare and is considered a bizarre exchange. Iceland, as noted in Chapter 3, is a small, technologically developed nation with few crime problems. The widespread practice of trial marriage is no doubt one reason why prostitution has been unnecessary.[5]

The United States

As with the world generally, there is no way of making fairly accurate estimates of the incidence and prevalence of prostitution in the United States. Rather, most estimates have to do with the numbers of men who had had relationships with prostitutes and the amounts of money spent on prostitution. The latest estimates are that $10 billion is spent annually on prostitution in the United States. There are thought to be in excess of half a million full-time prostitutes and many more part-time workers.[6]

Most men do not use the services of prostitutes with any regularity. Kinsey and his associates found that 70 percent of adult males in the United States had had at least one sexual encounter with a prostitute. Only 15–20 percent had had "regular" contact, that is, more than a few times a year over five years or more.[7] The proportion of males who first experienced coitus with a prostitute declined from 25 percent in the 1950s to 7 percent in the 1960s.[8] This is often attributed to the increase in sexual freedom in the United States in recent times.

Prostitution appears to be more prevalent in the southern and western sections of the country than in the East and Midwest, and it seems to flourish more, proportionate to population, in small cities and towns than in large urban areas.[9]

Arrest rates for prostitution are not necessarily at all indicative of the actual extent of prostitution. But there are in any event tangible figures that tell something of the society's response to this form of deviance. In 1987, the FBI estimated that there were 100,950 arrests for prostitution and commercialized vice.[10] Of those, 65 percent were females and 35 percent were males (homosexual prostitutes, pimps, customers, and so on).[11] Somewhat under half of those arrested for prostitution were blacks (40.8 percent), although blacks made up but 12 percent of the total population.[12] Arrests for prostitution rose by one-quarter the period 1978–1987. Arrests of persons under the age of 18 years remains about the same, while for those age 18 and over the increase was 25.6 percent.[13] The arrests of females of all ages for prostitution rose by 20.3 percent during that period, while the arrests for males of all ages (homosexual prostitutes, pimps, and so on) rose by 34.9 percent.[14]

THE FORMS OF PROSTITUTION

From the point of view of sex roles, the two major forms of prostitution are heterosexual relations between female sellers and male buyers and homosexual relations between male sellers and buyers. However, each of these can take a number of forms based on other criteria. A commonly used classification system is described in the following sections.[15]

Streetwalkers and Bar Prostitutes

Streetwalkers are the most common type. The woman solicits customers, usually strangers, on the street. Male homosexual prostitutes may similarly solicit males on the street. Streetwalking is the poorest paid form of prostitution; it also holds the lowest status. These prostitutes are poorly educated; they may be aging and considered unattractive, although this is by no means a rule. The risks of streetwalking are great. Exposure to venereal disease and apprehension by the police are commonplace. The streetwalker is financially exploited by her pimp; subjected to violence and forced into degrading sexual behavior by her clients. Depression, low self-esteem, and emotional exhaustion are typically experienced by a streetwalker.[16]

Bar prostitutes are usually young women, although they may be young men, who are part-time prostitutes. Often they are bartenders or cocktail or food waitresses as well. They may be employed by the bar, tavern, or cocktail lounge in legitimate jobs. Again, they may be working for these establishments in the sense that they drink with customers and cajole them into paying for numerous drinks. They may pay the establishment owner a part of what they earn in prostitution, or they may simply operate on their own, using bars as places for quiet soliciting. These prostitutes are very often transients moving from town to town or city to city, taking odd jobs and prostituting as they go. They most often operate in the southern, midwestern, and western regions of the United States. Bar prostitutes almost invariably drink heavily; they are usually poorly educated and have few close ties. While far from being immune to arrest, they are arrested less often than streetwalkers because they are less visible and may be protected by establishment owners, especially if they have an arrangement for splitting fees with them. Their income and social standing are low, but tend to be somewhat higher than that of streetwalkers.

Whorehouse Prostitutes

Whorehouses, cathouses, brothels, bordellos, parlor houses, and pleasure houses are all forms of the same phenomenon: a place where management and labor (prostitutes) supply sex to customers on a fee basis. Usually the prostitute gets a "cut" of each fee. The madam oversees the daily operation of the business. She may "own" the business or work for a higher management. Drinks may or may not be served. Customers may be admitted only if they are known by the madam or referred by regular customers. The madam arranges the daily schedule and mediates disputes which arise among the girls. While madams tend to view the prostitutes as dependent and indecisive, they nonetheless treat them with compassion and tolerance.[17]

Again, anyone may be admitted unless he appears to be "down-and-out," highly intoxicated, belligerent, or a "plant" of the police. Often, however, there is some sort of arrangement between the police and the management: the prostitutes will receive regular medical checkups, will not practice if they have venereal disease; the police may regularly make token arrests of the madam or prostitutes while the business continues on in regular fashion.

Prostitutes seldom stay more than a few months at a given house since regular customers tend to insist on variety and will go elsewhere if new prostitutes are unavailable. Some houses operate until the early hours of the morning. Most close by early evening. This helps to avoid having to deal with drunken and assaultive customers. It also minimizes raids by the police if police protection is absent. Police "crackdown" and vice squads operate at night as a rule. Prostitutes who work in houses are usually full-time workers, earn more money than streetwalkers or bar prostitutes, and have more status.

Truck Stops, Roadside Lounges, Motels/Hotels

Truck stops, roadside lounges, motels, and hotels are legitimate businesses where prostitution is commonly practiced.[18] Prostitution is an ancillary service provided by the management to its transient clientele. The prostitutes frequently work a circuit and return to the same location every three to four weeks. As much as half of the prostitute's earnings are paid to the business owners for the use of a room and the right to work in their establishments. In smaller truck stops or roadside lounges, the prostitutes may also serve as waitresses or bar maids.

It is common for truck stop and roadside lounge prostitutes to develop a relatively stable core of patrons. As a result, the risk of physical injury or disease is greatly reduced. This, however, is not the case for motel-hotel prostitutes who do not benefit from the level of protection typically provided by truck stop or roadside lounge employees.

Massage Parlor and Photography Studio Prostitutes

Massage parlors as places of prostitution have in recent years had great vogue in the United States. It is common practice for the massage to be accompanied by masturbation of the customer by the masseuse or by sexual intercourse between customer and masseuse. Fees are usually based on services provided with specific amounts for massage, masturbation (called a "local"), coitus, fellatio, anal intercourse, and so on. A combination of services may readily exceed $50 or $60. As a consequence, customers are usually middle and upper class, white-collar and professional men. The "therapists" are typically young adult females with some training and a license as a masseuse. They are likely to have regular medical check-ups. They are of all social classes. Their income is fairly substantial, based usually on a fixed percentage of what their customers spend. Their status is higher than that of workers in whorehouses but lower than that of call girls, who will be discussed next.

Some photographic studios are basically similar. Clients take photographs of nude or seminude female "models" and negotiate fees for various forms of sex. Heterosexual photographic studios and massage parlors have their homosexual counterparts where clients and prostitutes are both male. Rarely if ever are homosexual and heterosexual services combined under one roof. Clients who insist on bisexual services must as a rule patronize more than one establishment.

Call Girls

Call girls depend on the telephone. They are called by regular clients, friends of clients, or procurers who arrange meetings with clients. Clients are almost always "checked out" by other clients, friends, procurers, or the call girls themselves. Call girls meet clients at their own or their clients' dwellings or at hotel rooms. Many are extremely busy, have answering services, and move by taxi, as do legitimate photographic models, from one appointment to another within a given urban location.

Call girls tend to see themselves as high-status professionals, not as prostitutes. They live in respectable areas, charge high fees, have well-to-do clients, and are at home in expensive restaurants. They follow an ethical code which stresses protection of clients: they do not mention clients' names to other persons, and they do not "recognize" clients in settings where recognition might embarrass clients. Many are highly educated, speak well, and make good, if temporary, companions for business executives and professional men, especially those who are traveling. Call girls compose the affluent, upper-middle class of prostitution. Some eventually marry their clients, a rarity in the types of prostitution previously discussed.

"Super call girls" are the elite of prostitution. These are young women who have connections in "high places." They cater to powerful business executives, wealthy professionals, visiting dignitaries, and the just plain rich. They are considered the most attractive of call girls. They speak and dress well, seem at home in upper-class circles. Their fees are high, often $1000 or more "a sitting." They might be considered topflight free-lancers who are on call to some of the large corporations, certain government agencies, and an occasional "old-boy" network of influential men.

Exclusivity and Independence of Prostitutes

Gale Miller has used other sets of criteria to classify prostitutes.[19] Two major criteria, Miller holds, are the extents to which prostitutes are *exclusive* about what types of clients they will service and whether they are *affiliated with an organization or work independently*. The prostitutes, female heterosexual or male homosexual, who work the street cater to almost anyone who has the requisite money. They are not organizationally affiliated but work on their own. They are similar to the previously mentioned streetwalkers and compose the lowest-status group of prostitutes. The exclusive, independent prostitutes are the call girls and super call girls, the upper crust of the occupation. They work on their own, are choosy about their clients, and charge high fees.

The nonexclusive, organizationally affiliated prostitutes are the prostitutes employed in whorehouses, massage parlors, and photography studios. While some customers are weeded out by the management, exclusivity is low. The women, or male homosexual prostitutes, are usually paid on a percentage basis, make a modest income, and have little status. The last form, the exclusive, organizationally affiliated prostitute, is the most rare. These are much like call girls except that they work in affluent houses of prostitution catering to prestigious, wealthy clients. They hold exceptionally high status in the profession.[20]

CHARACTERISTICS OF PROSTITUTES

Age, Sex, Race, and Class

Most prostitutes are in their twenties, although some are 70 and above. Call girls and workers in whorehouses, massage parlors, and photography studios are usually under 35, and very few are over 40. Those who continue in prostitution after 40 often become streetwalkers. There are, however, occasional reports of whorehouses for the elderly, staffed by senior citizens. Teenage prostitution is widespread, although how widespread is impossible to say.[21] Some teenage prostitutes operate on their own; others are members of the "stables" of pimps.

Male prostitutes are almost always homosexuals who cater to other males. Their numbers in relation to the numbers of female prostitutes is, again, exceedingly difficult to estimate. Some estimates put the proportion of all prostitutes in the United States who are males as high as one-quarter. Teenage male prostitutes are common as are teenage female prostitutes. Called "chicken hustlers," these boys are usually found in large cities, often runaways from parents living elsewhere. They are generally trained by pimps who pay them a small cut of the fees received.[22]

It is generally believed that blacks are heavily represented among the prostitute population.[23] This is very likely true for both female and male prostitutes. Most prostitutes come from the lower socioeconomic classes, but there are distinct exceptions. Female prostitutes are occasionally college-educated; in many instances they consider prostitution a sign of liberalism, and they engage in prostitution for excitement, for "kicks," as well as for money.[24] Most upper-middle-class prostitutes are free-lancers who work the streets or operate as call girls.

Family Background and Personality Factors

In the remainder of this chapter, reference is generally to female prostitutes. Male homosexual prostitution is discussed further in the next chapter. There is little doubt that *most* female prostitutes grow up in economically impoverished families.[25] There is, however, disagreement over whether poverty is a factor in generating female prostitution.[26] Certainly the great majority of females with few economic means do not become prostitutes. Yet it seems only reasonable to think that poverty, together with a lack of education and of job skills, is a distinct contributing factor in much female prostitution. One belief which should be laid to rest is that poor girls are sold into prostitution. "White slavery" is a rarity, very nearly a total myth, in this and most societies.

There is some tendency for female prostitutes to come from backgrounds where there has been parental strife, where parents are separated or divorced, where the mother has a history of promiscuity, and/or where the father has brutalized the daughter and made sexual advances.[27] Involuntary sexual intercourse during childhood is found in over three-quarters of street prostitutes and two-thirds of those in brothels.[28] There is evidence that in certain families parents have sown the seeds for secondary or career deviance in their daughters by labeling them at an early age as promiscuous, "sluts," "whores," for real or imagined sexual transgressions.[29]

Moreover, while not a necessary condition for prostitution, it is altogether usual for female prostitutes to have had contact with the organized world of prostitution prior to actually becoming a prostitute. They have had friends who were prostitutes, worked in jobs sometimes on the fringe of prostitution such as cocktail waitressing and bartending, and many have known men who were pimps.

Female prostitutes do not appear to be generally distinguished by personality characteristics. However, dislike of men because of early brutality at the hands of fathers does seem to be a recurring theme. In any event, many researchers are convinced that the sex role is far more critical in the development of prostitution among females than are personality attributes.[30] The female role has in many societies, the United States included, traditionally involved a measure of trading sexual access for economic gain. Edwin Lemert argues that our culture is conducive to female prostitution in a number of ways.

> Being in an inferior position from the standpoint of power and control over material rewards in our culture, it is not unnatural that women should re-

sort to sex as a means of redressing the status differential. This is perceived in the gamut of reactions from the salesgirl who "charms" a male customer into purchasing goods, through the sale of war bonds with kisses by actresses, to the sexual submission of a secretary to her boss in order to hold her job.[31]

Moreover, the very marriage relationship itself may contribute to a climate psychologically conducive to prostitution. If one female trades sex in marriage for goods, money, and status, then another may reason that attempting to do so outside of marriage is a reasonable alternative.

A major problem for female prostitutes in the United States revolves around the relative absence of close, affective relationships with other persons. Some may find support from other prostitutes and madams in whorehouses. Others may be in love with their pimps. Still others may be fond of some of their clients. But most female prostitutes are detached from familial relations, unmarried, and without children of their own. They frequently move from one community to another. They seldom have friends and lovers. They are psychologically isolated. In addition, they are in a socially stigmatized occupation. The stigma may not be as severe as it once was because of the blurring in recent decades of the distinction between the "good girl" and the "bad girl." Nevertheless, the marginality, the psychological isolation, and the social disapproval inherent in the role of the prostitute very likely take a heavy toll on the females who fill that role. Research on the stressful effects of prostitution on those who practice it, female or male, is rare indeed. This is in itself one testimony to the discredited nature of the role.

CAREERS IN PROSTITUTION

Stages in Career Development

Nannette Davis analyzed the lives of youthful streetwalkers.[32] She saw the development of a career in prostitution as involving three stages. The first begins in adolescence and entails *negative labeling* by other persons. The girl has promiscuous affairs, acquires a "bad" reputation, and is rejected socially. The final point in this stage is the first actual act of prostitution. The second stage involves *learning the skills and values of the occupation of prostitution* and of *taking on a self-image as prostitute*. The girl learns to satisfy a wide range of client desires in terms of the nature and context of sexual acts. She overcomes her fear of clients who are sadistic or masochistic. She learns to cope with police harassment. She learns how to handle drunken clients and those who will not pay. She substitutes a business ethic for an earlier one of excitement and promiscuity. Throughout this process, the would-be professional prostitute "*normalizes*" the role of prostitute. She does this by accepting the role as appropriate for her and gradually evaluating the life of a prostitute as acceptable and rewarding. With this accomplished, the female enters the third and final stage, that of the *professional prostitute*.

Many prostitutes receive training in various ways. Some learn in a hit-or-miss fashion from friends who are streetwalkers. Some are recruited into whorehouses by acquaintances and under the general oversight of the madam are taught how to handle customers. Call girls are often trained over a period of several weeks by other call girls who provide them with on-the-job training with overflow clients. Pimps may train females to enter their stable of prostitutes. The relationship between the pimp and his prostitutes is a complex one and is outlined below. An interesting aspect of most forms of training is that it revolves much more around gaining social, interactional skills for dealing with clients than it does with sexual practices per se. Females are taught how to approach clients, how to extract the fee, how to move the interaction along so that valuable time is not wasted, how to avoid emotional entanglement, how to cope with special problems (police, drunken or violent clients), and how to protect the privacy of higher-status clients. It is usually assumed that whatever form of sexual activity is required will come naturally.

The Role of the Pimp

The pimp is an entrepeneur of sorts who lives on the efforts of from one to as many as 20 prostitutes. He is most often black, in his twenties, exceedingly well dressed, lives in "style," and treats his stable of women with tyrannical authority. His prostitutes give him their earnings, and he is likely to be violent with them if they do not bring in sufficient money. At times he is affectionate, treating the prostitutes as his "wives." They seem to be drawn to him, crave his affection, and accept his violence as just.[33] The ideal arrangement appears to be one black male pimp with a stable of several or more white women. Customers are often white. The pimp and his friends, usually other pimps, are said to gain satisfaction in exploiting white men through the use of white women. In direct contrast to conventional culture, the pimp does not work but is supported by his "wives" who do. The pimp spends countless hours grooming himself. As one prostitute said of her pimp, "The way he does nothing is *beautiful*."[34]

Training of a female by a pimp to be a prostitute is termed "turning her out."[35] In the first step, the pimp is affectionate to a young woman, but he is careful to ensure that she commits herself emotionally to him while he does not to her. The second step is to alter the woman's value system so that she sees prostitution as a morally efficient way of gaining money. He uses her emotional commitment to him to accomplish this, giving her affection for compliance and punishment for noncompliance. Gradually she becomes a submissive, efficient member of his stable. Throughout, she has gained informal training in how to make money rapidly "on the street." This training is usually done by the "bottom woman."

Other Related Roles

The bottom woman[36] is the most influential prostitute in the pimp's stable. She is the "foreman" of the stable. She recruits for the pimp, sees to the training of recruits, and in general controls the other prostitutes. The *madam* plays a somewhat similar role in the setting of the whorehouse, overseeing the prostitutes there. However, rather than being connected to a pimp, she is her own boss or the manager for an absentee boss.

Gagnon suggests various other related roles.[37] *Steerers,* who are usually men, direct potential customers to prostitutes and whorehouses. Most cities have their hotel desk clerks and bellhops, bartenders, and taxicab drivers who do this sideline work. There are also the *profiteers,* owners and managers of apartments and hotels. In the case of apartments, the prostitute is charged a higher rent in order to be left free to ply her trade. Regarding hotels, the customer is charged a day's rate for an hour's use of a room. Gagnon also suggests that there is a group of *professionals* who legally make a living in connection with prostitution. Those include physicians who give medical examinations to prostitutes, social workers, and researchers on deviant sex practices. There are also the journalists and crusaders who make a living out of attacking prostitutes. Then there are the members of the criminal justice system who profit from prostitution: police who receive payoffs, lawyers who defend the prostitutes in court, prosecuting attorneys, bail bondsmen, correctional personnel, and so on.

Finally, there is the *customer.* Harold Greenwald, a psychiatrist, classified male customers of female prostitutes into three groups.[38] First are the "occasional Johns." These are usually young, unmarried men who are away from home, either tourists or military personnel. They seek out prostitutes in groups, often for a lark. "Habitual Johns" want an affectionate, continuing relationship with one prostitute. They try to mix talk and sex, often to the annoynace of the prostitute who is interested in "turnover." They give prostitutes presents in order to provide for themselves the illusion of a love relationship. Third, there are the "compulsive Johns." These are often married men who perceive sex as dirty and unfit for "good" women. They compulsively seek out prostitutes for so-called unnatural or peculiar sex acts. Many can achieve orgasm only with prostitutes.

Certain customers use prostitution as a form of *conspicuous consumption*. Certainly most men who frequent whorehouses and massage parlors do not, yet those who buy the services of the super call girls may insist on "only the best." The traveling business executive or professional who takes his "date" out for the evening to a fine restaurant or an exclusive nightclub may be more intent on conspicuous public display than clandestine sex play. And the host company that provides the visitor with the "best that money can buy" may hold the view that funds are well spent when the company's image is burnished by such conspicuous consumption.

Ideology and Other Aspects of the Career

Those who are "in the life," that is, professional female prostitutes, have developed a coherent ideology which insulates them at least in part from the stressful effects of the stigma society attaches to prostitution.[39] First, they believe that prostitution is necessary. It helps to hold the families of the customers together by "taking the pressure off" the marital relationship and providing the husband with a "no-strings-attached" sexual freedom. In the process, it reduces sex crimes such as rape and incest, the ideology runs. Moreover, prostitutes provide therapeutic services to their clients by catering to deviant sexual needs and in some instances by listening to the client's woes. Finally, the prostitutes' ideology holds that they are no worse than anyone else, and in the respect that they are not hypocritical as is the straight world, they are in fact morally superior. Professional prostitutes believe that society is a gigantic system of exploitation and that while they may exploit their customers, the customers, the official authorities, and the power structure exploit them.

In recent years, prostitutes have coupled ideology with political action. Prostitutes in France have gone on strike in protest over harrassment by government officials. In the United States, prostitutes have organized into unions and political groups, among them COYOTE or "Call Off Your Old Tired Ethics," sometimes termed "The Loose Women's Organization," and PONY, "Prostitutes of New York." They press for equal rights for prostitutes and sometimes win support from feminist groups.

To some extent prostitutes have their own argot. This includes phrases for describing how to "work Johns," how to recruit and train other prostitutes, and euphemisms to be used in conversing about genitalia with customers.[40] Prostitutes have traditionally worn heavy, bright cosmetics and abbreviated clothing. Of interest is Lemert's contention that in recent times in the United States, much of the behavior of prostitutes has made its way up the socioeconomic status hierarchy and been "appropriated by the middle-class woman."[41] Lemert links this to revolt by females against their traditional roles as homebodies.

While there is debate on the matter, certainly drug addiction and alcoholism are at least moderately severe problems among prostitutes. Some must drink in order to do their job, as is true of those who work for owners of cocktail lounges. Others drink to overcome anxiety in their job. Some drug addicts enter prostitution to gain quick money for drugs. Others find escape from the stigma and stress of their work. One major source of stress is the threat of assault. Prostitutes are prone to be assaulted by disgruntled customers, occasionally by those who employ them, and in the course of harrassment by police. Prostitution may not be the oldest profession, it may not be the most dangerous profession, but it is an ancient and in many respects unhealthy line of work.

EXPLANATIONS OF PROSTITUTION

Two central questions regarding prostitution are these: Why does it become institutionalized in so many social and cultural settings? And why do some women (and men) enter prostitution and others do not? Regarding the first, prostitution, if it exists in a given society and it usually does, tends to be a highly institutionalized form of deviance. There are numerous customs and values for effecting this form of economic exchange. Seldom do individuals operate as prostitutes apart from a subculture of prostitution. Very often they operate as independent free-lancers rather than employees. This is the case in many other occupations such as journalism, medicine, plumbing, and so on. But independent, self-employed workers in given lines of work generally follow the insitutionalized customs and values of their occupation. The same is true of prostitution.

Regarding the second question, why women become prostitutes, Kingsley Davis points out that the especially interesting question is why in fact so few enter prostitution.[42] His answer in very broad terms is that the monetary rewards which prostitutes gain are really in return for the loss of social esteem which is brought about by their work rather than for their sexual skills. And for women generally the monetary gain does not outweigh the loss of esteem.

Social Integration

Kingsley Davis has been the leading proponent of social integration as an answer to the first question, why prostitution develops and becomes institutionalized in a society.[43] His position is that prostitution contributes to preservation of the moral order and therefore to integration of the society. How can this be? It contributes to the purity of marriage and to feminine virtue (among nonprostitutes). Prostitution does this by institutionalizing work for "immoral" and therefore stigmatized persons, that is, prostitutes.

Men away from home, men who do not have a physically compatible relationship with their wives, and men who desire deviant (fellatio, etc.) sexual activity can buy the services of prostitutes. The sexual relationship with the prostitute is socially defined as meaningless in the emotional sense, not involving affection, and not enduring. It is not a threat to marriage and the family. Moreover, Davis contends, it means that these men will not seek out and destroy the virtue of moral women. In the process, prostitution not only preserves the sanctity of marriage and the family, but it also is one social way of defining its opposite, that is, what is virtue and who are the virtuous.

It does appear that in some societies—in Asia, for example, where prostitution is widely institutionalized—"respectable" females are seldom promiscuous. When prostitution is not widely institutionalized, there may be a tendency, as in some Western societies, for females generally to enter into extramarital sexual relationships. At the same time, certainly there are societies which have institutionalized other ways of handling sexual problems, without moral disintegration: trial marriage, easy divorce, polygamy (several wives to one husband). Prostitution can be one way, then, of contributing to preservation of the moral order and thereby to social integration. There are numerous ways of achieving those ends, however; and prostitution need not, in a given society, necessarily be one of them.

Does social integration bear on why some women enter prostitution and others do not? There is some evidence, as indicated earlier, that prostitutes come from marginal, impoverished homes where the means for achieving cultural success goals are meager. Prostitution is one way of attempting to gain success goals of money and material goods. While there is stigma attached as well, there is always the possibility, however remote, of becoming an affluent, super call girl who covertly moves in prestigious circles. This possibility may be so unlikely as to be all but nonexistent for many young women. However, an unrealistic dream may be as strong a motivating factor as a realistic one.

Cultural Supports

Beyond question, Sutherland's concept of differential association[44] and Cloward and Ohlin's formulation of deviant opportunity structures[45] play important parts in explaining which women enter prostitution. It is all but impossible to become a prostitute without association with at least some of those directly involved: other prostitutes, madams, pimps, steerers, massage parlor and photography studio personnel, and so on. Even streetwalking purely on one's own is likely to be abortive over time unless there are associations with the other prostitutes. They may well resent an outsider moving in on their territory and take appropriate action.

This raises the question of the significance of recruitment into opportunity structures and requisite role learning if one is to become more than a very occasional prostitute. Prostitution is an occupation and, like most occupations, those who practice it exercise considerable control over who enters the occupation, how they are trained, and how they function once in the occupation. The previous discussions of the forms of prostitution and of careers in prostitution made clear that not only are contacts with workers in prostitution necessary if one is to become a prostitute, but usually there is an element of recruitment involved as well. Only those who are young and physically attractive are recruited. Other prostitutes, madams, or pimps invite the woman to "try out" as it were. There is a training period. This may be brief and casual or may extend over a considerable period and be rather complex. Even seemingly haphazard training is far less hit-or-miss than it appears to the outsider. Training may not be rigorously organized, but it is likely to involve bits of knowledge and practice crucial to success as a prostitute. And success means not only satisfying customers. In most settings and forms of prostitution, it also means getting along with others in the trade whomever they may be: sister prostitutes, madams, pimps, steerers, managers, sometimes police as well. Success means adequately learning the role of the prostitute and thereby gaining access to the institutionalized opportunity structure of prostitution.

Social Disorganization and Conflict

Prostitutes often work the so-called disorganized areas of the cities. The sections where prostitution is widespread have traditionally been termed "red-light districts." For generations past, the red light in the window signified sex for sale. But these "disorganized" areas are really not so disorganized, it turns out. Rather, they are organized in a *different way* from the middle- and upper-class areas, according to the customs and rules of the underlife of the city. And it is in the whorehouses that these two worlds meet, for the customers are often of higher status than the sellers. Moreover, much prostitution thrives in areas not categorized as disorganized: in massage parlors and photography studios in middle-range business areas, in uptown hotels of repute, in

moderately or very affluent apartment complexes. Social disorganization, then, may sometimes be a significant factor in prostitution but
this is by no means always so.

Thio's power theory has relevance to prostitution in two main respects.[46] The powerful bring about the institutionalization of prostitution as a form of higher-consensus deviance. Some of the powerless
are forced through poverty to take on the roles of prostitution, pimps,
madams. They are, to some extent at least, prosecuted for doing so
while lower-consensus, "covert" prostitution flourishes. By the latter,
Thio means the system in which wives and mistresses enter into marriage and liaisons with higher-status men for gain. They trade their
bodies for economic and prestige rewards. This lower-consensus deviance may very well be more widespread than ordinary, disreputable
prostitution, Thio holds. It is covert, it escapes stigma, and the rewards
are great.

Societal Reaction

Societal reaction theory is clearly relevant to prostitution as generally conceived, that is, higher-consensus prostitution. It is not relevant,
however, to the lower-consensus type which Thio sees among the
powerful. As has been stressed, ordinary, that is, higher-consensus,
prostitution is seldom an individualistic form of deviance. It is highly
institutionalized. Individuals enter the world of prostitution and become career prostitutes, which means learning the customs and values
of the subculture of prostitution. It means accepting prostitution as a
suitable line of work and developing a self-concept as a prostitute. This
involves the reactions of others. It involves their defining the individual as a potential prostitute, as a novice, then as a professional. In
Lemert's terms, becoming a prostitute, taking on the role of prostitute,
is secondary deviance.

Societal reaction does not apply to Thio's formulation of lower-
consensus prostitution among the well-to-do. Because of low visibility
and the lack of consensus about whether such prostitution is negative
deviance, the societal reaction process does not operate. Others do not
define and react to the woman as a prostitute. Hence she does not
come to define herself as such. This highlights a recurring problem of
Thio's power formulation in relation to deviance. His theory best explains what he considers to be deviance among the powerful. The societal conception of deviance differs from Thio's in that by his definition there is low social consensus about what he sees as higher-status
deviance. Therefore Thio's power theory explains mainly what *he* defines as deviance.

SUMMARY

Prostitution is an economic exchange of sexual relations for money or goods which seldom involves an enduring, close, stable relationship between participants. Both soliciting for prostitution and the sexual act itself may be considered crimes. With rare exceptions the practice of prostitution continues in most societies. One study showed that seven of every 10 American men have had at least one sexual encounter with a prostitute. Fewer than one in five men, however, regularly have relations with a prostitute. Prostitution appears to be especially prevalent in the southern and western regions of the United States and low in the East and Midwest. Of the 90,000–100,000 persons arrested for prostitution and commercialized vice in a given year, about seven in 10 are women and about 4 in 10 are black. However, arrests for prostitution are rising faster for males than females.

The various types of prostitutes are streetwalkers and bar solicitors, those employed by a whorehouse, those employed in a massage parlor or photography studio, and call girls. Streetwalkers are the most common type. They are drawn from the lower classes, are poorly educated, and are the poorest paid prostitutes. Bar prostitutes are from similar backgrounds and are often transient, but their income and status are somewhat higher than that of streetwalkers. Whorehouse prostitutes also tend to move from one house to another to ensure variety for the customers. Madams oversee the business practices in the house, make arrangements with the police, protect the prostitutes from drunken or assaultive customers, and provide for medical check-ups. Recently, massage parlors and photography studios have become prominent in the sex-for-sale business. A variety of sexual services may be performed by the masseuse or photographic model for a commensurate fee. Call girls are considered the elite of prostitution. They are usually well educated, articulate, sophisticated, and attractive. Their clients include business executives and professional men who compensate them extremely well. High-ranking prostitutes also include those who work in whorehouses that cater exclusively to the wealthy.

Prostitutes are invariably young, in their twenties or early thirties; many are teenagers, most of whom have left home. Blacks are disproportionately involved in prostitution; so too are economically deprived individuals. Parental strife, promiscuous mothers, and brutalizing, incestuous fathers are common factors in the backgrounds of prostitutes. A general disdain of men is characteristic of many prostitutes. Prostitutes tend to be psychologically isolated, often without familial or affective ties with others.

Careers in prostitution usually involve three stages: (1) negative labeling as a result of early promiscuity; (2) learning the skills and values of the occupation of prostitute and adopting the self-image of a prostitute; and (3) becoming a professional prostitute. Pimps may assist in the socialization of a young girl into the role of prostitute. This is known as "turning her out." Initially, a pimp is affectionate toward her and thereby establishes her emotional dependence on him. Gradually he convinces her that prostitution is a morally efficient way of gaining money. Further training in working the street is handled by the "bottom woman," "the foreman" of the pimp's stable of prostitutes.

The ideology that justifies prostitution to professional prostitutes is that (1) it hold families together by "taking the pressure off" the marital relationship; (2) it reduces sex crimes; (3) it provides for deviant sexual needs; and (4) prostitutes as a group are no worse than anyone else.

Major theories of prostitution have attempted to explain why it becomes institutionalized and why some women (and men) enter prostitution whereas others do not. Social integration theory holds that by preserving the moral order, prostitution contributes to the integration of society. Prostitution preserves marriage by providing meaningless outlets for deviant sexual activity. Prostitution also provides employment for economically deprived persons. Subcultural opportunities are important to young women who seek careers in prostitution. To be a successful prostitute requires training and support provided by subcultures of persons engaged in the sex-for-sale business. More visible, poorly paid, often addicted and physically and psychologically abused prostitutes work in areas of cities marked by disorganization and conflict. These powerless individuals are most apt to be harrassed by the police and at least temporarily placed in custody. Prostitutes who cater to the affluent are in turn protected by them from such practices.

Prostitution is widespread in society but arrests are infrequently made. Acquittal of defendants is common. Survey data show that females, blacks, and the poorly educated take a harsher view of prostitutes than do males, whites, and the better educated. Little is done to prevent prostitution, but efforts are made to keep its practice within manageable bounds.

REFERENCES

1. For a useful discussion, see Kingsley Davis, "Sexual Behavior," in *Contemporary Social Problems*, eds. Robert K. Merton and Robert Nisbet (New York: Harcourt Brace Jovanovich, 1976), pp. 245–252.
2. Vern L. Bullough, *The History of Prostitution* (New Hyde Park, NY: University Books, 1964).

3. Edwin M. Lemert, "Prostitution," in *Problems of Sexual Behavior*, eds. Edward Sagarin and Donald E. J. MacNamara (New York: Crowell, 1968), p. 92.
4. David, *op. cit.*, p. 249.
5. Personal observation by one of the authors, Palmer.
6. Gale Sheehy, *Hustling: Prostitution in Our Wide Open Society* (New York: Delacorte Press, 1973).
7. Alfred C. Kinsey et al., *Sexual Behavior in the Human Male* (Philadelphia: Saunders, 1948).
8. Lester Graham, *No More Morals: The Sexual Revolution* (New York: Pyramid Books, 1971), p. 141.
9. Lemert, *op. cit.*, p. 80.
10. Federal Bureau of Investigation, *Crime in the United States, 1987* (Washington, D.C.: U.S. Government Printing Office), 1988.
11. *Ibid.*, p. 165.
12. *Ibid.*, p. 182.
13. *Ibid.*, p. 168.
14. *Ibid.*, p. 169.
15. Partially follows the classifications set forth by Alex Thio, *Deviant Behavior* (Boston: Houghton Mifflin, 1978), pp. 172–176; and Lewis Diana, *The Prostitute and Her Client* (Springfield, IL: Charles C Thomas, 1985).
16. Diana, *op. cit.*
17. Diana, *op. cit.*, pp. 16–17.
18. Diana, *op. cit.*, pp. 16–17.
19. Gale Miller, *Odd Jobs: The World of Deviant Work* (Englewood Cliffs, NJ: Prentice-Hall, 1978), pp. 126–133.
20. An adaptation of Miller, *ibid.*
21. *Ibid.*, p. 137.
22. Robin Lloyd, *For Money or Love* (New York: Ballantine Books, 1976).
23. Lemert, *op. cit.*, p. 70.
24. Kate Coleman, "Carnal Knowledge: A Portrait of Four Hookers," *Ramparts*, Vol. 10, December 1971, pp. 19–28.
25. Diana, *op. cit.*, p. 45.
26. Clinard thinks not: Marshall B. Clinard, *Sociology of Deviant Behavior* (New York: Holt, Rinehart, and Winston, 1968), p. 513.
27. Diana, *op. cit.*, p. 45; Harry Benjamin and R. E. L. Masters, *Prostitution and Morality* (New York: Julian Press, 1964); Marsha Rosenbaum, *Women on Heroin* (New Brunswick, NJ: Rutgers University Press, 1981).
28. Rosenbaum, *op. cit.*
29. Lemert, *op. cit.*, p. 97.
30. *Ibid.*, p. 74; Clinard, *op. cit.*, p. 510.
31. Lemert, *op. cit.*, p. 74.
32. Nannette Davis, "The Prostitute: Developing a Deviant Identity," in *Studies in the Sociology of Sex*, ed. James M. Henslin (New York: Appleton-Century-Crofts, 1971).
33. Diana Gray, "Turning-Out: A Study of Teenage Prostitution," *Urban Life and Culture*, Vol. 1, January 1973, pp. 401–425; Christina Milner and Richard Milner, *Black Players* (Boston: Little, Brown, 1972).
34. Quoted in Thio, *op. cit.*, p. 184.
35. Milner and Milner, *op. cit.*
36. *Ibid.*
37. John H. Gagnon, *Human Sexualties* (Glenview, IL: Scott, Foresman, 1977).
38. Harold Greenwald, *The Elegant Prostitute* (New York: Walker, 1970), pp. 221–236.
39. James H. Bryan, "Occupational Ideologies and Individual Attitudes of Call Girls," *Social Problems* 13(4): 441–450, 1966; Norman R. Jackman, Richard O'Toole, and Gil-

bert Geis, "The Self-Image of the Prostitute," *Sociological Quarterly*, 4(2): 150–161, 1963.

40. Bryan, *op. cit.*; Gagnon, *op. cit.*
41. Edwin M. Lemert, *Social Pathology* (New York: McGraw-Hill, 1951), p. 253.
42. K. Davis, *op. cit.*
43. *Ibid.*
44. Edwin H. Sutherland and Donald R. Cressey, *Criminology* (Philadelphia: Lippincott, 1974).
45. Richard C. Cloward and Lloyd E. Ohlin, *Delinquency and Opportunity* (Glencoe, IL: Free Press, 1960).
46. Thio, *op. cit.*

7

Homosexuality

DEFINITION AND PREVALENCE

Defining Homosexuality

As is the case with prostitution, homosexuality is difficult to define clearly. Some researchers distinguish between homosexual behavior and homosexual identity.[1] Homosexual behavior refers to erotic physical stimulation between two persons of the same sex. Homosexual identity concerns an individual's self-conception as a homosexual individual, as one who prefers homosexual relationships although he or she may also engage in heterosexual relationships, or not engage in sexual activity at all.

Numerous sociologists and psychologists have taken the view that individuals cannot be dichotomized into the two simple categories of heterosexual and homosexual.[2] At one end of a continuum are individuals who engage only in heterosexual relations and see themselves as heterosexual persons. Then there are those who are mainly heterosexual, view themselves as heterosexual, but occasionally engage in homosexual relations. Some men in one-sex communities such as prisons are examples as are some male prostitutes who service other males. In the middle range are individuals who engage in both heterosexual and homosexual relations and conceive of themselves as bisexual. Next there are persons who have only homosexual relationships but do so clandestinely and often hold a semiformed identity as a homosexual. Finally are those men or women who have "come out," made their homosexuality public, participate in homosexual subcultures, and hold a distinct self-image as a homosexual. Many more persons are to be found near the heterosexual than the homosexual end of the continuum. Most of the evidence suggests that homosexual behavior and identity are considerably more rare among females than males.

Laws vary widely regarding homosexuality. In most countries, homosexual behavior between consenting adults in private is not a criminal violation. Soliciting or engaging in homosexual relationships with minors often is a crime. So is homosexuality between adults when it is in public view. But heterosexual relationships with minors or in public are crimes also in most jurisdictions.

Criminal laws against homosexuality are stringent in the United States compared to other countries. In most states homosexuality between consenting adults, even in private, is a crime. Exceptions are Illinois, Oregon, Connecticut, Hawaii, and Colorado. Soliciting or engaging in homosexuality with minors is a crime in all states as is homosexuality in public. Penalties range to as high as ten years or more imprisonment. Usually laws apply to both sexes but are enforced much more in cases of males than females. English law is considerably more lenient. Homosexuality is not a crime as long as it is carried out in private between consenting adults.

Prevalence

Prevalence of homosexuality is even more difficult to determine than prevalence of prostitution. It is frequently a more clandestine sexual activity than prostitution. Also, where laws against homosexuality exist, they are as a general rule less likely to be enforced than those regarding prostitution. In any case, surveys of societies around the world do indicate that homosexuality is common in many societies and very nearly universal in the sense that it is found to at least a limited extent in a large majority of societies.

Bryan Magee lists some famous men who were homosexuals[3]: Socrates, Plato, Julius Caesar, probably Alexander the Great and William of Orange; also Frederick the Great, Charles XII of Sweden, Marlowe, Tschaikowsky, Kitchener, Rimbaud, Verlaine, Proust, Walt Whitman, Oscar Wilde, and Andre Gide.

Kingsley Davis reports that "historically, in all complex societies, there were people who engaged in homosexual practices."[4] Male homosexuality was in some respects highly approved in ancient Greece. It was fairly common although not necessarily approved in ancient Rome. Davis concludes that "complex societies seem to tolerate a certain amount of homosexual behavior (and literary praise of it) without giving it respect."[5]

Clelland Ford and Frank Beach analyzed homosexuality in 77 nonliterate human societies around the world and in a wide variety of animal species.[6] In about one-third of the human societies homosexuality was very rare and distinctly unacceptable. In about two-thirds of those societies, homosexuality was at least somewhat common among certain members and was tolerated or socially approved. Ford and Beach report as follows[7]:

> Among all the societies in which adult homosexual activities are said to be very rare, definite and specific social pressure is directed against such behavior. The penalties range from the lighter sanction of ridicule to the severe threat of death. The Mbumdu make fun of all homosexual practice, although it is said to occur secretly among both men and women. Homosexual play among Alorse children is frowned upon although it may not be punished, but adult homosexuality is strongly discouraged. One ethnographer has described an eighteen-year-old Goajiro boy who insisted upon dressing like a girl and working with the women. This individual was tolerated by the women, but men treated him with derision. Overt homosexuality was not observed among the Goajiro. Homosexuality in both sexes occurs in Haiti, particularly in urban areas, but it is socially condemned. Masculine and feminine inversions are known to take place in rare instances among the Manus. The only form of homosexuality known to exist in Bali is that connected with prostitution. The Kwoma considered homosexual sodomy (anal intercourse) unnatural and revolting. The Rwaia Bedouins are so strongly opposed to homosexuality that they sentence male or female offenders to death.
>
> Homosexual behavior is reported to be very rare among the Siriono. This is of particular interest because these people have no known social sanctions that would prevent such practices. As a matter of fact, in this culture sexual relationships are particularly free. The Siriono thus appear to be an exception to the general statement made above that all societies in which homosexual activities are rare direct specific social pressure against such behavior. The major anxieties in the culture center about food rather than sexual behavior. Holmberg, who lived with a band consisting of about 100 Siriono natives, found no instances of overt homosexual behavior. One bachelor appeared to show some homosexual tendencies, but he was never seen to make overt sexual advances toward other men.
>
> The most common form of institutionalized homosexuality is that of the "berdache" or "transvestite." The berdache is a male who dresses like a woman, performs women's tasks, and adopts some aspects of the feminine role in sexual behavior with male partners. Less frequently a woman dresses like a man and seeks to adopt the male sex role.
>
> In some societies the man who assumes the feminine role is regarded by other members of the community as a powerful shaman. Among the Siberian Chukchee such an individual puts on women's clothing, assumes feminine mannerisms, and may become the "wife" of another man. The pair copulate per anum, the shaman always playing the feminine role. In addition to the shaman "wife," the husband usually has another wife with whom he indulges in heterosexual coitus. The shaman in turn often supports a feminine mistress; children are often born of such unions. The shaman enjoys considerable prestige and has a position of power in the community. He is believed to have been involuntarily transformed by supernatural power and some men fear being changed even though the procedure might enhance their standing.
>
> Among the Koniag, some male children are reared from infancy to occupy the female role. They learn women's crafts, wear women's ornaments,

and become skilled in wifely duties. When he is older such a male becomes a wife of one of the more important men of the community. He is usually credited with magical powers and accorded a great deal of respect.

Male homosexual behavior in other societies most frequently involves anal intercourse. In many cases this behavior occurs within the framework of courtship and marriage, the man who takes the part of the female being recognized as a berdache and treated like a woman. In other words, a genuine mateship is involved. In some societies, however, this kind of sexual behavior, instead of being confined to a relatively small number of individuals, is practiced by a large part of the population, and the relationship is more appropriately classified as a liaison.

Among the Siwans of Africa, for example, all men and boys engage in anal intercourse. They adopt the feminine role on strictly sexual situations and males are singled out as peculiar if they do not indulge in these homosexual activities. Prominent Siwan men lend their sons to each other, and they talk about their masculine love affairs as openly as they discuss their love of women. Both married and unmarried males are expected to have both homosexual and heterosexual affairs. Among many of the aborigines of Australia this type of coitus is a recognized custom between unmarried men and uninitiated boys. Strehlow writes of the Aranda as follows: ". . . Pederasty is a recognized custom. . . . Commonly a man, who is fully initiated but not yet married, takes a boy ten or twelve years old, who lives with him as a wife for several years, until the older man marries. The boy is neither circumcised nor subincised, though he may have ceased to be regarded as a boy and is considered a young man. The boy must belong to the proper marriage class from which the man might take a wife." (Strehlow, 1915, p. 98)

Keraki bachelors of New Guinea universally practice sodomy, and in the course of his puberty rites each boy is initiated into anal intercourse by the older males. After his first year of playing the passive role he spends the rest of his bachelorhood sodomizing the newly initiated. This practice is believed by the natives to be necessary for the growing boy. They are convinced that boys can become pregnant as a result of sodomy, and a lime-eating ceremony is performed periodically to prevent such conception. Though fully sanctioned by the males, these initiatory practices are supposed to be kept secret from the women. The Kiwai have a similar custom; sodomy is practiced in connection with initiation to make young men strong.

More rarely reported than sodomy are mutual masturbation and oral-genital contacts between males. Manual stimulation of the genitals of one young boy by another is described only among the Hopi; childhood sex play apparently consists far more frequently of attempts to copulate with another member of the same sex. For the Wogeo, however, homosexual relations between adult males seem confined to mutual manual manipulation of the sexual organs. In Africa, Dahomean and Nama men practice mutual masturbation as the only form of homosexual behavior. Tikopia men manipulate their own genitals in the presence of other members of the same sex, although mutual masturbation apparently never occurs.

Ford and Beach reached the general conclusion that their data on humans and lower animals as well

suggest that a biological tendency for inversion of sexual behavior (homosexuality) is inherent in most if not all mammals including the human spe-

cies. At the same time . . . homosexual behavior is never the predominant
type of sexual activity for adults in any society or in any animal species.[8]

Found in most if not all human societies, then, homosexuality is
never more prevalent than heterosexuality. It is incompatible with marriage, family, and the conception of offspring. The last is necessary if
a society is to perpetuate itself and the first two, marriage and the
family, appear to be necessary for the adequate development of children. Moreover, homosexuality is in some respects incompatible with
socialization of children. Models for learning one sex role or the other
are likely to be absent in homosexual settings.

Regarding the United States, Kinsey and his coresearchers concluded that 17 percent of white males and 13 percent of white females
had some homosexual experience over their lives. They found that 4
percent of white males and 1 percent of white females were exclusively
homosexual from adolescence onward.[9] Paul Gebhard reached the conclusion that between 2 and 5 percent of adult males in the United States
were distinctly homosexual.[10]

CHARACTERISTICS OF MALE HOMOSEXUALS

Age, Race, and Class

Ford and Beach report that in nonliterate societies around the world
homosexuality is more common among adolescents than adults.[11] This
is the case for both male and female homosexuality. However, in many
respects homosexuality within the two sexes is greatly different. Therefore, the remainder of this chapter is concerned with male homosexuality, with the exception of a section which focuses directly on homosexuality among females.

The belief that male adult homosexuals prey on male children and
young adolescents is largely myth. Males usually seek out other adult
males for sexual purposes. As a male grows older he may very well
engage in sex with a younger male but only rarely with a child. One
partial exception is that a significant proportion of male homosexual
prostitutes are teenage boys, who are in much demand.

Researchers agree that homosexuals come from all socioeconomic
classes and occupational strata. High-status homosexuals tend more than
those of lower status to keep their homosexuality secret. They fear the
loss of status if discovered. Schur points out that homosexuality is revealed more often in some occupations than others: ballet and chorus
dancing, interior decoration, fashion design, hairdressing.[12] The word
revealed is critical since it may be that in other occupations there is more
concealment of homosexuality.

It is not clear whether in the United States homosexuality is more prevalent among blacks or whites. It is a common research finding that there is considerable homosexuality *between* black and white males. And within races, there is a good deal of homosexuality between males of higher and lower status. Some conclude that homosexuality is therefore democratic. Yet male sex relations across class and caste lines tend to be covert rather than overt. Moreover, as Schur contends, there may be an implicit bargain struck between white and black: the black provides the higher-status white with sex in return for companionship.[13] This may also be the case with higher- and lower-status males of the same race.

Family Background and Personality

Some researchers hold that homosexuality is simply a form of sexuality just as heterosexuality is. The predisposition to homosexuality, it is argued, is genetically determined.[14] Others take the view that homosexuality is a pathological condition brought about largely by abnormal family conditions in early life. The evidence is mixed. Certain studies, such as those of Irving Bieber and his colleagues, point to an irrational castration fear developed during the male's early years.[15] The boy grows up fearing the insertion of the penis in the female vagina will result in its loss. Others view homosexuality quite differently, as an outgrowth of complex social interactions and subcultural learning.[16]

Certainly male homosexuals have grown up in families of all economic levels and of highly varied racial and ethnic backgrounds. There does seem to be evidence that one of two conditions existed in the past experience of the male homosexual in the United States: The first has to do with early family relationships and the second with later associations. Regarding the former, the young boy may have had a weak, distant relationship with a passive yet hostile father who presented a poor male role model or who was absent from the home; simultaneously the boy may have had a close emotional attachment with a dominating mother who demanded in return for affection that the boy internalize the female role.[17] Regarding the second condition, the male youth or man may have found himself in a one-sex setting conducive to homosexuality, such as a boys school, a reformatory, the military, or a prison. Many males who enter into homosexual relationships in these settings later return to heterosexuality, but others do not; or the male adolescent or young adult may have been recruited into a homosexual subculture and rewarded with friendship and perhaps material gain for engaging in homosexual behavior.[18]

Some male homosexuals have overt female role characteristics of walking, talking, so on. Others do not at all and cannot by appearance, mannerisms, or speech be distinguished from male heterosexuals. There is, however, fairly general agreement that male homosexuals suffer considerable or greater anxiety and stress because of their deviation from cultural norms. All in all, homosexuality in the United States is defined as "bad." This leads to a negative self-image. It does appear that the more homosexuals "come out," publicly declare their homosexuality, and become integrated into a homosexual community, the less stress they experience.

Far more male homosexuals are or have been conventionally married (to a female) than is generally realized. The figure is often put at 25 percent.[19] Some married homosexuals are bisexual; others have seldom if ever had sexual relationships with their wives. Still others are essentially heterosexual: when unable to engage in sexual relations with their wives—due to being away from home, spouse's illness, and so forth—they seek out quick, impersonal homosexual relations as a pragmatic solution to a problem. This all reinforces the view that homosexuality is a complex, diverse form of deviance of many dimensions.

SUBCULTURES OF MALE HOMOSEXUALITY

The Diverse, Amorphous Nature of Subcultures

Homosexuality may be quite individualistic or it may be institutionalized to a considerable extent. Varying degrees of both exist in the United States. There are two kinds of male homosexual communities: (1) networks of individuals who know each other and interact from time to time but are spread out through a city; and (2) actual homosexual neighborhoods as in San Francisco; Fire Island, New York; and Provincetown, Massachusetts. Institutionalized subcultural forms are several. There are the public restrooms or "tearooms," small enclaves of homosexual customs with rapidly changing players. There are the gay bars and coffeehouses where homosexuals meet openly. There are male homosexual places of prostitution (discussed below) and the Turkish baths. There are the subgroups of homosexuals within some boys schools, prisons, military organizations, and the like.

All of these subcultural forms have a somewhat amorphous quality. They exist but they are not as well formed as many other deviant subcultures. Several are, of course, clandestine and customs of self-protection can give the illusion of ambiguity. But many clandestine subcultures are very clearly formed, for example, professional theft, hard drugs, and some institutionalized forms of prostitution. The tenuous nature of homosexual subcultures is in good measure a function of an important characteristic of relationships between male homosex-

uals. Those relationships tend to be highly unstable.[20] Only very seldom are they close and enduring. One reason advanced for this is that
since homosexuality is socially defined as bad, homosexuals tend un-
consciously to define each other as bad and so to avoid stable, long-
lasting relationships with each other.[21] Also, having been geared in a
culture which values male dominance, it is difficult for one of two males
to accept a dependent position vis-à-vis another. When both strive to
be dominant, conflict inevitably arises.

The instability of homosexual relationships may be one reason for,
or a result of, the considerable promiscuity in male homosexuality. Many
men have had sexual relations with hundreds and even thousands of
other men. Men may go from one to another male because of the inability to form lasting attachments. Again, promiscuity can work against
the establishment of an enduring relationship. Very likely these two
processes operate simultaneously and reinforce each other.

Even where "marriage" occurs between male homosexuals, there
are institutionalized arrangements for promiscuous relationships. One
form is "open marriage" wherein partners are able to carry on "extramarital" sexual liaisons providing they do not develop into love affairs.
A second form is "three-way marriage" where the two partners from
time to time together seek out one or more additional males to provide
sexual diversity.[22]

The ambiguous nature of homosexual subcultures and the instability of relationships means that socialization of males into homosexuality tends to be sporadic and haphazard. There are, to be sure, occasional homosexual "tutors" who frequent the gay bars and offer to train
newly self-proclaimed homosexuals in the argot, the varieties of sexual
experiences, and the self-protective measures of the homosexual world.
But such persons are rare. More usually, if there is any training, it
takes the form of hit-or-miss instruction between temporary partners
or reading of homosexual literature.

Gay Bars and Tearooms

The gay bar is the symbol of male homosexual defiance of conventional morality. It is a public place where homosexuals gather and by
doing so proclaim their sexual preference. At the same time it is a "back
place," out of the mainstream and consequently out of the limelight of
disapproval of the "straight" world. Homosexuals often "come out"
there; it is a rite of passage. There are gay discos, gay restaurants, gay
beachclubs, gay bars for homosexual couples. But it is the gay singles
bar that predominates as the epitome of gay disdain for the straights
who oppose their life-style, since a major function of these bars is to
provide a setting where male homosexuals can effect liaisons.

Observers note the seemingly cheerless, speechless quality of many gay singles bars. There is little conversation and little overt movement. Men communicate by eye and facial expressions. They size each other up. Two may, from far corners of the room, silently effect the beginning of a sexual relationship. This in itself is not unlike that which may occur in a heterosexual singles bar. However, the two males seldom later converse within the confines of the bar. Instead, after a time they silently meet at the door and once outside make arrangements as to where to go for sexual purposes.[23]

Defiance toward the straight world may be expressed in the gay bar when a heterosexual mistakenly enters. He may be subjected to clear if subtle "status degradation" through the verbal and facial expressions and gestures directed toward him. He is accorded a welcome in reverse. There may well be in this an element of revenge against the straight world where the homosexual often meets with basically similar derision and ostracism.

In sharp contrast to the public nature of the gay bar is the essentially covert, private nature of the men's restroom, called "tearoom" by homosexuals. Technically a public place, it offers a high degree of anonymity. Laud Humphreys make an extensive analysis of the "tearoom trade," reported in a book with that title. He describes the setting and the action[24]:

> There is a great deal of difference in the volumes of homosexual activity that these accomodations shelter. In some, one might wait for months before observing a deviant act (unless solitary masturbation is considered deviant). In others, the volume approaches orgiastic dimensions. One summer afternoon, for instance, I witnessed twenty acts of fellatio in the course of an hour while waiting out a thunderstorm in a tearoom. For one who wishes to participate in (or study) such activity, the primary consideration is one of finding where the action is.
>
> I have chosen the term "purlieu" (with its ancient meaning of land severed from a royal forest by perambulation) to describe the immediate environs best suited to the tearoom trade. Drives and walks that separate a public toilet from the rest of the park are almost certain guides to deviant sex. The ideal setting for homosexual activity is a tearoom situated on an island of grass, with roads close by on every side. The getaway car is just a few steps away; children are not apt to wander over from the playground; no one can surprise the participants by walking in from the woods or from over a hill; it is not likely that straight people will stop there at all. According to my observations, the women's side of these buildings is seldom used.
>
> Active tearooms are also identifiable by the number of automobiles parked nearby. If two or more cars remain in front of a relatively isolated restroom for more than ten minutes, one may be reasonably certain that homosexual activity is in progress inside. This sign that the sexual market is in operation is an important one to the participants, who seldom enter a park restroom unless the presence of other unoccupied cars indicate that potential partners are inside. A lone arriver will usually wait in his auto

until at least one other has parked nearby. That this signal is obscured when a golf course, zoo, or other facility that draws automobiles is located in close proximity may help explain the popularity of the isolated restroom.

Another means of recognizing the active tearoom requires closer inspection. Here, I refer to the condition of the windows and doors. Men who play the tearoom game must be able to know when someone is approaching. A door that squeaks or sticks is of great assistance; however, the condition of the windows is even more important. If they are of opaque glass, are nailed shut, or have no broken panes, the researcher may presume that the facility is seldom used for homosexual encounters.

Throughout most homosexual encounters in public restrooms, nothing is spoken. One may spend many hours in these buildings and witness dozens of sexual acts without hearing a word. Of fifty encounters on which I made extensive notes, only fifteen included vocal utterances. The fifteen instances of speech break down as follows: Two were encounters in which I sought to ease the strain of legitimizing myself as lookout by saying "You go ahead—I'll watch." Four were whispered remarks between sexual partners, such as "Not so hard!" or "Thanks." One was an exchange of greetings between friends.

The other eight verbal exchanges were in full voice and more extensive, but they reflected an attendant circumstance that was exceptional. When a group of us were locked in a restroom and attacked by several youths, we spoke for defense and out of fear. This event ruptured the reserve among us and resulted in a series of conversations among those who shared this adventure for several days afterward. Gradually, this sudden unity subsided, and the encounters drifted back into silence.

Barring such unusual events, an occasionally whispered "thanks" at the conclusion of the act constitutes the bulk of even whispered communication. At first, I presumed that speech was avoided for fear of incrimination. The excuse that intentions have been misunderstood is much weaker when those proposals are expressed in words rather than signalled by body movements. As research progressed, however, it became evident that the privacy of silent interaction accomplishes much more than mere defense against exposure to a hostile world. Even when a careful lookout is maintaining the boundaries of an encounter against intrusion, the sexual participants tend to be silent. The mechanism of silence goes beyond satisfying the demand for privacy. Like all other characteristics of the tearoom setting, it serves to guarantee anonymity, to assure the impersonality of the sexual liaison.

Tearoom sex is distinctly less personal than any other form of sexual activity, with the single exception of solitary masturbation. More will be said of this in the concluding chapter of the book. For now, let me indicate only what I mean by "less personal": simply that there is less emotional and physical involvement in restroom fellatio—less, even, than the furtive action that takes place in autos and behind bushes. In those instances, at least, there is generally some verbal involvement. Often, in tearoom stalls, the only portions of the players' bodies that touch are the mouth of the insertee and the penis of the insertor; and the mouths of these partners seldom open for speech.

Only a public place, such as a park restroom, could provide the lack of personal involvement in sex that certain men desire. The setting fosters the necessary turnover in participants by its accessibility and visibility to the "right" men. In these public settings, too, there exists a sort of democracy that is endemic to impersonal sex. Men of all racial, social, educational, and physical characteristics meet in these places for sexual union. With the lack of involvement, personal preferences tend to be minimized.

Homosexual Organizations and Ambiguous Ideology

Gay organizations abound in the United States. Most are male, a few female. Some are militant such as the Gay Liberation Front and Gay Activists Alliance; others are not, such as the large Mattachine Society (the name refers to masked jesters in medieval courts who always spoke the truth). These organizations have gained membership and power in recent years for several reasons. The success of the black movement gave other minorities the courage to try. The Kinsey Report of 1948 brought male homosexuality out of the closet.[25] And there has been in the United States in recent decades a growing tolerance of sexual deviance. Great strides have been made by gays in gaining rights of employment and in achieving respectability generally. "Gay is good" is not without its heterosexual supporters. Many colleges and universities now have "gay studies" programs. Gays are especially incensed at the idea that they are "sick" and have experienced considerable reward over the recent decision of the American Psychiatric Association to remove homosexuality from its list of psychiatric disorders.

Despite more political power than at any time in the past in the United States, gay males still suffer much exploitation and abuse.[26] They are easy prey as criminal victims, especially regarding assault and robbery. Seldom do they turn to the police whom they see as distinctly unsympathetic. Assault may result in the homicidal death of the homosexual. In some areas, heterosexual males make a sport of beating up and robbing homosexuals. Gays are also especially susceptible to blackmail because of fear of exposure, job loss, and so on. And, of course, there is the psychological stress of either social disapproval if they have "come out" or the burden of secrecy if they have not.

Isolation is a primary reason for male homosexuals entering the gay subculture. Once they have, they are on the path to becoming secondary or career homosexuals. Having become such, they experience psychological support from other gays and stress may very well lessen. Thus is there a rewarding, compelling quality to moving from individualistic to institutionalized homosexuality. Yet the degree of ambiguity in the ideology of the homosexual community remains. The sex role is a master role in every society: when its norms are overthrown, the social fabric is threatened. If special allowances are made for the homosexual, a special role created—medicine man, spiritual leader, seer—then life may be altogether tolerable. If not, as in the United States, then homosexuals, even with subcultural supports, are likely to possess a personal identity, value system, and ideology which fundamentally reflect the deep chasm between personal inclination and public rejection.

A telling finding regarding the position of the male homosexual in the United States has to do with the response of 300 homosexuals to the question of whether or not they would want a son to be homosexual. "No" was the answer of 83 percent; "yes" of 2 percent; the remaining 15 percent said that was a matter for the son to decide.[27]

Male Homosexual Prostitution

Female homosexual prostitution is extremely rare in the United States and most other societies. One form of quasi-prostitution among female homosexuals is the "companion" who is employed by the wealthy woman. They live together, conducting a well-hidden homosexual relationship. But female homosexual streetwalkers, bar girls, call girls, massage parlor personnel, are all but unknown. Quite the opposite is the case regarding male homosexual prostitution.[28] Precisely how prevalent this is is very unclear. It is certain, however, that it is fairly common. Every medium and large city in the United States appears to have its hustlers (male streetwalkers) and call boys. In many cities there are gay brothels and also massage parlors and Turkish baths which specialize in prostitution among males.

This form of negative deviance is, generally speaking, prohibited by law as are heterosexual prostitution and homosexuality without prostitution. There are sporadic arrests, "round-ups" and harrassment of male prostitutes by the police as in cases of female prostitutes. The aim seems to be similar: to contain the problem rather than to eliminate it.

The main forms of male homosexual prostitution are parallel to those of female heterosexual prostitution. There are the hustlers, independents, who ply the streets and gay bars. There are the young men who work in the all-male brothels. There are the men employed as masseurs and attendants in Turkish baths, often working on a commission basis. And there are the call boys and super call boys. The former may be on their own or work for a call boy organization. The latter almost always are part of a call house which arranges appointments with wealthy, prestigious men. There is, in addition, the transvestite male homosexual prostitute. He does not have a counterpart in female prostitution. He wears women's clothes, poses as a female prostitute, and works the heterosexual bars or street. He sometimes deludes the male customer into believing that he is being serviced by a female.

The hustlers and brothel workers usually consider themselves het-erosexuals who work as prostitutes purely for the money. The call boys are likely to be self-confirmed homosexuals. Those who work in mas-sage parlors and Turkish baths may see themselves as homosexual, heterosexual, or bisexual. Whatever their self-concept, male prostitutes as a rule have short careers since their male customers have a strong preference for youthful physical attractiveness. There is little call for aging male homosexuals except for the brief encounters in the tearoom.

The chicken hustler is a teen-age boy, sometimes no more than 12 or 13, who as a street hustler or call boy caters to men termed "chicken hawks," who want only boys. Usually he is separated from his family and lives alone in the city. He is physically attractive, "beautiful" to male adult homosexuals. He is not necessarily exclusively homosexual himself. Often he is taken under the wing of a pimp, who trains him much as pimps do the members of their stable of female prostitutes. He is befriended by the pimp who gives him affection in return for total cooperation, brutality for anything less. Often he is trained by another boy, already a veteran in the pimp's stable. As with the train-ing of female prostitutes, the emphasis is on learning how to interact efficiently with the customers rather than with training in sexual prac-tices per se. Usually the chicken hustler's career is short. Customers want "fresh" boys. In many instances the chicken hustler later marries heterosexually and leads a straight life.

EXPLANATIONS OF MALE HOMOSEXUALITY

Explanations of male homosexuality are less convincing than those regarding most forms of negative deviance. That is also true of expla-nations of female homosexuality, to be discussed in the next section. Certainly one underlying reason is the considerable degree of dissen-sion among members of a given society such as ours, and across soci-eties, as to whether homosexuality is in fact negative deviance. More-over, research on homosexuality has not been abundant. Consequently, there is but a weak empirical base on which to construct theories of this form of deviance.

Over past decades, biological and psychiatric theories of male ho-mosexuality have been dominant over sociological theories. Biological explanations have stressed one or another form of inherited disposition to sexual relationships with other males. Psychiatric explanations have tended to focus on the development of some type of fear related to the opposite sex or the individual's own male sex role.[29] While psychiatric approaches have a certain limited validity in some instances, they fail to take into account the social and cultural forces that determine in many instances whether persons are heterosexual or homosexual throughout their lives or at a certain period in their lives.

Social Integration and Cultural Supports

Explanations of male homosexuality sometimes point to the homosexual's deviation from society. However, this usually is seen as a result rather than a cause of sexual aberration: social disapproval by others leads to the alienation. There are nonetheless some indications that low social integration and anomie are generating forces of male homosexuality. On the one hand, when heterosexual freedom increases, so does homosexuality. It may be that the more anomic are social conditions, the more do sexual mores break down and the more do individuals "do their own things," including homosexuality.[30] On the other hand, anomic individuals, alienated and outside the mainstream of society, may express their rage by rebellion against the established order which approves of heterosexuality and disapproves of homosexuality.[31]

More likely is the reasoning that if conditions of low social integration and anomie pervade the family environment, then the seeds are sown for developing boys to learn homosexuality. If fathers are forced by failure in the economic marketplace either to admit defeat and become passive role models or to be absent from the home, and if mothers are consequently forced to be dominant in the home, then sons may seek to emulate their mothers sexually as well as otherwise.

Regarding cultural support explanations, subcultures of male homosexuality are moderately well formed in this and many other societies.[32] The frustrated, alienated youth, uncertain in sexual identity, may find in older male members of homosexual subcultures compatible role models who provide the behavior patterns and values of homosexuality and affection as well. At the same time, it is clear that access to institutionalized opportunity structures and learning of subcultural values and customs are not necessary for homosexuality to occur. All that is required is that persons of the same sex stimulate each other erotically.

However, as we have seen, subcultures and opportunity structures of male homosexuality exist often in fairly full-blown form. They have their functions, mainly two. While subcultures and opportunity structures may function as socialization mechanisms for new "recruits" to homosexuality, far more often their value is felt after individuals have begun to engage in homosexuality. They provide "moral support" for persons who have followed a disvalued (in this society) form of sexuality. And they provide a group mechanism for coming out, for making public one's homosexuality and thus removing the burden of secrecy.

The old adage that there is strength in numbers is certainly true regarding male homosexuality. Informal but cohesive homosexual communities, gay bars, homosexual organizations both militant and otherwise, even homosexual literature, all provide important supports for those stigmatized by their sexual preference. And the evidence shows that there can be a powerful long-term reward in these mutually supportive efforts. Male homosexuals who have come out, gone public, and remained so have less psychological problems than others. Group and cultural supports are effective mechanisms for coping with adverse public reactions to male homosexuality.

Conflict and Societal Reaction

Thio attempts to explain male homosexuality in terms of power conflict theory.[33] Overt homosexuality is found mainly among the powerless, he contends, and covert homosexuality among the powerful. The powerful have the means to cloak this sexual deviance in secrecy. Public scrutiny and prosecution of the supposed overt homosexuality of the powerless serves to further hide the homosexuality of the powerful by distracting attention from it. The problem here is that in fact there is not a direct connection between social class or racial position and whether male homosexuality is private or public. At any given status level, some male homosexuals want their sexuality to be known and others do not.

Thio goes on to contend that powerful men are especially prone to "experience subjective deprivation from their unrestrained and difficult-to-fulfill desire to become great winners in a highly competitive 'masculine' culture."[34] They hold unrealistically high "expectations for success in the institutionalized game of heterosexual conquest. Not being able to realize this expectation, they may be driven to achieve success in the deviant homosexual conquest."[35] This seems to stretch the facts to the limits of belief. If males have great power, then by Thio's own reasoning about rape, males should certainly be able to effect coercive sexual conquests of females.[36]

If a homosexual subculture is not at hand, then young males may begin mutually to create one as a defense against negative labeling, loneliness, and uncertain identity. Thus does adverse societal reaction to negative deviance contribute to the institutionalization of that deviance.

Immersion in a male homosexual subculture may lead to the development of an identity as a homosexual. It may facilitate the internalization of the role of homosexual. Uncertainty and ambiguity over who one is may be decreased through socialization into the customs and values of male homosexuality. Feelings of insecurity, alienation, and despair may be lessened through the support of others with similar problems and similar participation in the subculture.[37] Some males who repeatedly enter into homosexuality become secondary or career deviants in this way. Yet many do not, and for them this explanation is unsatisfactory. As noted earlier, theories of deviance are not especially applicable to male (or female) homosexuality.

One line of reasoning as to why this is so may be that males who have homosexual relations experience early in life one of two forms of psychological problem. The first involves an aversion to females because of some type of trauma associated with them. Often related to this, sometimes as a reaction formation, is a strong identification with males and the male role. The second type of problem is in some ways the opposite: it has to do with a desire to take on the female role, to play out sexually and otherwise (female mannerisms and so on) the part of a female. This will result from a close identification with a dominant female figure in childhood, usually the mother. Frequently there is concomitantly an aversion to the male role because of adverse experiences with a passive male figure, often the father. In any case, the first centrally concerns an aversion to females and the female role, and a consequent turning to other males for affection, support, and sex. The second involves a closeness to a desire to be *like* females, and the seeking by the male of a female emotional and sexual relationship with a male. It may well be that different explanations are required for each.[38]

Female Homosexuality

Female homosexuality—lesbianism—is in this and most other societies far less widespread than male homosexuality.[39] It is usually less visible also, making comparisons regarding prevalence especially difficult. Ford and Beach in their analysis of 76 nonliterate societies reported evidence of female homosexuality in but 17 societies.[40] In about 50 of the societies, male homosexuality was distinctly in evidence. As noted earlier, Kinsey and his colleagues found that in the United States, 13 percent of white women, as compared to 37 percent of white men, had had one or more homosexual experiences. One percent of the white females, in contrast to 4 percent of the white males, were exclusively homosexual during and after adolescence.

Most societies do not have the strong taboos and criminal laws against lesbianism that so many have against male homosexuality. Lesbianism is as a rule considered a form of negative deviance but not one which especially threatens the social organization and society's members. Most jurisdictions in the United States do not have explicit criminal laws outruling female homosexuality. Even when laws do exist, police very seldom make arrests. Kinsey in his research in the 1940s and early 1950s found no cases in the United States, beginning with colonial times, in which females had been convicted of homosexuality. And he found in his large sample of women subjects but four instances where police had questioned their activities as being possibly homosexual.[41]

Adolescent girls sometimes slide without awareness into initial acts of homosexuality. They are fond of another girl. They find themselves "petting" with the other girl much as they do with boys. They may even reach orgasm. They in no way conceive of the relationship as homosexual. They find the relationship comforting. They continue to date boys; they pet. They may enter into intercourse with males. Later they may marry. They may (or may not) pick up, that is continue, the earlier homosexual pattern. They may gradually take on a hidden career as a homosexual, living with another woman as "a friend" yet having her as a lover. Frequently the lesbian's job is a major link with the straight world. She may well be accepted as a heterosexual on the job, even asked to go on and accept dates, while her private life is clearly homosexually oriented. Others tend not to be suspicious of female homosexuality as they are of male homosexuality.

Lesbianism is generally less institutionalized as a deviant sexual form than male homosexuality. (The fact that one type of deviance is less prevalent than another does not in itself mean that it is less institutionalized. Professional theft is, for example, less frequent than shoplifting in the United States. Yet the former is far more institutionalized than the latter.) Certainly in the United States, subcultures of lesbianism are less well formed than those of homosexuality among males. While women may go to gay bars, this is much less frequent than among males. There are gay women's organizations (the Women's Gay Movement is one), but they are few in number, have relatively small memberships, and are less active than male organizations. Female "careers" in homosexuality, secondary deviance of this type, are less marked than for men.

Of course, there is some institutionalization of lesbianism. Women do not always enter into homosexuality in a purely individualistic way. But they are far more private about their sexual deviance. They tend more than men to enter into hidden homosexual marriages, to avoid promiscuity, and to stay out of the public eye generally. In contrast to men, women stress love over sex in homosexual relationships as they do in heterosexual relationships. They tend in both forms of sex to be monogamous to a greater extent than men.

The female role in the general sense is less divorced from homosexuality than the male role in this and many other societies. Females are socialized at an early age to be pleasant and affectionate toward both sexes. They do not have to "prove" their femininity, as males do their masculinity, by conquering the other sex. They can without disapproval make comforting, affectionate gestures to members of their own sex. They do not find switching back and forth between heterosexuality and homosexuality—in other words bisexuality—as conflicted as many males do. Intimate relations with other females do not require as great a role shift as intimate relations with other males do for men.

Females who find themselves in one-sex settings frequently engage in homosexuality.[42] If later they return to a dual-sex setting, they usually resume heterosexual relationships. Women's prisons are a primary example. Researchers have found that in female prisons in the United States homosexuality is threaded through much of everyday life. Homosexual relationships among inmates determine who controls what to a large extent. In male prisons, homosexual relations are also widespread. But, unlike female prisons, sheer physical power plays a dominant part in social control of inmates by other inmates.

The occupation of "stripper" is one where considerable female homosexuality is found.[43] To a greater extent than is generally realized, strippers are isolated from males. They travel around the country in female troupes. Men tend to approach them for sex only, not for dates. They resent that. Also, they see themselves as distinct from prostitutes in many cases and will not engage in sex for money. Stripping is fairly hard work. Strippers sometimes find solace in each other. They may provide for each other affection and comfort through erotic physical contact.

If explanations of male homosexuality are less than adequate, this is even more so regarding female homosexuality. We do know that the female role tends to be less incompatible with homosexuality than the male role. And we do know that female homosexuality is more easily tolerated by societies than male homosexuality. We also know that, generally speaking, female homosexuality, at least repetitive "career" homosexuality, is less prevalent than male career homosexuality. Very likely a useful explanation of lesbianism will be based on a combination of anomie and role theory. It may well be that the more anomic are females and the more uncertain is their identity in the female role, the more likely they will be to engage in homosexuality.

SUMMARY

Homosexual behavior refers to erotic physical stimulation between two persons of the same sex. Homosexuals may restrict their sexual relations to those of the same sex or engage in such relations with members of either sex. Homosexuality is far more common among males than females.

Laws against homosexual behavior tend to be more stringent in the United States than elsewhere. In most states homosexuality is a crime even when practiced in private between consenting adults. In many countries, Great Britain, for example, this is not the case.

Homosexuality continues to exist in most societies around the world. Homosexual behavior, however, is never more prevalent than heterosexuality. Less than 5 percent of adult males in the United States and 1 percent of adult females are homosexual. In most societies homosexual behavior is practiced more by adolescents than adult males. Homosexuality cuts across all social classes but is more visible in certain occupations than in others. Many homosexual contacts occur between persons of different races and social classes.

Distinctive familial relationships mark the early lives of male homosexuals. Their fathers were hostile yet passive toward them as children; their mothers, on the other hand, were emotionally close to them but domineering. Affection was given for feminine behavior by the child. Time spent in one-sex institutions—boys schools, reformatories, the military, and so on—is also conducive to homosexuality.

There are two main kinds of homosexual subcultures: the first involves networks of individuals who know each other and interact from time to time but are spread throughout a city; and the second involves exclusively homosexual neighborhoods. These subcultures are tenuous owing to the unstable nature of the homosexual relationship. There are struggles for dominance, and promiscuity is quite high. Socialization into a homosexual subculture is as a result haphazard.

Gay bars and tearooms are two kinds of meeting places for homosexuals. Homosexuals who have "come out" may choose to meet in bars to arrange "dates" or sexual encounters. Homosexuals who wish to remain out of public attention meet in "tearooms" or public men's rooms for anonymous sexual contacts with other hidden homosexuals.

Homosexual organizations—the Gay Liberation Front and Gay Activists Alliance, among others—have risen in attempts to establish ideological support for homosexuality. Nonetheless, homosexuals in general are still faced with a fundamental split between personal sexual preference and societal rejection.

Forms of male prostitution parallel those of female prostitution. There are hustlers, "chicken hustlers" (young boys) and independents who work the streets and gay bars, masseurs and Turkish bath attendants, call boys, and transvestite homosexual prostitutes. Call boys see themselves as confirmed homosexuals; others, such as "chicken hustlers," do not.

Social integration explanations of homosexuality suggest that fathers who are occupational failures may either leave home or become passive role models for their sons. As a result, mothers may become dominant in the home and their sons may emulate them sexually. There are no direct links between social class and race and homosexuality. However, homosexuals drawn from the more powerful segments of society are better able to hide their sexual deviance. While subcultures of homosexuals seldom actively recruit new members, they do provide moral support to self-proclaimed homosexuals.

Early lives of homosexuals tend to involve two kinds of psychological problems. The first manifests itself as an aversion to females because of traumatic experiences with them. The second problem, opposite from the first, involves close female identification and the desire to take on female mannerisms and sexual proclivities. Overly strong ties with a dominant mother and aversion to a passive father combine to bring about this psychological dilemma.

Lesbianism, female homosexuality, is far less common than male homosexual behavior. Criminal laws prohibiting female homosexuality are rare and where they do exist are seldom enforced. Lesbians are less organized, less apt to form subcultural arrangements, and generally less visible than male homosexuals. As with males, females in one-sex settings are more prone to homosexual behavior than otherwise.

REFERENCES

1. For example, Marshall B. Clinard and Robert F. Meier, *Sociology of Deviant Behavior* (New York: Holt, Rinehart, and Winston, 1985); also, Richard R. Troiden, "Becoming Homosexual: A Model of Gay Identity Acquisition," *Psychiatry* 42:362–373, 1979.
2. Alfred C. Kinsey *et al.*, *Sexual Behavior in the Human Male* (Philadelphia: W. B. Saunders, 1948), p. 638.
3. Bryan Magee, *One in Twenty: A Study of Homosexuality in Men and Women* (New York: Stein and Day, 1966), p. 46.
4. Kingsley Davis, "Sexual Behavior," in *Contemporary Social Problems*, eds. Robert K. Merton and Robert Nisbet (New York: Harcourt, Brace, Jovanovich, 1976), p. 252.
5. *Ibid.*, p. 253.
6. Clellan S. Ford and Frank A. Beach, *Patterns of Sexual Behavior* (New York: Harper, 1951), pp. 125–143.
7. *Ibid.*, pp. 129–133.
8. *Ibid.*, p. 143.
9. Kinsey *et al.*, *op cit.*, pp. 474–475.
10. Paul H. Gebhard, "Incidence of Overt Homosexuality in the United States and Western Europe," in *NIMH: Task Force of Homosexuality: Final Report and Background Papers*, ed. J. M. Livengood (Rockville, MD: National Institute of Mental Health, 1971).
11. Ford and Beach, *op. cit.*, p. 143.
12. Edwin M. Schur, *Crimes Without Victims* (Englewood Cliffs, NJ: Prentice-Hall, 1974), p. 93.

13. *Ibid.*, p. 92.
14. Alan P. Bell, Martin S. Weinberg, and Sue K. Hammersmith, *Sexual Preference: Its Development in Men and Women* (Bloomington: Indiana University Press, 1981).
15. Irbin Bieber *et al.*, *Homosexuality* (New York: Basic Books, 1962).
16. See Ronald L. Akers, *Deviant Behavior* (Belmont, CA: Wadsworth, 1985); also, Kenneth Plummer, *Sexual Stigma: An Interactionist Account* (London: Routledge and Kegan Paul, 1975).
17. Bieber *et al.*, *op cit.*; also, Alan P. Bell and Martin S. Weinberg, *Homosexualities: A Study of Diversity Among Men and Women* (New York: Simon and Schuster, 1978).
18. Barry M. Dank, "Coming Out in the Gay World," *Psychiatry*, 34(2), May 1971, pp. 180–197.
19. Barry M. Dank, "Why Homosexuals Marry Women," *Human Sexuality*, 6, August 1972, pp. 14–23.
20. Bell and Weinberg, *op. cit.*, 1978.
21. Martin Hoffman, *The Gay World* (New York: Basic Books, 1968).
22. Carol A. B. Warren, *Identity and Community in the Gay World* (New York: Wiley, 1974).
23. For general discussion, see Hoffman, *op. cit.*
24. Laud Humphreys, *Tearoom Trade* (Chicago: Aldine, 1975), pp. 6–8, 12–13.
25. Kinsey *et al.*, *op. cit.*
26. See Schur, *op. cit.*, pp. 82–85.
27. Gilbert Geis, *Not the Law's Business* (Washington, D.C.: U.S. Government Printing Office, 1972), pp. 26–27.
28. Regarding the discussion below, see Harry Benjamin and R. E. L. Masters, *Prostitution and Morality* (New York: Julian Press, 1964), p. 290; David Pittman, "The Male House of Prostitution," *Transaction*, 8(5–6), March/April 1971, pp. 21–27; Robin Lloyd, *For Money or Love* (New York: Ballantine Books, 1976); Charles Winick and Paul M. Kinsie, *The Lively Commerce* (New York: New American Library, 1971).
29. Bieber *et al.*, *op. cit.*
30. For related discussion, see Davis, *op. cit.*, p. 256.
31. Robert Lindner, "Homosexuality and the Contemporary Scene" in *The Problem of Homosexuality in Modern Society*, ed. Hendrik Riutenbeck (New York: Dalton, 1963).
32. Evelyn Hooker, "The Homosexual Community," in *Sexual Deviance*, eds. John H. Gagnon and William Simon (New York: Harper and Row, 1967), pp. 167–184.
33. Alex Thio, *Deviant Behavior* (Boston: Houghton Mifflin, 1978), pp. 219–220.
34. *Ibid.*, p. 219.
35. *Ibid.*, p. 220.
36. *Ibid.*, Ch. 6.
37. Martin S. Weinberg and Colin J. William, *Male Homosexuals: Their Problems and Adaptations* (New York: Penguin, 1975).
38. Clinard, *op. cit.*, pp. 550–557; see also Michael Schofield, *Sociological Aspects of Homosexuality* (Boston: Little, Brown, 1965).
39. For a useful discussion, see Jack H. Hedblom, "The Female Homosexual: Social and Attitudinal Dimensions," in *The Homosexual Dialectic*, ed. Joseph A. McCaffrey (Englewood Cliffs, NJ: Prentice-Hall, 1972); William Simon and John H. Gagnon, "The Lesbians: A Preliminary Overview," in *Sexual Deviance*, eds. John H. Gagnon and William Simon (New York: Harper and Row, 1967).
40. Ford and Beach, *op. cit.*, p. 133.
41. Kinsey *et al.*, *op. cit.*
42. David A. Ward and Gene G. Kassebaum, "Homosexuality: A Mode of Adaptation in a Prison for Women," *Social Problems*, 12(2), Fall 1964, pp. 159–177.
43. Charles H. McCaghy and James K. Skipper, Jr., "Lesbian Behavior as an Adaptation to the Occupation of Stripping," *Social Problems*, 17(2), Fall 1969, pp. 262–270.

8

Mental Illness

The Meaning of Mental Illness

Problems of Definition

Individuals who manifest certain forms of deviant behavior are designated as mentally ill. These behaviors usually vary considerably within a given culture, and they certainly vary widely among cultures. Hearing voices when others do not, acting out compulsive rituals, refusal to communicate, upredictable bursts of anger—these are examples of deviant behaviors that qualify persons as mentally ill in many cultural settings. Certain forms of deviance are designated as criminal in a given society. These are not usually viewed as indicative of mental illness unless they are accompanied by other behaviors, for example, compulsions, which are taken to be symptoms of mental illness. Still other forms of deviant behavior are seen as eccentric but not necessarily as mental illness. Eccentricities are behavioral peculiarities which often are not viewed as especially disruptive. The well-dressed man who wears an old piece of rope for a belt displays an eccentricity. So does the person who barks like a dog on the beach but desists from doing so in crowded urban places. Deviant behavior that is not defined as criminal in a given society but which others do find disruptive constitutes one basis for defining individuals as mentally ill.

There is, however, a second especially important criterion for mental illness: a high level of anxiety which the individual finds difficult to bear. While anxiety may manifest itself in the disruptive behavior just mentioned, often it does not. There are great numbers of individuals who carry out their social role adequately, who are not disruptive to others, who nevertheless suffer greatly because of severe anxiety. They may feel anxiety directly. They may experience depression, an indirect result of anxiety, yet be able to carry out their jobs adequately. They may have very bothersome psychosomatic complaints due to anxiety. As long as they can carry out their social roles adequately and are not otherwise disruptive, these persons are not automatically defined as mentally ill. It is only when they seek help in the form of treatment from psychiatrists, psychologists, or other therapists that they are likely to be so designated.

Forms of Mental Illness

In the United States, four broad forms of mental illness are often distinguished: psychosis, neurosis, psychosomatic illness, and character disorders. The *psychoses* are those which are especially debilitating psychologically and which are characterized by an inability to interpret reality in the way that most individuals do. The psychoses may be due to organic factors and are then termed organic brain syndromes or disorders. Far more often there is no clear organic basis; they are then referred to as functional psychoses. In either case, psychotics are seen as "out of touch with reality" because they interpret the world quite differently from most of us. It is sometimes said that psychotic individuals are unable to understand that they are mentally ill while neurotics comprehend that they are. The psychotic person may *seem* to interpret reality as do others although at bottom he or she does not. This is held to be the case with some highly paranoid individuals who "act normal" in order to fool their supposed persecutors.

In some societies, certain forms of psychosis have been reversed. Some charismatic leaders were later viewed as psychotic. R. D. Laing, a British psychiatrist, holds that psychotics are the only truly normal individuals. In Laing's view, psychotics are the creative persons who are treated as mentally ill by others for their "heresies."[1] Hence, psychosis is usually seen as deviant but in certain cultures and by some individuals may be defined as positive rather than negative deviance.

The two main types of psychosis are schizophrenia and manic-depression. Subtypes of schizophrenia include disorganized, paranoid, catatonic (involves extreme psychological and physical withdrawal symptoms), undifferentiated, and residual. The disorganized schizophrenic suffers from disordered thought processes and inappropriate affective responses. The thoughts and emotional reactions of paranoid schizophrenics are not disorders; however, they suffer from highly developed delusions about reality. Catatonic symptoms include stupor, negativism, rigidity, excitement, or posturing. Persons with symptoms of distorted thinking who do not fit into any of the first three categories are diagnosed as undifferentiated schizophrenics. The residual category is reserved for those persons whose schizophrenic symptoms are in remission but who suffer minor psychiatric impairment.[2] Some authorities believe that schizophrenia is at least in part a response to contradictory demands on the individual that have been impossible to resolve, "double binds" to which the person has been subjected. The parent who advocates and rewards one type of behavior and as a role model for the child acts out the opposite type may create such a double bind.[3]

The two main types of psychosis in old age are depression and senile dementia. They involve a variety of symptoms usually associated with aged individuals: poor memory, confusion, undue suspicion, loss of control over urination and defecation. The senile psychoses are often due to some mixture of organic impairment and stressful life conditions, for example, loss of social roles.[4]

Manic-depressive psychosis is characterized by alternating periods of manic elation and severe depression. In the manic phase the individual wildly overestimates the likelihood and ease of carrying out complex tasks and of reaching high goals. Frenetic, round-the-clock activity is common. In the depressive phase the person tends to experience a profound sense of guilt and unworthiness and, in some cases, hostility toward others as well. Apathy and inactivity are characteristic of the depressive phase. Over time one phase may be more pronounced than the other, and severe depression may exist without alternating periods of obvious mania. It is extremely rare, however, for mania to be found without counterperiods of considerable depression.[5]

Anxiety disorders involve a multitude of behaviors and are divided into numerous subtypes. Four major subtypes of anxiety disorders include (1) anxiety states (including panic attacks); (2) obsessive-compulsive behavior; (3) phobic disorders; and (4) posttraumatic stress disorder.[6]

Anxiety in one way or another usually impairs the carrying out of the individual's social roles but does not lead to gross dysfunction. Karen Horney defined anxiety as "the feeling of an imminent powerful danger and of an attitude of helplessness toward it."[7] Behavioral symptoms are attempts, however inadequate in some instances, to cope with that anxiety. Symptoms may take the form of compulsive disorders such as very frequent washing of the body, ritualistic counting, checking of electrical switches over and over. They make take the form of obsessions—compulsive beliefs—about illness or of injuring oneself or others as examples. There may be phobias of heights, open spaces, animals, people, or many other aspects of the environment. Other symptoms include amnesia, disturbance of hearing or sight, hysteria, panic, and erratic bodily movements. Again there may be depression or high anxiety without other symptoms. The list is very long and includes many forms of behavior and psychological states which the individual is likely to realize are undesirable but feels he or she can do little about. The person is in touch with reality as the members of society in general construe that reality.

Psychosomatic disorders include a wide range of physical symptoms generated by anxiety. Examples are severe headaches and backaches, ulcerative colitis, asthma, and in some instances hypertension. Almost needless to say, most disorders which can be psychosomatic may also be the result of something other than anxiety. But the end result is often the same. Hypertension or an ulcer are "real diseases" regardless of the conditions that led to them.

The fourth category of mental illness is *character disorders.* These are behaviors which are usually viewed as antisocial. In some instances they are difficult to distinguish from neurotic symptoms. Generally there is believed to be less anxiety involved and a greater tendency for the individual to flagrantly disregard the social rules. "Character disorder" is a catch-all concept, and it is doubtful that it has utility either for diagnosis or treatment. Some psychiatrists and psychologists employ it and some do not. Certainly, character disorder designates a gray area of negative deviance between mental illness and either criminal or eccentric behavior.

Mental illness is, then, a term which designates a diverse set of conditions and behaviors which usually include high anxiety and behavior which impairs the carrying out of one's social roles. There may or may not be a divorce from reality as others know it. And there may or may not be a clear organic basis in the usual sense of that term.

INCIDENCE AND PREVALENCE

Around the World

As with many forms of deviance, determining the incidence or prevalence of mental illness is exceedingly difficult. Within a given culture, what constitutes mental illness varies from one group to another and among diagnosticians. Across cultures, what is socially defined as mental illness in one is not necessarily so defined in another. Even where there is agreement as to definitions, there remains the fundamental fact that much mental illness is unknown to researchers. Most statistics for the large, industrial societies concern *treated* mental illness: Those persons who have been treated in or out of mental hospitals for mental disorders are enumerated as mentally ill. Those who are not known to have been treated are seldom known officially or in research studies to have been ill. Important exceptions are those analyses which depend on self-reporting of symptoms by respondents "out in the community" regardless of whether they have been treated. Using those self-reported symptoms, conclusions are indirectly drawn, often by psychiatrists or psychologists, as to whether individuals have been or are mentally ill.

Most researchers on mental illness are in agreement that it is a universal phenomenon, that is, it appears to exist in all, or very nearly all, societies. Overall rates of mental illness vary greatly, however, from one society to another. Some societies clearly have a widespread prevalence, others a very limited prevalence. And the prevalence of specific types of mental illness shows great variation. Some societies have none of a given form. In others, a large majority of persons appear to suffer from what is considered in the United States to be a severe disorder.

Of course, this raises the matter of cultural definition. The Dobu of the South Pacific, for example, are a highly suspicious people, paranoid in our terms.[8] The vast majority of Dobuans show this characteristic. An island people with a limited food supply, they are exceedingly distrustful of each other in their everyday interpersonal relationships. For them, it is deviant not to be distrustful in a wide range of situations. Paranoia is institutionalized as a theme running through the acceptable culture. In terms of our cultural definition, the Dobu are paranoid. On the other hand, in almost if not all societies there are individuals who are considered mentally abnormal from the standpoint of the majority of that society's members. These persons are usually viewed as negative deviants, although on occasion they are seen as positive deviants.

In the United States

About 1,483,000 patients are treated for mental illness in hospitals and other psychiatric facilities in the United States each year. An additional 2,807,000 are treated in outpatient facilities such as mental health clinics, day treatment centers, and psychiatrists' offices.[9] Thus, approximately 4,300,000 individuals are treated for mental illness. (However, some of these are repeaters treated for more than one "episode" of illness.) The largest diagnostic category is schizophrenia. Manic-depressive disorders form the second largest category and alcohol disorders the third.[10]

The annual rate of inpatient treatment of mental illness in the United States is about 756 per 100,000 population. This means that each year for every 100,000 individuals, there are 756 "episodes" of treatment; somewhat fewer than 756 persons are treated since some receive treatment for more than one episode.[11]

Such figures are necessarily dependent on the mental hospitals and other facilities available. Hospitals can hold only so many patients. Psychiatrists can treat only so many clients. The "true" rate of mental illness is, of course, much higher than the "treated" rate. The best known study of true rates is the Midtown Manhattan Study. This report, published in 1962, provided the first clear evidence of the extent of mental illness in the population.[12] Of a population of 110,000 individuals within a section of the borough of Manhattan in New York City, a sample of 1660 were interviewed at length about symptoms of mental illness they had experienced and related matters. Psychiatrists then made indirect judgments about diagnoses as to mental health and illness on the basis of the interview data. Slightly under one-fifth, 18.5 percent, were judged to be "well" or mentally healthy. Almost 58 percent were classified as having mild neurotic or psychosomatic symptom. And 23.4 percent were judged to have severe, marked, or incapacitating symptoms.[13]

Most individuals no doubt suffer occasionally from symptoms that indicate mild neurotic states or psychosomatic distress. It is the 23.4 percent of the respondents who show severe symptoms which is the significant figure. Taken at face value, almost one quarter clearly suffered from mental illness. That figure is doubtful, however, since psychiatric diagnosis is an uncertain process and diagnosis from interview data may be more open to question than that obtained directly by the diagnostician in face-to-face conversation with the subject. Nevertheless, psychiatrists judged symptoms of about one-quarter of the sample of the Midtown Manhattan Study population to be indicative of severe mental illness.

DIFFERENCES BY SEX, AGE, RACE, AND RELIGION

Sex and Age

Females are treated more often than males for both physical and mental illnesses in the United States.[14] Known rates for schizophrenia are about equal for the two sexes. Females, more often than males, are treated for manic-depressive disorders and various neurotic conditions. Males are more likely to be treated for character disorders and antisocial behavior. Moreover, males are four times more likely than females to be treated for alcohol-related disorders.[15]

Researchers tend to think that it is the male and female roles which in considerable measure account for these differences. Walter Gove suggests that the role of married women is highly restrictive and this leads to depression and neurotic disorders.[16] Kessler and Essex, however, find that marriage may well provide a means of coping better with life stress and thereby reduces the likelihood of mental illness.[17] Nathanson found that women with preschool children and employed women had lower rates of treatment for mental illness than women with older children or with no children or women who were not employed.[18] There is good reason to believe that challenging role obligations foster mental health. On the other hand, the excessively competitive roles that males often carry out can be overdemanding rather than challenging. These may lead to character disorders, "rebellious" antisocial patterns of behavior, and alcoholism.

Regarding age, the findings are mixed. As expected, mental disorders related to organic deterioration increase with age. However, other psychoses (schizophrenia and manic-depression) and neuroses are highest among young adults.[19] Younger patients are especially likely to be treated in outpatient facilities. Aged patients are very likely to be institutionalized, often with organic brain syndrome. While most forms of mental illness can occur at most ages, schizophrenia usually becomes pronounced in early adulthood. Approximately two-thirds of those treated for schizophrenia are first treated between the ages of 15 and 35 years.[20]

The stresses and strains of competing for economic rewards and of raising families clearly take their toll. But so also do the changes that occur in later middle life and old age when the children leave home, income begins to decline, retirement looms, and social supports in general often dwindle.

Race and Religion

Most studies of rates of mental illness by race in the United States show higher rates for blacks than whites. However, much of this difference is accounted for by socioeconomic standing. Rates of mental illness increase as socioeconomic status decreases. More blacks than whites are of low socioeconomic status.[21]

As to particular forms of mental illness, blacks have higher rates than whites for schizophrenia, paranoia, various antisocial categories, and organic disorders. Whites have higher rates for manic-depression and most forms of neurosis. Again, these are related to social class: the lower classes show higher rates for the same forms as blacks; the higher classes show greater rates for the same forms as whites.[22]

Concerning the religious factor, the evidence suggests that in the United States, Jews have low actual or "true" rates of mental illness, Protestants middle-range rates, and Catholics high rates. Catholics are especially likely to have alcohol-related disorders whereas Jews suffer from the various neuroses.[23] Familial and community supports appear to help insulate Jews from mental disorders. The tendency for Catholics to be found in the lower socioeconomic levels may explain much of their higher rates. On the other hand, Jews are *treated* for mental illness more often than other groups.[24] This is probably because they are more likely to be economically well off and to seek professional help whenever mental problems arise.

Social Class and Mobility

Class

Social classes are composed of individuals of similar prestige. Members of a class tend to have many patterns of behavior in common. Those patterns tend to differ from the behavioral patterns of members of other classes. The child-rearing practices of social classes, the varying levels of social stress experienced in the various classes, and the types and extent of resources for coping with stress may all affect mental health and illness outcomes.

Hollingshead and Redlich in their New Haven study found a clear inverse relationship between rates of treated mental illness and social class standing.[25] Those researchers found that the highest social class made up 3.1 percent of the city's "normal" population but contained only 1.0 percent of those treated for mental illness. On the other hand, the lowest class, accounting for 17.8 percent of the "normal" population, had 36.8 percent of the treated or psychiatric patients.

The Midtown Manhattan Study[26] attempted to determine the true rates of mental illness, that is, of both treated and untreated illness. Proportionate to members in the classes, almost three times as many individuals born into the upper classes were classified as well as those in the lower classes; twice as many in the lower as in the upper classes were classified as impaired.

Findings of the Midtown Manhattan Study in regard to the present socioeconomic standing of subjects, rather than that of their parents, in relation to incidence of mental illness were even more starling. Four times as high a proportion of those in the lowest stratum as in the upper stratum were impaired. The percentage impaired in the lowest socioeconomic group was almost half, 47.3; the percentage in the highest group was but 12.5.[27]

The Dohrenwends surveyed 33 studies concerned with the relationship between social class and true rates of mental illness. They found that in 28 of the 33 populations studied, the lowest class had the highest rates of mental illness.[28] It is fair to conclude that mental illness is concentrated in the lower classes.[29] This is either because low social class standing generates mental illness much more than higher-class standing or because individuals who are becoming mentally ill move downward in the social class stratification system or because of a combination of the two.[30]

Type of mental illness clearly appears to be associated with social class. Hollingshead and Redlich in New Haven found that patients treated for the neuroses were concentrated in the higher classes and those for the psychoses in the lower classes.[31] The psychotic cases outnumbered the neurotic cases by about 3:1. Hence for both combined—all treated mental illness cases in the New Haven study—the concentration was in the lower classes.

There is strong evidence that schizophrenia as a major form of psychosis is especially likely to occur in the lower classes. On the other hand, manic-depressive psychosis is in some studies found to be more prevalent in the higher classes.[32] In general, it appears that the more internalized, "invisible" disorders, such as manic-depression, are characteristic of the more prestigious groups and those disorders with external behavioral symptoms—schizophrenia is a major example—are likely to be characteristic of lower-prestige groups. This notion is buttressed by findings that some neuroses, such as the obsessive-compulsive types, are prevalent in the upper classes while phobias and antisocial character disorders are likely to be found in the lower classes.[33]

Life is stressful in the lower classes, resources for coping with stress are relatively meager, and individuals with mental problems tend to drift downward in the stratification system. Moreover, child-rearing problems in the lower classes lead to a more rigid and therefore less innovative way of responding to life's problems. At the same time, there are weaker controls over the external expression of anxiety in the lower than in the upper classes.

Occupation, Education, and Status Inconsistency

As might be expected in the light of the foregoing findings, mental illness rates increase as occupational prestige decreases. Again, this does not necessarily mean that occupations of low prestige cause mental illness. Individuals with incipient or developed mental disorders may select or be selected into the low-prestige occupations. At the same time, certain specific occupations, some of high and some of lower prestige, have relatively high rates of treated mental illness. A 1977 study analyzed the hospital records of men and women in 130 occupations in Tennessee. The 12 occupations from which individuals were admitted to mental hospitals for psychiatric disorders, beginning with the highest rated, were the following[34]:

1. Health technicians
2. Waiters/waitresses
3. Practical nurses
4. Inspectors

  5. Musicians
  6. Public relations
  7. Clinical laboratory technicians
  8. Dishwashers
  9. Warehousemen
 10. Nurses' aides
 11. Laborers
 12. Dental assistants

It is striking that five are related to health care: health technicians, practical nurses, clinical laboratory technicians, nurses' aides, and dental assistants. In addition, two other similar occupations, health aides and registered nurses, ranked high on the list although below twelfth place. Work in hospitals and with the ill outside of hospitals can, of course, be stressful. Moreover, it is likely that persons with psychiatric problems gravitate to occupations where there is ready access to professional advice about those problems. There are no occupations of very high prestige on the above list, although there are a number of moderate prestige. Public relations is probably the highest in prestige. Inspectors are in a decidedly stressful role, and musicians are well known to be migrant persons lacking stability in the usual sense.

Educational level of attainment also shows a clear inverse relationship to treated mental illness: the lower the educational level, the higher the rate of treatment.[35] Various studies have also shown that individuals in the higher classes are especially likely to obtain treatment for mental disorders when they need it.[36] Hence the inverse relationship between education and class probably holds for untreated as well as treated mental illness.

Special interest attaches to the relationship between status inconsistency and mental illness. A major form of status inconsistency is dissimilarity in prestige between occupational and educational attainment. When one is especially lower than the other for given individuals, mental illness is probably more likely to occur, and in any case is more likely to be treated, than when they are of similar levels. A number of studies have found that the more educational level of attainment exceeds occupational prestige, the higher the rate of treated schizophrenia. In other words, those who are overeducated for their jobs tend more than other persons to develop schizophrenia.[37]

On the other hand, status inconsistency involving educational levels which are low in relation to occupational prestige tends to be associated with neuroses. Some researchers contend that here individuals feel guilt over having gained the rewards of high occupational status without the requisite education. In the previous case—high education, low occupational prestige, and schizophrenia outcome—the severe frustration of not gaining the monetary and prestige rewards or "pay-offs" for educational attainment may play a part in the generation of schizophrenia.[38]

Social Mobility

Status inconsistency is closely related to social mobility. The latter is movement up or down the social class scale. Persons of low educational attainment who achieve occupational prestige are likely to be successfully upwardly mobile. Those of high educational attainment who have low-prestige occupations are either downwardly mobile or were earlier blocked from upward mobility. There are, of course, persons who achieve high status through both occupational and educational attainment, and there are those who achieve high status without either, such as lower-class women who marry upper-class men. There are also persons who despite high educational and occupational attainment drift downward in the social stratification system.

There is evidence that those who develop mental disorders, especially schizophrenia, are more likely to be downwardly mobile that those who are mentally well. This was found in the Midtown Manhattan Study of true mental illness. Here individuals' prestige levels were compared with those of their parents as a measure of mobility.[39] The same general findings have been made in studies of treated mental illness.[40] However, whether downward mobility is a cause or effect of schizophrenia or both is unclear. It may well be that individuals who are developing schizophrenia become increasingly unable to carry out their social roles at the higher-prestige levels and so descend in the social scale to less demanding roles.

FAMILY EXPERIENCE AND STRESSFUL EVENTS

Heredity and Environment

Whether some individuals are genetically predisposed to mental disorders has never been clear. Studies of schizophrenia especially have focused on this issue. To an extent there is a tendency for schizophrenia to be characteristic of some families and not others. But that in itself does not demonstrate a genetic factor.[41] Hollingshead and Redlich in their New Haven study reported that 75 percent of subjects with schizophrenia did not have schizophrenic relatives.[42]

Very likely there is a genetic component in some forms of mental illness and not in others. When it is a factor, as it may well be in schizophrenia, it probably operates in conjunction with stressful experiences. That is, certain genetic predispositions may make individuals more vulnerable to stress; if stress is great, then genetic predisposition may increase the likelihood of some mental disorders such as schizophrenia. Certainly, there is much evidence that prolonged severe stress is associated with mental illness.[43] Childhood stress, occasioned by various types of family relationships, is one major form. Later stress, often taking the form of crisis within or without the family, is another.

Parent–Child Relationships and Socialization

Conflict between parents is a major source of stress for the child.[44] It is well known that mental illness rates are greater among persons whose parents were divorced than among those whose parents were not.[45] A variety of parent–child relationships of a stressful nature have been shown to be related to schizophrenia. Sanua reviewed various studies and concluded that mothers of schizophrenics were often domineering or rejecting or overprotecting. Fathers were indifferent, weak, or negligent.[46] Parents, especially mothers, of schizophrenics are notorious for placing them in double binds. The child is put in a "damned-if-you-do-and-damned-if-you-don't" position. The parent may demand one thing and reward the opposite. Or the parent may react negatively to whichever alternative the child chooses: "You smile at me when you're trying to get something out of me"; "You don't smile at me because you don't love me."

Theodore Lidz and his colleagues hold that three family conditions affect the development of children in such ways that schizophrenia later results[47]:

1. A deficiency in parental nurturing of the child which leads the child to have severe difficulty in achieving autonomy in the sense of adequate independence and ability to take responsibility.
2. Defective socialization of the child by the family as a social institution. The integrated development of the child, the learning of appropriate age and sex roles, and the achievement of an integrated ego structure are consequently blocked.
3. Defective transmission by the family of basic communicative and other instrumental cultural techniques to the child.

Rogler and Hollingshead studied families with and without schizophrenic husbands or wives in San Juan, Puerto Rico.[48] Their findings are quite different. The earlier lives of the schizophrenic spouses appeared to be similar to those of the nonschizophrenic spouses in regard to family relationships and socialization. It was in the 12 months preceding the explicit onset of the disease that the experiences of the schizophrenic persons differed from those of the nonschizophrenics. The incipient schizophrenics felt excessive pressures to conform, could not meet their normal role obligations, and became increasingly dependent on the members of their families. Rogler and Hollingshead describe the developing schizophrenics as inescapably trapped: the more they were unable to meet their role obligations, the more they were socially defined as *loco*, crazy, social outcasts.

Perhaps cultural differences explain those findings about schizophrenia in Puerto Rico as compared to the mainland United States. In any case, research on family experience and mental illness has focused especially on schizophrenia. But whether it has or not, the results present an ambiguous picture. One common thread is that at some point prior to the onset of illness—shortly before and long before—the individual experienced stress in one form or another and was unable to cope adequately with it.

Marital Status

Srole *et al.* in the Midtown Manhattan Study found that married men had relatively low rates of true mental illness.[49] Single men had rates somewhat higher than those of married men. Divorced males had the highest rates. Data were not available for widowed men of whom there were few in the study. For women, the findings were somewhat different. Single females typically had lower rates than married women. Divorced women showed a high rate, while widowed women did not. Getting married appears to immunize against mental illness to some extent for men but not for women.[50] Depression is more common in married women than married men.[51] For women, marital satisfaction, rather than simply being married, is a better protector against mental illness. On the other hand, divorce is fairly strongly associated with mental illness for both sexes.

Stressful Events

Considerable research has been carried out to determine which life events, either within or without the family, are especially stressful and may lead to mental illness. Those that require rapid role readjustment appear to be especially likely to generate mental disorders. The stress of social isolation and feelings of powerlessness are linked to mental disorders, especially paranoia.[52] Stressful events need not necessarily be those generally considered to be negative occurrences. For example, getting married and having a child have been found by a number of researchers to be stressful experiences, although most who marry or become parents probably construe those events positively.

Holmes and Rahe and Dohrenwend and Dohrenwend have been leaders of stressful event analysis.[53] They ranked events according to the amount of stress believed to be experienced from each. Losses of various kinds—loss of a spouse through death, loss of a spouse through divorce and through separation—head the list. Other important losses include loss of liberty and prestige because of a jail term, loss of a close family member other than a spouse, loss of job through firing, and loss of job through retirement. However, taking on the marital role and "gain of new family member" are considered stressful events as well.

The effects of stressful life events and social class combine to influence the vulnerability to mental illness.[54] There is evidence that stressful life events result in greater emotional pain for lower-class persons than those from other class backgrounds.[55] This differential response to stressful life events may help to explain the relationship of social class to mental disorders.

MEDICAL, SOCIAL INTEGRATION, AND CONFLICT EXPLANATIONS

The Traditional Dominance of the Medical Explanation

In recent centuries, mental disorder has in the main been seen as disease, as illness; hence the terms mental disease and mental illness. This means that mental disorder is seen as something an individual *has*, something located in the body. This view leads to the conclusion that *treatment* of the body is the cure for mental disorder.

The roots of this conception, often termed the medical model, appear to lie in the development of medical practice in classical Greece at about 500 to 300 B.C. The Greeks traditionally conceived of madness as due to the supernatural—the gods or the spirits of the underworld. Medical practice in classical Greece took a different view: madness was due to certain imbalances in the individual of the four humors—blood, phlegm, black bile, and yellow bile. The Middle Ages saw the return of the supernatural model and a way of joining that with the medical model: the devil entered the body and upset its physiological balance. This and hence madness were punishment for sin. Freud revised the supernatural-medical model by introducing the notion of the unconscious. Conflicts between the individual's basic drives for sex, aggression, and the like, and the demands of society and culture were repressed in the unconscious, causing mental illness. Freud was a physician, and he saw the unconscious as residing in the head—something to be treated but to be treated verbally rather than by medicine and surgery. He created the psychological-medical model of mental illness.[56]

More recently, emphasis has been placed on adverse interpersonal relationships as the source of mental illness[57] and on societal reaction to certain forms of deviance, that is, the labeling of some persons as mentally ill and the competent reaction to them by the group as if they were indeed mentally ill.[58] It would appear that in fact there is sometimes a partial medical basis for mental illness, especially in such extreme forms as schizophrenia. And it would also appear that who is mentally ill is often largely a determination of the group through the societal reaction process. Very likely the most usual case combines as generating conditions for mental illness adverse, stressful social experiences, societal reaction or labeling, and learning the role of mentally ill person. These conditions are likely to give rise to physiological change which provides a resultant medical effect. Often, then, medical treatment deals with physiological symptoms occasioned by social-environmental experience and hence is ineffective.

Social Integration

Social-environmental experience may be highly individualistic in the sense that it occurs idiosyncratically in the case of one person and not others in similar positions in the social system. More often, however, certain broad conditions of social integration, social disorganization, and social conflict produce stressful social-environmental experiences for whoever is located at the relevant junctures in the social system.

The evidence is considerable that levels of social integration which are either extremely low or high can give rise to anxiety and mental disorders. When individuals are detached from the group, as in cases of very low social integration, there is much uncertainty in life and there are few social supports. When, in Merton's terms, individuals experience anomie because of the inability to acquire the institutionalized means to achieve cultural success goals, they are likely to suffer severe stress and almost by definition to lack social supports to cope with that stress.[59] Hence, the economically deprived show high rates of both treated and true mental illness.

Extremely high levels of social integration lead to a different kind of stress. When individuals are excessively integrated into the social system, their individuality is submerged in favor of the group. Life is likely to be highly predictable. Social supports are very great: the emphasis on group cohesion necessitates that individuals care for one another's needs. Creative, innovative activity (positive deviance) is discouraged. Negative deviance is firmly discouraged. If it occurs, however, the individual is helped rather than punished by the group. Others support the person in avoiding repetition of the deviant act.

These conditions of high social integration do not necessarily have the benign outcome that they are so often assumed to have. Individuals have few explicit complaints about life. But they are apt to suffer psychological distress.[60] Symptoms are likely to be depression, anxiety, headaches, backaches—those associated with repressed aggression. Envelopment and smothering by the culture and social system impede and stifle self-expression. The consequent aggression is directed toward the self since there is no one else to blame; others are extremely helpful and cooperative. It is in these societies that suicide may also be high (see Chapter 9).

Mental disorders as an outcome of high social integration are especially likely to occur if the identity of the society or group is in danger of being eroded by nearby powerful groups. Highly integrated groups are unlikely to possess the flexibility and innovativeness required to cope with changing conditions, in this case the possibility of gradually being submerged by the neighboring groups. Thus, members of the highly integrated group suffer, in addition to blockage of individual expression, the threat of loss of group identity and therefore of individual identity since the latter depends so heavily on the former in the excessively integrated group. Yet norms of the group preclude aggression against the threatening group. Again, aggression is repressed and depressive symptoms arise.

Conflict

Social disorganization and social and cultural conflict have long been thought to be conditions that foster mental illness as well as other forms of negative deviance.[61] In the United States, mental illness rates are greater in lower-class neighborhoods than in others. Long believed to be socially disorganized, these areas may actually be well organized, although differently from others. Certainly, they are areas where residents encounter much stress in daily life and where resources for coping with stress are meager.

Culture conflict clearly can contribute to mental illness.[62] Individuals may be caught between two cultures when they move from one to another or when they are on the boundaries between cultures. Uncertainty over which norms and values to follow may lead to inappropriate behavior. And ambiguity over norms and values may in itself be stressful. Once behavior inappropriate to the cultural setting is acted out, labeling of the individual as peculiar together with stress may generate at least mild forms of mental illness. Of special interest is the fact that when migrants to a given culture live in ethnic enclaves, they frequently show little negative deviance. Which of the old ways are permissible and which are not is learned, and there exist the supports of close community ties for coping with stress.

Alex Thio elaborated a power conflict theory of mental illness which is though provoking if overstated.[63] It is his view that the powerless become psychotic while the powerful develop neuroses. The powerless tend to respond to the stress of being exploited by physically disruptive behavior such as aggression, inappropriate noise making, and gesturing. Those are labeled psychotic by the powerful. The lack of treatment facilities for the poor reinforces their psychoses. The powerful become neurotic in an unending quest for power. Their neuroses are manifested in less physically obvious ways: indirect economic and other exploitation of the poor. The cultural emphasis on psychosis as more severe, perpetuated by the powerful, draws attention away from their own neurotic disorders and places the focus on the disorders of the poor. It could be added that one manifestation of power hunger by the powerful is to persecute the poor by effectively labeling them as mad, that is, psychotic.

A major problem with power theory here is that it casts mental illness and the social processes that supposedly generate it in black and white terms: political power makes the poor and otherwise powerless psychotic and the wealthy and powerful neurotic. Yet there are powerful persons diagnosed as psychotic and powerless persons who are considered neurotic. Moreover, some individuals who hold moderate degrees of power are either psychotic or neurotic. On the one hand, the stress of exploitation by the powerful may drive the powerless to noncriminal but physically or otherwise blatantly disruptive behavior that is labeled psychotic. On the other hand, given certain adverse social-environmental experiences and possibly genetic predispositions, persons of any rank and degree of power may suffer the pains of severe anxiety, depression, and disorientation. The powerful are far from immune to psychosis, yet on balance they do probably experience less social stress than the powerless while possessing greater resources for coping with stress.

SOCIETAL REACTION AND CULTURAL SUPPORTS AS EXPLANATIONS

Societal Reaction

Thomas Scheff, a sociologist, is a leading proponent of the societal reaction explanation of mental illness.[64] He holds that certain nonconforming behaviors which are not considered criminal or otherwise officially designated as negative are labeled as "residual deviance." Included are compulsions, phobias, hallucinations, delusions, and such socially inappropriate behavior as talking to oneself in public. Almost all of us manifest these behaviors occasionally. If others find such behaviors especially disruptive or wish to aggress against the person who manifests them, they may attempt to label him or her as mentally ill or "peculiar" or "crazy."

If the person does not have the power to throw off or otherwise reject the label, then a process of learning the role of the mentally ill person begins. Others reward the person for agreeing to and conforming to the role of the mentally ill. Accepting the fact of one's mental illness and accepting treatment is a part of the process. Cultural stereotyping about mental illness provides a source of information concerning the mentally ill role for the labeled person who is expected to learn that role. The person is rewarded for carrying out the stereotypical prescriptions of what constitutes mental illness and punished through hostility and the threat or fact of incarceration for the refusal to do so. Thus, labeling of individuals for manifesting residual deviance leads to secondary deviance, that is, assuming the role and career of mentally ill or neurotic or crazy person.

Thomas Szasz, a psychiatrist, takes the view that mental illness is a myth.[65] He means that some individuals are labeled mentally ill and treated as such because their behavior is morally or otherwise unacceptable to the group. He holds that there is no such thing as mental illness within persons, only differences in behavior and conflict over those differences which result in some being treated as mentally ill. Involuntary treatment is thus a form of social control with psychiatrists and clinical psychologists the major agents of control. While the positions of Szasz and Scheff are basically similar, Szasz places greater emphasis on moral conflict while Scheff stresses the process of becoming a secondary or career deviant.

R. D. Laing, a British psychiatrist, takes the position that those portrayed by society as the most seriously mentally ill, that is, abnormal, persons are actually the most normal.[66] For Laing, societies that kill millions in war and deprive millions through economic politics have turned reality on its head, made the sane seem insane and the deranged normal. Inner space versus outer space and a certain form of highly informal political conflict explain this paradox. Inner space has to do with thought, imagination, dreaming, and so on. The person designated as mentally ill is, for Laing, acting in relation to his or her inner space while others are oriented to outer space, reality as we usually construe it. Thus, the person is seen as behaving inappropriately.

Yet inner space is where true self-expression, true mental breakthrough occurs, according to Laing. Those oriented to inner space may themselves be terrified of it. This is because the culture provides so few guidelines to it and condemns those who publicly express their preoccupation with it. In the politics of everyday life, especially in the family, individuals are singled out by others, often their family members, as troublesome. They retreat to inner space, are further condemned for it, and labeled as mentally ill or mad. They become the scapegoats for the "normals." The latter satisfy their needs to aggress by perpetuating the illusion of madness in the former. This process can indeed occur. Yet there are many who suffer severely from mental illness which is the result of quite different factors.

Laing and Szasz stress societal reaction and labeling in the social manufacturing of mental illness, as does Scheff. However, they emphasize the component of political conflict more than does Scheff. Walter Gove, a sociologist, has been a leader in refuting the societal reaction and labeling explanation of mental illness.[67] He contends that the majority of persons who are mentally ill would be so irrespective of labeling. Many of them suffer greatly, and they need care and help. In some instances, they are so beset by emotional problems that they are unable to seek help, and hence it may be necessary to provide what is commonly referred to as involuntary treatment.

Cultural Supports

Threaded through the societal reaction approach to mental illness is a recognition of the cultural learning of the role of the mentally ill person in the society at large and in the mental hospital especially. And in fact, whether or not societal reaction is involved in given instances of mental illness, there are available in most societies cultural prescriptions as to how neurotic and psychotic persons are expected to act. There may be a number of different mental illness roles, and these may vary considerably from one society to another. But some are likely to exist in a given society, and it is likely to be quite possible to learn them. There are role models in myth, in literature, and in everyday life. And if one is institutionalized for mental illness, there is, so to speak, a large, well-organized support system in the mental hospital for learning he role of the mentally ill.

Given all the evidence, it seems reasonable to conclude that societal reaction and labeling and cultural transmission as well *may* play crucial parts in who becomes mentally ill. To some extent, that is, mental illness may be fabricated and forced on individuals by the group. It may under certain conditions be learned as is other behavior. But it is equally reasonable to conclude that there are indeed many individuals who because of genetic predisposition or adverse environmental experience other than labeling are subject to severely painful and debilitating emotional disorders and behavioral derangements. The stresses of excessively low or high social integration or of cultural or political conflict can generate these disorders and derangements. There is also the possibility, often overlooked by students of mental illness, that negative labeling in early life can combine with other stresses and with conditions conducive to the cultural learning of mental illness to produce disordered states.

It remains that extreme forms of mental illness are fearsome phenomena and can involve behavior which is disruptive to social life as we know it. Hence, while unfortunate, it is not surprising that group members react with hostility to the mentally ill. Neither is it surprising that there is a tendency to create mentally ill persons. As always, the conditions of existence and of individuals are defined by their opposites. We know in part what society is and who is sane by the conception of insanity and the presence of the insane.

SUMMARY

As with other forms of deviance, mental illness is culturally defined. What is considered mentally aberrant behavior in one culture may not be in another. Noncriminal behavior which is socially disruptive is often taken to be evidence of mental illness. Debilitating anxiety is another sign of mental disorder.

There are four broad types of mental illness: psychosis, anxiety disorders, psychosomatic illness, and character disorder. Psychosis is the most severe form of mental illness and is characterized by an inability to interpret reality in a way consistent with other persons. Psychosis may be organically based or functional, the latter being due to environmental factors. The two main types of psychosis are schizophrenia and manic-depression. Common forms of schizophrenia are multiple-personality syndromes, paranoia, and catatonia. All involve lack of contact with reality. Manic-depression is characterized by alternating periods of euphoria and deep depression. A common denominator of the various forms of neuroses is anxiety severe enough to impair the carrying out of important social roles. Psychosomatic disorders are physical problems due to prolonged anxiety. Character disorders involve antisocial behaviors which fall between criminal behavior and severely mentally ill behavior.

About five million people are treated for mental illness each year in the United States, more than one-third of whom are hospitalized. The most prevalent form of mental illness for which patients are treated is schizophrenia; the second most prevalent is manic-depression; and the third, alcohol disorders. The Midtown Manhattan Study, in an attempt to determine the true prevalence of mental illness, found that about one in four persons had severe, marked, or incapacitating symptoms of mental disorder.

Females are more often treated for physical and mental illness than males in the United States. They are most likely to be treated for manic-depressive and neurotic disorders. Men are treated more than women for character disorders, antisocial behavior, and alcohol-related problems. Schizophrenics are equally likely to be men or women.

Persons between the ages of 25 and 55 are most apt to be treated for mental illness. The very old and the very young are least likely to be treated. Blacks have higher rates of mental illness than white. Much of the differential in rates of mental illness is accounted for by social class. The lower the social class, the higher the rate of mental illness. Catholics have distinctly higher rates of mental illness than Protestants or Jews. Downwardly mobile persons are more apt to be mentally ill than those who experience career or other success.

Various lines of evidence suggest genetic predisposition to certain forms of mental illness. Strong links have also been found between stressful life events and mental illness. Conflict experienced within the family is particularly stressful for children. Marriage seems to insulate men from mental illness; the highest rates are found among those who are divorced or single. However, for women marriage does not protect against mental illness.

The disease concept of mental illness has dominated thought about etiology. More recent investigations of mental illness have centered on sociological and social-psychological causation. Extremes of social integration tend to produce stress for the individual and may result in mental disorder. Systematic blockage of cultural goals or overfacilitation of their attainment may both create debilitating conditions for the individual. Social conflict and disorganization may also produce mental illness. Disruptive life styles, conflicting cultural norms, and lack of resources for coping with stress make certain subcultural socioeconomic groups more vulnerable to mental disorder.

The labeling of eccentric or inappropriate behavior by powerful social-control agents is a strong inducement to accept the role of the mentally ill. Once that role has been accepted, the career of the mental patient has begun. Rewards are granted for exhibiting behaviors consistent with the role; punishments are inflicted for denial of one's mental illness. Certain behaviors are defined in most cultural groups as engaged in only by mentally deranged persons. Inevitably someone will behave in those ways or will be encouraged to do so. Mental illness is thereby perpetuated and "normal" behavior is brought into sharper focus.

REFERENCES

1. R. D. Laing, *The Politics of Experience* (New York: Ballantine Books, 1967).
2. Bruce Pfohl and Nancy Andreasen, "Schizophrenia: Diagnosis and Classification," in *American Psychiatric Association Annual Review*, Vol. 5, eds. Allen J. Frances and Robert E. Hales (Washington, D.C.: American Psychiatric Press, 1986).

3. Gregory Bateson, Don D. Jackson, Jay Haley, and John Weakland, "Toward a Theory of Schizophrenia," *Behavioral Science* 1 (4):251–264, 1956.

4. Dan Blazer, "The Epidemiology of Psychiatric Disorder in the Elderly Population," in *Psychiatry Update,* ed. Lester Grinspoon (Washington, D.C.: American Psychiatric Press, 1983), pp. 87–95.

5. Hagop Akiskal, "The Bipolar Spectrum: New Concepts in Classification and Diagnosis," in *Psychiatry Update,* ed. Lester Grinspoon (Washington, D.C.: American Psychiatric Press, 1983), pp. 271–292.

6. Robert L. Spitzer and Janet B. W. Williams, "Diagnostic Issues in the DSM-III Classification of the Anxiety Disorders," in *Psychiatry Update,* ed. Lester Grinspoon (Washington, D.C.: American Psychiatric Press, 1984), pp. 392–401.

7. Karen Horney, *The Neurotic Personality of Our Time* (London: Routledge and Kegan Paul, 1937), p. 61.

8. Ruth Benedict, *Patterns of Culture* (Boston: Houghton Mifflin, 1934).

9. U.S. Department of Health and Human Services, *Health United States, 1985* (Hyattsville, MD: U.S. Government Printing Office, 1985), p. 101.

10. National Institute of Mental Health, *Summary Report of the Research Task Force of the National Institute of Mental Health* (Washington, D.C.: U.S. Department of Health, Education and Welfare, 1975).

11. U.S. Department of Commerce, Bureau of the Census, *Statistical Abstracts of the United States, 1986* (Washington, D.C.: U.S. Government Printing Office, 1985).

12. Leo Srole and Anita Fischer, eds. *Mental Health in the Metropolis: The Midtown Manhattan Study* (New York: New York University Press, 1978).

13. *Ibid.*

14. Ronald C. Kessler, James A. Reuter, and James R. Greenley, "Sex Differences in the Use of Psychiatric Outpatient Facilities," *Social Forces* 58 (2):557–571, 1979.

15. Bruce P. Dohrenwend, "Sociocultural and Social-Psychological Factors in the Genesis of Mental Disorders," *Journal of Health and Social Behavior* 16(4) (December 1975):365–392; and Ronald C. Kessler, Roger L. Brown, and Clifford L. Broman, "Sex Differences in Psychiatric Help-Seeking: Evidence from Four Large-Scale Surveys," *Journal of Health and Social Behavior* 22(1):49–64, 1981.

16. Walter R. Gove, "The Relationship between Sex Roles, Marital Status, and Mental Illness," *Social Forces* 51(1):34–44, 1972.

17. Ronald C. Kessler and Marilyn Essex, "Marital Status and Depression: The Importance of Coping Resources," *Social Forces* 61(2):484–507, 1982.

18. C. A. Nathanson, "Illness and the Feminine Role: A Theoretical Review," *Social Science and Medicine* 9(2):57–62, 1975.

19. Bruce P. Dohrenwend, Barbara S. Dohrenwend, Madelyn S. Gould, Bruce G. Link, Richard Neuberger, and Robin Wunsch-Hitzig, *Mental Illness in the United States: Epidemiological Estimates* (New York: Praeger, 1980).

20. H. M. Bahegian, "Schizophrenia: Epidemiology," in *Comprehensive Testbook of Psychiatry,* Vol. 2, eds. Alfred M. Freedman and Harold I. Kaplan (Baltimore: Williams and Wilkins, 1975).

21. George J. Warheit, Charles E. Holzer, and Sandra A. Arey, "Race and Mental Illness: An Epidemiologic Update," *Journal of Health and Social Behavior* 16(3):243–256, 1975; Bruce J. Gallagher, *The Sociology of Mental Illness* (Englewood Cliffs, NJ: Prentice-Hall, 1980); and William C. Cockerham, *Sociology of Mental Disorder* (Englewood Cliffs, NJ: Prentice-Hall, 1981).

22. Barbara S. Dohrenwend and Bruce P. Dohrenwend, *Social Status and Psychological Disorder* (New York: Wiley, 1969); Bruce P. Dohrenwend, "Social Status and Psychiatric Disorder: An Issue of Substance and an Issue of Method," *American Sociological Review* 31(1):14–34, 1966, also D. M. Kole, "A Cross-Cultural Study of Medical-Psychiatric Symptoms," *Journal of Health and Social Behavior* 7(3):162–174, 1966.

23. Leo Srole and Thomas S. Langner, "Protestant, Catholic, and Jew: Comparative Psychopathology," in *Changing Perspectives in Mental Illness*, eds. Stanley C. Plog and Robert B. Edgerton (New York: Holt, Rinehart and Winston, 1969).

24. Bertram H. Roberts and Jerome K. Myers, "Religion, National Origin, Immigration, and Mental Illness," in *The Mental Patients: Studies in the Sociology of Deviance*, eds. Stephen P. Spitzer and Norman K. Denzin (New York: McGraw-Hill, 1968).

25. August B. Hollingshead and Frederick C. Redlich, *Social Class and Mental Illness* (New York: Wiley, 1958).

26. Srole and Fischer, *op. cit.*

27. *Ibid.*, p. 309.

28. Bruce P. Dohrenwend and Barbara Snell Dohrenwend, "Social and Cultural Influences on Psychopathology," *Annual Review of Psychology 25:* 417–452, 1974.

29. Allan V. Horwitz, *The Social Context of Mental Illness* (New York: Academic Press, 1982); and Dohrenwend *et al.*, *op. cit.*, 1980.

30. August B. Hollingshead and Frederick C. Redlich, "Social Stratification and Psychiatric Disorder," *American Sociological Review* 18(2):163–169, 1953.

31. *Ibid.*

32. David Mechanic, "Social Class and Schizophrenia: Some Requirements for a Plausible Theory of Social Influence," *Social Forces* 50(3):305–309, 1972.

33. S. M. Miller and Elliot G. Mishler, "Social Class, Mental Illness, and American Psychiatry: An Expository Review," *Milbank Memorial Fund Quarterly* 37(2):174–199, 1959.

34. National Institute for Occupational Safety and Health, *Proceedings of Occupational Stress Conference* (Washington, D.C.: U.S. Government Printing Office, no date [approximately 1978]).

35. Richard L. Meile, David R. Johnson, and Louis St. Peter, "Marital Role, Education, and Mental Disorder Among Women: Test of an Interaction Hypothesis," *Journal of Health and Social Behavior* 17(3):295–301, 1976.

36. Richard A. Kulka *et al.*, "Social Class and the Use of Professional Help for Personal Problems, 1957–1976" (Paper delivered at Annual Meeting of the American Sociological Association, San Francisco, 1978).

37. D. Stanley Eitzen and Jeffrey H. Bair, "Type of Status Inconsistency and Schizophrenia," *The Sociological Quarterly* 13(1):61–73, 1972.

38. *Ibid.*

39. Srole and Fischer, *op. cit.*

40. R. J. Turner, "Social Mobility and Schizophrenia," *Journal of Health and Social Behavior* 9(3):194–203, 1968.

41. Seymour Kessler, "The Genetics of Schizophrenia: A Review," *Special Report: Schizophrenia, 1980* (Washington, D.C.: U.S. Department of Health and Human Services, 1981).

42. Hollingshead and Redlich, *op. cit.*

43. Gerald L. Klenan, "The Psychiatric Revolution in the Past 25 Years," in Walter R. Gove, ed. *Deviance and Mental Illness* (Beverly Hills, CA: Sage, 1982); and Seymour S. Ketz, "The Biological Roots of Schizophrenia," in *The Sociology of Mental Illness*, eds. Oscar Grusky and Melvin Pollner (New York: Holt, Rinehart and Winston, 1981).

44. P. L. Berkman, "Life Stress and Psychological Well-Being," *Journal of Health and Social Behavior* 12(1):35–45, 1977; and Joan H. Liem, "Family Studies of Schizophrenia: An Update and Commentary," *Special Report: Schizophrenia, 1980* (Washington, D.C.: U.S. Department of Health and Human Services, 1981).

45. Hugh Carter and Paul C. Glick, *Marriage and Divorce: A Social and Economic Study* (Cambridge, MA: Harvard University Press, 1976).

46. V. D. Sanua, "Sociocultural Factors in Families of Schizophrenics," *Psychiatry* 24(3):246–265, 1961.

47. Theodore Lidz, Stephen Fleck, and Alice Cornelison, *Schizophrenia and the Family* (New York: International Universities Press, 1965), p. 362.
48. Lloyd H. Rogler and August B. Hollingshead, *Trapped: Families and Schizophrenia* (New York: Wiley, 1965).
49. Srole and Fischer, *op. cit.*
50. William C. Cockerham, *Sociology of Mental Disorder* (Englewood Cliffs, NJ: Prentice-Hall, 1981).
51. Walter R. Gove and Michael Geerken, "The Effects of Children and Employment on the Mental health of Married Men and Women," *Social Forces* 56(1): 66–76, 1977.
52. John Mirowsky and Catherine E. Ross, "Paranoia and the Structure of Powerlessness," *American Sociological Review* 48(2):228–239, 1983.
53. T. Holmes and R. H. Rahe, "The Social Readjustment Scale," *Journal of Psychosomatic Research* 11:213–218, 1967; and Barbara S. Dohrenwend and Bruce P. Dohrenwend, eds. *Stressful Life Events: Their Nature and Effects* (New York: Wiley, 1974).
54. Ramsey Liem and Joan H. Liem, "Relations among Social Class, Life Events and Mental Illness: A Comment on Findings and Methods," in *Stressful Life Events and Their Contexts*, eds. Barbara S. Dohrenwend and Bruce P. Dohrenwend (New Brunswick, NJ: Rutgers University Press, 1984).
55. Ronald C. Kessler and Paul D. Cleary, "Social Class and Psychological Distress," *American Sociological Review* 45(3):463–478, 1980.
56. Information in this paragraph based in part on Bernard J. Gallagher III, *The Sociology of Mental Illness* (Englewood Cliffs, NJ: Prentice-Hall, 1980), pp. 39–54.
57. Laing, *op. cit.*
58. Thomas Scheff, *Being Mentally Ill* (Chicago: Aldine, 1966).
59. Robert K. Merton, "Social Structure and Anomie," in Robert K. Merton, *Social Theory and Social Structure* (Glencoe, IL: Free Press, 1957), pp. 131–160.
60. Joseph W. Eaton and Robert J. Weil, *Culture and Mental Disorders* (Glencoe, IL: Free Press, 1955).
61. Robert E. L. Faris, *Social Disorganization* (New York: Ronald Press, 1948).
62. Thorsten Sellin, *Culture, Conflict and Crime* (New York: Social Science Research Council, Bulletin No. 41, 1938).
63. Alex Thio, *Deviant Behavior* (Boston: Houghton Mifflin, 1978).
64. Scheff, *op. cit.*
65. Thomas Szasz, *The Myth of Mental Illness* (New York: Harper and Row, 1961).
66. Laing, *op. cit.*
67. Walter Gove, "Societal Reaction as an Explanation of Mental Illness: An Evaluation," *American Sociological Review* 35(5):873–884, 1970.

9

Suicide

THE MEANING AND INCIDENCE OF SUICIDE

The Meaning of Suicide

Suicide is the intentional, that is, nonaccidental, killing of the self. Hence, suicide and criminal homicide are similar in that death is brought about intentionally, although in the one case the target of the violent act is the self and in the other another person. In some societies, such as Japan and India, suicide has traditionally been institutionalized. In most societies it tends to be individualistic deviance, as does homicide. Whether taking one's own life is in fact deviance will, of course, depend on the context in which it occurs and whether it is in the line of culturally prescribed duty. The wife who throws herself on the funeral pyre of her husband because custom requires it is not acting in a deviant way. Neither is the soldier who, following orders, goes on a "suicide mission" and never returns.

On the other hand, the fact that suicide is somewhat common under certain circumstances does not automatically put it outside the realm of deviance. It may not be especially unusual for college students in some societies to kill themselves if they fail final examinations. Unless the culture demands that they do so, this is deviance. It is institutionalized deviance to the extent that students who do kill themselves respond to similar conditions, such as failure on examination, by resorting to similar means for taking their lives.

Rates around the World

Suicide rates are calculated in the same way as homicide rates: the number of deaths per 100,000 population per year. Rates for suicide, however, are less reliable than those for homicide. There is the well-

Much of this chapter is adapted from Stuart Palmer, *The Violent Society* (New Haven, CT: College and University Press, 1972), Part 2.

recognized tendency to list officially some suicides as deaths due to other causes in order to spare the feelings of family members and friends. Very likely in many countries, among them the United States, suicide rates are at least half again as high as official statistics indicate. Since we do not know with any accuracy the extent to which official rates are based on underenumeration of actual suicides, we must use the official rates, keeping in mind their drawbacks.

The average recorded suicide rate for countries around the world is about 12. Rates range from a high of over 40 to a low of under 1.0. In comparing rates of suicide for the late 1970s and early 1980s for 50 countries, the United States had a rate of 11.6, about equal to the world average. Hungary showed the highest rate, 43.5; and Kuwait the lowest, 0.1. According to these figures, Hungarians are over 400 times more likely to kill themselves than Kuwaitians. There are few consistent sets of characteristics that distinguish countries with very high or low suicide rates from others. However, there is a tendency for the high-suicide countries to be advanced in the technological sense and in some instances also to be within the satellite orbit of Russia. The low-suicide countries are without exception ones with low levels of technological advancement.

In Chapter 3 it was shown that high-homicide countries tend to be characterized by low levels of technological advancement as are low-suicide countries. Conversely, low-homicide countries are likely to be technologically advanced and so are high-suicide countries. It was also noted in Chapter 3 that among nonliterate societies, those with much emphasis on reciprocity in everyday life, that is, on patterns of mutual facilitation of role playing, tended to have low homicide rates and high suicide rates, while societies which do not stress reciprocity and instead emphasize competition and conflict tend to have low suicide rates. Smith and Hackathorn report that in primitive and peasant societies suicide is highest (1) in stable and agricultural societies rather than ones that rely on hunting and gathering; (2) where extremes of emotional expression are permitted, either overly restrained or highly demonstrative; and (3) when individual pride and shame are stressed.[1]

All in all, high incidences of suicide and low incidences of homicide appear usually to be related to social systems which are not in the throes of technological change and its consequent turmoil and which emphasize reciprocity and cooperation. Conversely, low incidence of suicide and high homicide seem to characterize societies with much change, turmoil, conflict, and competition.

Rates in the United States

The suicide rate has been quite stable in the United States since 1940, between 10 and 13. In 1945, it was 11.2; in 1955, 10.2; in 1965,

11.1; in 1975, 12.1; and in 1981, 11.8. During the 1930s the rate was significantly higher, for example, 17.4 in 1932.[2] There is a tendency for suicide to increase in times of economic depression and to decrease in times of prosperity.[3] Overall, the United States has a history of moderate suicide rates, that is, about equal to world averages, and of high criminal homicide rates, far above averages for the world.

Highest suicide rates are found in the western region of the United States and the lowest are concentrated in the northeast and midwest. In 1981, the five states with the highest suicide rates were: Nevada, Colorado, New Mexico, Montana, and Wyoming. The lowest rates were found in: North Dakota, Massachusetts, Illinois, New Jersey, New York, and Hawaii.

Traditionally, the urban centers of greatest population density have shown the highest suicide rates. This has been thought to be due to the impersonality of social relationships and the social disorganization and anomic conditions of urban life. Gibbs and Martin tested this explanation and found it wanting.[4] They argued that residential mobility was a universal common denominator of social disorganization. They investigated the relationship of residential mobility to suicide and found the following: the less, rather than the more, that people move, the more prone they are to suicide.[5] It appears that the social disorganization hypothesis is more applicable to homicide and other crimes than to suicide.

SEX, AGE, AND RACIAL DIFFERENCES

Sex and Age

In most societies, male suicide rates exceed female rates by several times. The disparity in male–female suicide rates in the United States is decreasing for persons 35 years of age and over. However, among the young (persons 15–24 years of age), sex differences are increasing. This trend is mainly due to the sharp rise in suicide among young white males.[6]

In recent decades, the suicide rate among youthful persons has increased dramatically while that among the elderly has decreased. For example, from 1960 to 1980, for persons aged 15–24 years, the rate of suicide showed a 237 percent increase in the United States; for persons aged 65 years and over, the rate declined.[7]

Race, Age, and Sex in Relation to Each Other

In the United States, white suicide rates are two to three times black rates. As was seen in Chapter 3, black homicide rates, in contrast, are 12 times white homicide rates. Blacks, usually in the lower socioeconomic strata, are more exposed and socialized to patterns of violence toward others than are whites. Blacks suffer greater relative deprivation in the pursuit of cultural success goals. On the other hand, whites are more likely to suffer *loss* of status and other success goals than blacks (mainly because blacks are unlikely to have attained those goals in the first place). And whites appear more than blacks to have been socialized away from patterns of violence toward others. Therefore, if whites suffer severe frustration, especially due to social loss, they are prone to direct their consequent rage against themselves. Blacks, if they experience sufficient relative deprivation, are more prone than whites to attack others, sometimes homicidally.

When age, sex, and racial variables are analyzed in relation to each other, differences in rates are particularly striking. Statistics on suicide by race in the United States are often available only for two categories, white and nonwhite. However, the nonwhite figures are fairly indicative of black rates since blacks compose about 92 percent of the nonwhites in this country. (Whites account for 85 percent of the entire United States population and blacks for 12.)

The highest suicide rates are for older white males. The next highest are for younger adult males who are also white. Rates for white females are in general low while the rates for nonwhite females are lowest. Except for the 5- to 14-year-old category, where all rates are low, nonwhite females 65 and older show the lowest rate, 2.3, of any race–age–sex grouping. White males aged 65 and over have the highest rate, 35.7, which is 15 times greater than the nonwhite females 65 and older. It is these elderly white men who are most likely to suffer loss of success goals: loss of job through forced retirement or illness; loss of status or prestige through loss of income; loss of loved ones through death.

EDUCATION, OCCUPATION, AND PRESTIGE

Education

Data on the educational levels of attainment of those who commit suicide are seldom available. However, one national study done in the United States does show a clear inverse relationship between level of education of males and death by suicide: as education increased, the likelihood of suicide decreased. Men with less than eight years of school committing suicide was almost twice that of men with some college. Educational attainment is an excellent measure of status or prestige. Therefore, one can say that suicide increases as prestige decreases.[8]

Occupation

There is some tendency for suicide rates to be high for persons with occupations of both high and low prestige and low for those with middle-range prestige occupations. Lambert and co-workers' analyses of occupational status and male suicide shows that higher rates of suicide are found in the lower-status occupations.[9] This trend in occupational status and suicide is maintained over the three decades studied.

Clearly, suicide rates are greatest for farm workers, laborers, and operatives, all low-prestige groups. The next highest rate is for craftsmen and service workers. On the other hand, professionals, an even higher prestige group, have the lowest rate.

The results of a 20-year study of suicide in Tulsa, Oklahoma, however, provide evidence for the concentration of suicide in the high occupational prestige categories as well as the low. The highest suicide rates were for the professionals and managers, the occupational groups of greatest prestige, next highest rates for service workers and operatives, low-prestige categories, and lowest rates for the middle-prestige groups of clerical and sales workers. (Laborers were not included in the study.)[10]

The main conclusions to be drawn are that suicide is a lower-prestige and to some extent an upper-prestige phenomenon while criminal homicide (see Chapter 3) is distinctly a lower-prestige phenomenon. Those of middle-range prestige relatively seldom commit either form of lethal killing.

Downward Social Mobility

Loss of status or prestige in the social structure, that is, downward social mobility, has long been thought to be a factor in suicide. Warren Breed conducted a study in New Orleans of 103 white male suicides and 206 control subjects matched for sex, race, and age.[11] Breed found that suicides came from the lower occupational prestige groups more often than the controls (who closely paralleled occupational data for all white males in the city). Three times as many suicides as controls were in the lower strata and only three-fifths as many were in the upper strata. As to mobility, Breed's results show that the suicides' occupational prestige was higher than that of their fathers in only 25 percent of the cases as compared to 38 percent of the controls. The occupational prestige of the suicides was lower than the fathers in 53 percent of cases as compared to 31 percent for the control group.

Breed's data show that 33 percent of the suicides who were employed full time and 50 percent of the suicides who were not employed full time were downwardly mobile; these results are in striking contrast to the 5 percent of the controls who were downwardly mobile. On the other hand, the suicides were slightly more upwardly mobile than the controls; 17 percent of the suicides employed full time and 9 percent of those employed part time were upwardly mobile as compared to 12 percent of the controls. The upwardly mobile suicides tended to be in the more prestigious occupations. However, Breed found that it was the suicide victims in these occupations, as compared to the victims in other occupational prestige categories, who had experienced the highest rate of loss of income prior to suicide. That is, these men tended to be failing in relation to the society's success goals even though they still retained their relatively prestigious occupations. In a more general sense, Breed reported large differences between income gain and loss over the two years preceding the suicides for the entire suicidal group as compared to the control group. Income decreased for 51 percent of the suicides and 11 percent of the controls; it increased for 8 percent of the suicides and 35 percent of the controls; income remained about constant for 41 percent of the suicide group and 54 percent of the control group.

Taking Breed's study as a whole, the conclusions are clear that in his samples, suicides were "failures" in terms of societal goals and "losers" in relation to their fathers and in relation to what they themselves had earlier achieved occupationally. The findings tend to clarify to some extent the moderate confusion that exists as to whether suicide is associated with both high and low extremes of occupational prestige or with the latter only: those suicidal individuals in the lower strata frequently arrived there by moving down the occupational prestige ladder. Those in the higher strata seem often to have been on the verge of such downward movement.

FAMILY EXPERIENCE

Childhood Socialization

The family is the initial primary group responsible for the socialization of the child. Experiences within the family are crucial to early development and tend to have lasting effects. The control or appropriate expression of aggression is in large measure learned in the course of interaction within the family. Henry and Short attempted to account for the direction, either inward or outward, that aggression may take.[12] They found that children who are psychologically punished, that is, are deprived of parental affection, tend to blame themselves when things go awry. As a consequence, such persons are less likely to strike out against whoever or whatever is the source of their frustration and are more likely to withdraw and direct aggression inwardly. In the extreme, they make take their own life.

Quite often parents unwittingly induce guilt in children by communicating to them that their behavior causes great suffering to the parents. For example, if a child fails in school or is involved in a schoolyard fight, a parent may say, "How could you do this to me, your own mother; what are you trying to do, kill me?" In such instances parents are presumably attempting to induce appropriate behavior in their children by setting themselves up as the "real" victims of the children's failure to perform in a socially preferred manner.

On the other hand, children who are physically punished tend to regard the agent of their frustrations as external to them and tend to direct aggressions outward. Persons who are physically mistreated tend not to internalize guilt about their misdeeds but rather identify the source of frustration as outside themselves. Such persons are less likely to take their own lives and more apt to respond in an assaultive manner to those who attempt to thwart them.

Gold also related the type of punishment experienced by children to the direction of aggression.[13] He reasoned that certain persons were more likely to be physically punished than others: boys more than girls, enlisted men in the military more than officers, those from rural areas more than urban places, and nonwhites more than whites. The findings of his study showed that persons who have experienced physical punishment as children have lower rates of suicide than those who are more apt to be psychologically controlled in early life.

Loss of Loved Ones

More than others, suicidal persons have experienced loss of individuals close to them. Half of those who commit suicide lost in childhood one or both parents through divorce, separation, or death. This contrasts with estimates of 17 to 33 percent for the general population.[14] Dorpat and his colleagues summarized the research on such losses as follows:

> This study reports on broken homes in childhood as related to the suicidal behavior of an unselected and consecutive series of 114 subjects who completed suicide and a series of 121 subjects who attempted suicide in King County, Washington. Fifty percent of the subjects who completed suicide and 64 percent of those subjects who attempted suicide came from broken homes. The incidence of death of a parent was highest for the completed suicide group and was the most common cause of a broken home. In contrast, the most important cause of a broken home in childhood for the attempted suicide group was divorce, the incidence being significantly higher than in the completed suicide group. Almost half of those who had come from broken homes in the completed suicide group had lost both parents;

whereas, nearly two thirds of those who had broken homes in the attempted suicide group had lost both parents. This research supports the theories of Bowlby and Zilboorg that parental loss in childhood predisposes to depression and suicide later in life. The recent loss of a love object was a frequent precipitating factor in both the attempted and the completed suicide groups. It is hypothesized that unresolved object loss in childhood leads to an inability to sustain object losses in later life. This in turn leads to depressive reactions culminating in suicide behavior.[15]

Moreover, suicides have lost mother or father or both in adulthood to a much larger extent than the general population; the respective percentages are on the order of 45 for suicides and 20 for others.[16] Rushing writes that 27 percent of a group of suicides lost a family member in the years immediately preceding their death and many more lost some "love object" individual outside the family just before committing suicide.[17]

Marital Status

Further, suicides have frequently experienced disruption of social relations from other sources. Many have been living alone prior to suicide—perhaps as high a percentage as 25 compared to 7 percent for the population in general.[18] Granting that the word of those who attempt suicide may be questioned, Rushing cities two studies that bear on the matter. In one, about half of the subjects stated that the main reason for the suicide attempt was friction with someone close to them. In the other study, 37 percent pointed to various types of disruptions in social relations as the major cause of attempted suicide.[19] There is much evidence that because of such losses, especially in early life, suicidal persons are overly dependent individuals.[20] They need the assurance of others so greatly that in their desperate demands for it, they drive others away from them, thereby closing the door to help.

Loss or absence of the marital role—single, never married, divorced, widowed—is linked to suicide.[21] The divorced are at greatest risk for suicide; and the married, the lowest risk. Rates for females, although low by male standards, follow roughly the same relative patterns.[22]

These differences are significant. They point to the loss of marital roles through divorce or death of the spouse as a factor of much importance in suicide and especially so for men. Apart from the sheer loss of a role, the dissolution of a marriage generally means a loss of support for both partners or for the surviving spouse. That support may take the obvious form of providing comfort for the other spouse. However, it may take an opposite form: the support that is a consequence of unreciprocity between spouses. Marital partners may grow used to, and come to depend on, daily fighting, arguing, bickering. Again, support may be a combination of these two diverse forms.

Over their life history, suicidal persons have suffered one severe loss and then another—of persons and of roles especially. They are hurt; their frustrations are great. Moreover, they have lost role models: a parent or grandparent, an older sibling, a friend. They have had the models, but some of them have departed abruptly. Their world is likely to be a mixture of what seems to them extremes of stability and instability. Their environments—both external and internal—are ones of considerable harmony punctuated by either inexplicable or impersonal losses. The death of someone close may be inexplicable. The layoff from the job or the retirement may be impersonal in the sense that all in a given seniority group are laid off, or all in a given age group are retired.

Suicidal persons test their precarious environments frequently. They try to ascertain whether or not significant others will be there tomorrow. It is their conception of the world, based on very good personal evidence, that other persons on whom one might depend can disappear from one moment to the next. Thus they test, seek total commitment from others, to ensure that those others will be there tomorrow. But it cannot be known with any certainty that they will be there.

PERSONALITY FACTORS

Identity

Attempts at suicide are in part the means of trying to recapture a lost identity or to build a new identity. While many of those who commit suicide are not known to have made previous attempts, attempts have been made by a much higher proportion of those who actually commit suicide than by the general population. In one study, Shneidman and Farberow found that 75 percent of suicidal victims either attempted or threatened suicide.[23] In another study, Rushing reports that 29 percent of suicides previously made verbal threats that they would kill themselves.[24] In many of these cases, either of oral communication or of actual attempts at death, the suicidal individuals have by their behavior tried to communicate to others the likelihood of impending disaster, the need for help, their desperate search for identity; and they have failed.

The completed suicidal act is itself not infrequently a last attempt to gain identity.[25] Individuals may believe firmly that by their violent act they will create a new life, a new identity. They imagine they will cut all ties with the past and after the cleansing rite of suicide begin again (although often with the same people they previously knew). They take control of their own destinies. And they do in fact gain a certain identity, that of a suicide.

Hope and Aspirations

The personality of a potential suicide is marked by an overwhelming sense of hopelessness and helplessness. The future is dark with despair. No change is seen as either possible or likely to occur that would make life worth continuing. Farber noted that with the loss of hope there is a concomitant loss of a sense of competence.[26] Competence is the feeling that one has some control over one's life, some influence to alter things to one's own advantage. A sense of competence is often lost with the death of a loved one or loss of job or health. If a person's sense of competence is low, even minor threats to "acceptable life conditions" can trigger suicidal behavior. When one's feeling of competence and hope is strong, these conditions must be in graver jeopardy for suicide to be generated.

A consistent finding in suicide research is that victims are not on average significantly more or less intelligent than nonsuicides.[27] However, suicidal individuals tend to set unattainable or unrealistic goals for themselves. These goals are then relentlessly pursued with all alternate goals blocked out. Failure to attain the one objective often precipitates a crisis situation. For example, a student who wants to become a medical doctor but cannot pass a course in organic chemistry might well consider other careers. Perhaps reluctantly, most students would change their course of study. The suicidal person is more apt to adhere rigidly to the plan to attend medical school, reasoning "If I can't be a doctor I don't want to be anything. I'd rather be dead." Suicide is always an option.

Mental Illness

One cultural myth holds that persons who kill themselves are crazy. However, estimates of mental illness among suicide victims vary widely, from 5 to 94 percent.[28] It is generally conceded that an individual does not have to be insane to commit suicide. And those who suffer from various mental disorders are not equally likely to kill themselves. It is nonetheless true that persons who have been hospitalized for mental illness have considerably higher suicide rates than the general population. Maris in his study of suicide in Chicago finds that four out of 10 suicide victims had previously been hospitalized for mental illness compared to only 3 percent of persons who died a natural death.[29] Overall, psychotics are more prone to suicide than neurotics.

Among those who have been diagnosed psychotic, depressives, especially manic-depressives, have the highest rates of suicide, and alcoholics and individuals with personality disorders the lowest. It should be noted, however, that other studies report that 31–36 percent of alcoholics kill themselves.[30] Manic-depressives who commit suicide are usually either in or moving toward the depressive phase of their illness. Severe depression is usually associated with a fatalistic view of life. Death, even at one's own hand, is seen as preferable to the darkness of depression. Neurotic individuals are more apt to attempt suicide with no clear intention of dying.

Menninger wrote that neurotic persons

> seldom die young, and despite frequent threats of suicide, rarely resort to it. . . . The neurotic patient rarely mutilates himself irrevocably. Substitute and symbolic forms of self-mutilation are, however, very common. . . . In the neuroses self-castration is usually achieved indirectly, for example, by impotence, financial failure, marital disaster, venereal disease.[31]

This is not to say that neurotic individuals never commit suicide, but they are less likely to do so than those afflicted with most other emotional disorders.

SITUATIONAL FACTORS

Motives

Hendin lists six major motives for suicide: retroflexed murder, that is, murder of another turned against the self; reunion with a loved one; rebirth of the self after death; self-punishment; seeing oneself as already dead; and retaliatory abandonment, that being when the suicidal victim abandons forever one who has abandoned him.[32] Dublin suggests the following as precipitating motivations in suicide: ill health, fear of insanity, disappointment in love, illicit sex relations, belief that life is futile, hopeless poverty, unemployment, altruism, and greed.[33]

In Palmer's study of nonliterate societies, three major types of motives were ascribed to suicidal individuals by other members of the society: self-condemnation, fear, and anger toward others, the first two being decidedly the most prevalent.[34] Everything considered, these various motives reflect frustration, especially over interpersonal losses, consequent aggression and, to a lesser degree, self-blame.

Methods

Shooting, hanging, cutting, poisoning, gassing, drowning, jumping from heights are among literate societies nearly universal methods of committing suicide.[35] Firearms recently replaced poisons and gas as the leading means of death. In the United States males use firearms over 60 percent of the time, hanging and strangulation as well as poisoning and asphyxiation a seventh of the time. Until recently, poisoning and asphyxiation were the leading methods for females, employed in about 40 percent of the suicidal cases. However, firearms and explosives are used now by females slightly more so than poisoning and far more than hanging and strangulation. As is true for homicide, females, less familiar than males with the use of firearms, tend more than males to employ other means.

There is considerable variation in method from one society to another. Methods most common in Canada, Australia, and New Zealand are similar to those used in the United States. However, in England and Scotland the most usual methods, in descending order of frequency, are poisoning, gassing, hanging, drowning; firearms are infrequently used because they are banned. In Denmark poisoning is the most frequent form of self-killing, while in Sweden it is hanging; firearms are seldom employed in either country.[36] In a sample of 54 nonliterate societies, hanging, poisoning, drowning, and jumping from high places were common methods.[37] The use of weapons—knives, spears, firearms—was unusual although these were generally available.

Drugs and Alcohol

Drugs and alcohol are often used to escape the pain of daily existence. Excessive use of either may be a response to chronic personal difficulties. The same disruption in social relations which tend to generate suicide may account for excessive drug or alcohol use. The ultimate escape from the vexations of life is, of course, suicide.

Nonetheless, the relationship between drinking and suicidal behavior remains problematical. Research shows that between 15 and 64 percent of suicide attempters and as many as 80 percent of completed suicides were drinking prior to the self-destructive act.[38] Ten percent of persons who attempt or complete suicide are found to be problem drinkers.[39] And problem drinkers are reported to attempt suicide four to six times more frequently than persons in the general population.[40] Alcoholics are found to be particularly vulnerable to suicide. Between 6 and 12–15 percent of alcoholics are found to commit suicide, while only 1 percent of the population at large does so.[41]

Except when taken concomitantly with barbiturates, excessive alcohol consumption rarely is the immediate cause of death. It may, however, facilitate the act of suicide by reducing inhibitions against

self-destruction. Rushing suggested that the consequences of alcoholism, loss of job, divorce, depression, and so on often precipitate tendencies toward suicidal behavior.[42]

ATTEMPTED SUICIDE AND HOMICIDE-SUICIDE

Attempted Suicide

It is extremely difficult to determine whether an act is an attempt
at suicide or accidental, even more difficult than to determine whether
an actual suicide has occurred. As a consequence, statistics on the incidence of attempted suicide are probably less accurate than those for
completed suicide. Nonetheless, from the data available, Hendin concluded that attempted suicide occurs about 10 times more often than
suicide.[43]

Alex Pokorny's[44] study of suicide and attempted suicide found that
between the ages of 15 and 39, a greater percentage of persons *attempted* rather than *committed* suicide, but that after age 40, a much
greater percentage actually committed suicide. There were, in fact, four
times as many suicides as attempted suicides for ages 50 and over.
Females were almost three times more likely than males to attempt
suicide, while males were three times more likely than females to actually kill themselves.

Regarding race, Pokorny found that blacks, who made up slightly
over one-fifth of Houston's population, accounted for less than one-
tenth of the completed suicides and also less than one-tenth of the
attempted suicides. Whites composed three-quarters of the city's population and accounted for over nine-tenths of both the completed and
attempted suicides.

Homicide Followed by Suicide

In relation to homicide alone, some societies have much homicide-
suicide, others relatively little. The United States is in the latter category. Guttmacher reports that in Baltimore 6 percent of those who
murdered later killed themselves.[45] Wolfgang found in the Philadelphia study that 4 percent of the offenders committed suicide shortly
after commiting homicide. Durrett and Stronguist put the figure at 2
percent for several cities in the South.[46] In sharp contrast, Siciliano's
research on homicide in Denmark gives the finding of 42 percent.[47]
And the percentage in England is about 33.[48]

One of the most extensive studies of homicide followed by suicide is the English study by D. J. West.[49] He compared a sample of 148 homicidal-suicidal cases with a sample of 148 homicidal cases. In both groups about half of the offenders were judged to be suffering psychological abnormalities—especially depressive disorders—to such an extreme extent that the juries' findings were of insanity or diminished responsibility. The occupational prestige of homicide-suicide offenders was remarkably similar to that of the general population while the homicidal group showed a distinct preponderance of individuals in the lower-prestige strata.

In the same study, offenders and victims in homicide-suicide cases were found to be familially related significantly more often than in homicide alone. Suicidal offenders tended to kill multiple victims more often than other offenders. Those victims were more likely to be family members than single victims, and they were especially likely to be the offenders' children. All in all, homicide-suicide was found to be largely a domestic affair. Of the 138 cases, 53 mothers killed their children; 62 fathers killed their children; and three women killed their husbands or lovers.

Forty-one (41) percent of the offenders in West's homicide-suicide sample were females in contrast to but 12 percent of the homicidal cases. Young offenders were more common in the homicide cases than in the homicide-suicide cases: 49 percent of the homicide offenders were under age 30 as compared to 18 percent of the homicide-suicide offenders. However, females who committed both homicide and suicide tended to be younger than females who committed homicide only. Fewer of the homicide-suicide offenders had previous criminal records than the purely homicide cases. Both types of cases tended to take place late at night. Homicides occurred most frequently on Saturdays and homicide-suicides on Mondays.

Wolfgang found that white homicidal offenders committed suicide more frequently than black offenders. "Although whites are one fourth of all offenders, they significantly make up half of the homicide-suicides."[50] He found also that "males comprise 83 percent of all homicide offenders, but make up 22 of the 24 homicide-suicides."[51] He stated, "Of all homicides, half of the victims were killed violently; whereas among homicide-suicide cases three quarters met death violently. . . ."[52]

As for the part played by alcohol, Wolfgang noted:

Alcohol was present in the homicide situation in the Philadelphia study in as many as 6 or 7 out of 10 homicides in general, but in only 3 out of 10 homicides followed by suicide. . . . Perhaps the lower incidence of alcohol in homicide-suicide situations indicates a greater likelihood of premeditation by the offender.[53]

Regarding arrest records: "One third of homicide-suicide offenders have a previous arrest record compared to nearly two thirds of all offenders."[54] As for age of the Philadelphia offenders, Wolfgang reported this:

> The median age of those who committed suicide (38.3 years) is about 7 years older than that for all offenders (31.9 years), while the median age of victims of the homicide-suicide group (30.1 years) is about 5 years younger than that for all victims (35.1 years).[55]

Finally, Wolfgang stated that in Philadelphia the proportion of close personal attachments between offenders who committed suicide and their victims was significantly higher than that between other offenders and victims.

Broadly speaking, the findings of West in England, of Wolfgang in Philadelphia—and of Siciliano in Denmark as well—are similar. West concluded:

> As far as they go, the statistics available in these three communities all fit the hypothesis that murderers who kill themselves, compared with murderers in general, form a less socially deviant group, and that their relationships to their victims are more often close and intimate.[56]

SOCIAL INTEGRATION EXPLANATIONS

Social and Status Integration

Many sociologists consider Emile Durkheim's book *Suicide*, published in 1897, to be the first full-scale empirical study in sociology.[57] That great work has led to an enormous amount of creative research and theory building in regard to suicide specifically and deviance generally.

In his analysis of suicide, Durkheim placed great stress on social integration, yet the meaning he assigned to the term has never been completely clear to others. As suggested in Chapter 2, he seems to have meant the degree to which a society or group is characterized by agreement about basic life values. Durkheim saw egoistic suicide as due to a widespread, perpetual absence of social integration and social regulation. Anomic suicide was a consequence of sudden decreases in individual's integration into society. Hence the anomic form is actually a variant of the egoistic. Durkheim held further that social integration and regulation and altruistic suicide are positively related, that is, as integration and regulation become excessive, the extent of the institutionalization of suicide for "the good of society" increases. Durkheim believed, then, that the extremes of both high and low social integration and regulation led to suicide.

Like Durkheim, Powell wrote of both excessive social integration and disintegration as giving rise to suicide.[58] He suggested that two opposite types of anomie result from these extremes. One is a consequence of the individual's dissociation from the culture, the other of his envelopment by it. "Both render the individual impotent and thus both give rise to self-contempt which in extreme cases eventuates in suicide."[59] Envelopment by the culture might be construed to imply excessive reciprocity in role relationships and dissociation from the culture to imply extremes of unreciprocating relationships. Extremes of either—reciprocity or unreciprocity—would then be seen as forces behind suicide.

Gibbs and Martin, using Durkheim's work as a departure point, set forth a status integration theory of suicide.[60] Their central idea was that the degree of status integration, of status positions being closely associated in a population, is related to the degree of suicide. The Gibbs and Martin conceptualization is essentially one of role conflict cast in status terms. Its major thrust is that as social integration, measured in terms of status integration and role conflict, decreases, suicide increases.

Social Structuring, External Restraint, and Anomie

Straus and Straus took the position that a more closely structured society, where reciprocal duties are stressed and enforced and variation in individual behavior is not tolerated, will have a higher incidence of suicide and a lower incidence of criminal homicide.[61] Straus and Straus clearly believed that in a closely structured society, homicide is not a culturally permissible solution to conflict whereas suicide is. Their position is a straightforward statement of the hypothesis that suicide increases as reciprocity in role relationships grows greater.

Henry and Short argued that suicide is characteristic of high-prestige groups and homicide of low-prestige groups.[62] They held that as prestige increases, there is a decrease in the strength of the relational system, that is, in the extent to which individuals are involved in social or cathectic relationships with others. Further, they took the position that as prestige increases, there is a decrease in the strength of external restraint—the degree to which behavior is required to conform to the demands and expectations of others. To summarize their position: as prestige of individuals becomes greater and external restraints and the strength of the relational system decreases, homicide also decreases, whereas suicide increases.

When behavior is subjected to strong external restraint by virtue either of subordinate status or intense involvement in social relationships with other persons, it is easy to blame others when frustration occurs. But when the restraints are weak, the self must bear the responsibility for frustration.[63]

Strong external restraints mean conflict among individuals while weak restraints imply an absence of conflict.

One aspect of Merton's anomie theory of deviance has special relevance for the study of suicide.[64] Retreatism in Merton's formulation refers to rejection of both cultural goals and institutionalized means. Included within this category are the behaviors of certain psychotics, alcoholics, drug addicts, and vagabonds—people who in a certain sense have given up on society and dropped out. This conception of retreat can be extended and broadened to include suicide. Having been unable to attain or having lost the culturally prescribed success goals and the means to them, the individual may respond to the consequent anomie by the ultimate form of retreat, of dropping out—suicide.

In summary, Durkheim was the first to stress the relationship between social integration and suicide. He held that both excessively high and low social integration and regulation generate suicide. Powell also concluded that high or low integration leads to suicide. Gibbs and Martin hypothesized that only low social integration gives rise to suicide. Straus and Straus took the position that high social structuring and, by implication, high social integration and regulation were conditions for suicide. The Henry and Short approach emphasized that low social regulation, that is, low external restraints, and a weak relational system (low integration) were critical factors in suicide. This might also be said to be true of Merton's retreatist behavior as a reaction to anomie: if retreat is taken to include suicide, then suicide results from a lack of social regulation (and integration) which is inherent in retreat. Thus some theorists predict that suicide will result from excessively low integration, some from excessively great integration, and some from both. We shall attempt to resolve these apparent contradictions after considering other approaches to the explanation of suicide.

SOCIAL DISORGANIZATION AND CONFLICT EXPLANATIONS

Social Disorganization

Maurice Halwachs was among the first to stress a connection between urbanization and suicide.[65] His was essentially a subcultural formulation. He saw the urban subculture as one of particularly great conflict in patterned social relations. Broadly speaking, in the Halwachs formulation, conflict in social relations leads to suicide.

Ruth Cavan,[66] Calvin Schmid,[67] and others have pursued with tenacity and ingenuity the possibilities of relationships between the lower-class core areas of cities and suicide. Viewing those areas as highly disorganized, Cavan found that they give rise to high suicide rates. For Cavan, it was disorder and instability that spelled suicide, not order and stability. Schmid's results were essentially similar. Faris summed up the case for the "social disorganization school":

> Suicide therefore usually reflects a failure of social control over the behavior of the person, and . . . is connected with various indications of individualism and detachment. It is therefore, in our society, clearly a phenomenon of social disorganization.[68]

However, relatively recent research and reinterpretation of earlier research indicated that what were traditionally viewed as disorganized areas of the city are in fact often quite highly organized.[69] Skid-row areas, for example, are characterized by much smoothly functioning, patterned interaction despite the high rate of turnover of the population, as are to some degree various types of tenement areas, ghetto and otherwise, in large cities. Reciprocity is far from absent in so-called disorganized areas. In some cases it may have been the researchers' ethnocentric, moralistic attitude that led them to characterize as disorganized areas with high rates of suicide and of other forms of deviance.

A closely related matter is the consistent finding that downwardly mobile individuals congregate in "disorganized" areas, and that those individuals are especially prone to suicide.[70] As noted earlier, Breed and others found a distinct tendency for downward occupational mobility to be associated with suicide.[71] Wood's findings in Ceylon pointed to the threat of downward mobility as a crucial variable. Stressing the need to combine the individual's subjectively felt condition with observations of the objectively observed social system, Wood found suicide to be largely a high-status phenomenon. Speaking of Ceylon he wrote: "Not high status per se, but relatively high status in conjunction with stress from an insecure achieved position is the structural component of a high suicide rate."[72]

Conflict

Miller's thesis that certain lower-class behavioral patterns are defined and prosecuted as criminal by the higher classes bears little on suicide.[73] While in some jurisdictions suicide and attempted suicide are crimes, in practice they are not treated as such. The situation is similar in regard to Quinney's social reality theory which holds that the definition and adjudication of crimes is a political process in which the lower socioeconomic groups suffer at the hands of the higher socioeconomic groups.[74] It was not Quinney's intent to address the matter of suicide.

In contrast, Thio attempts to apply his power theory to suicide.[75] He reasons that taking one's own life is voluntary among higher-status, relatively powerful individuals, but that lower-status persons lacking power are coerced into suicide. He contends that powerful persons, being used to luxury, have high expectations and low tolerance for suffering. This intensifies their disappointment when under adversity and may generate suicide. Powerless individuals, in contrast, seldom voluntarily react to adversity with suicide. Rather, society is structured by the powerful to induce or coerce them to participate in their own deaths. The powerless may commit suicide out of fear of the power structure or slowly kill themselves out of economic necessity (continuing to work in environments which cause black or brown lung disease, for example).

Undoubtedly, some low-status persons are coerced into suicide in one way or another. However, individuals who are either forced directly to take their own lives or who continue to expose themselves to hazardous conditions because of economic necessity can hardly be considered to have committed suicide. No doubt some higher-status persons have low tolerance for frustration and kill themselves. But most who commit suicide have suffered severe losses of status, loved ones, and self-esteem. To have power and social standing inevitably means vulnerability to loss. One can sympathize with the plight of the oppressed without concluding that suffering is fundamentally different for one category of humans than others. Power theory has more potential for explaining the gray area between suicide and homicide—coerced death, it might be called—than either suicide or homicide as usually defined.

Cultural Support and Societal Reaction Explanations

Cultural Support

Differential Association

Sutherland's differential association[76] and Cohen's reaction formation[77] theories hold essentially that negative deviance—crime and delinquency in particular—are learned in association with other persons who act out law-violating values and behavior patterns. This general approach has been seen as having little if any relevance to suicide. Suicide is usually seen as individualistic behavior (not institutionalized) that does not depend on subcultural learning. The one general exception has been the clear recognition that in some traditional societies (Japan and India), killing the self under certain conditions is socially expected and approved. This is conformity to overall cultural prescriptions, not deviance from them.

However, some suicide in some societies is to some extent at least institutionalized negative deviance. It is behavior which is widely disapproved by the society under any conditions. Yet it is prevalent in certain parts of the social structure and under certain conditions. It tends to follow certain patterns in its execution. For example, widowed persons in the United States are quite prone to take their own lives, especially in the years immediately following the deaths of their spouses. This is not at all behavior which is socially expected or approved. But it is fairly prevalent, and it occurs more at certain levels in the social structure and in some regions more than others. It is more prevalent in the upper and lower classes than in the middle classes. It occurs more among whites than blacks. It is far more prevalent among widowed males than widowed females. And it occurs more in the western and northern states than in the southern states.

Subcultures of Violence

It may be that rudimentary patterns and values for taking one's own life and for less extreme forms of self-aggression develop in subtle ways. In other words, *subcultures of self-violence* may exist which are fundamentally similar to the subculture of violence (toward others) suggested by Wolfgang and Ferracuti.[78] This is a conception that has not been pursued to any significant degree and deserves attention.[79] Urban skid-row areas where downwardly mobile unemployed men congregate may be one breeding ground of subcultures of self-violence. Here men who have lost prestige in the society, who have lost family ties, who have lost jobs, interact with each other in highly cooperative fashion. They may develop patterns of values of self-violence—alcoholism, poor health practices, suicide attempts—as ways of simultaneously distracting themselves from, and ending, their plight.

Mental hospitals constitute another possible site of subcultures of self-aggression. Increasingly, hospital policies restrict admission, except for the senile, to the mentally ill who are diagnosed as dangerous to self or others. If patients are judged to be especially dangerous to others, they are likely to be consigned to a special part of the hospital. (They may also be dangerous to themselves.) This leaves those who are diagnosed as self-dangerous to interact among themselves. Thus can arise patterns of self-destructive, possibly suicidal, behavior.

Societal Reaction

Societal reaction theory has been applied to suicidal behavior only to a limited degree.[80] It has considerable potential, however, as one explanation of certain forms of suicide. Once individuals speak of the possibility of killing themselves or make suicidal attempts, certain processes of social control may come into play which can induce suicidal behavior. These include labeling of the individual as suicidal by family members and friends and by physicians, psychiatrists, psychologists, social workers, and hospital personnel. They also include placing the individual in a local environment—such as a hospital room under observation—which implicitly labels him or her as a potential suicide. Isolation of the individual in such an environment, which is also common, can contribute to depression, which in turn can contribute to suicidal behavior. These matters are discussed further in the social control section of this chapter. The important point to note here is that any indication of suicidal behavior by a person can set in motion a labeling and reactive process by others that may indeed create a self-fulfilling prophecy of completed suicide.

TWO OTHER EXPLANATIONS

Phenomenological

Jack Douglas has been a leader in an attempt to direct explanation of suicide away from conventional social scientific lines and toward phenomenology.[81] This approach to understanding the world and our place in it stresses, insofar as human behavior is concerned, the pivotal value of the *meaning* the individual attaches to his or her behavior. Douglas points out that individuals attach certain meanings to their future acts of suicide, often as these are influenced by cultural meanings of suicide which are widely held in society.

Our society attaches three general, cultural meanings to suicide: (1) suicide is meaningful; (2) the suicidal individual's social situation is in some way flawed; and (3) the suicidal individual is also in some way flawed. From these, suicidal persons construct personal meanings of suicide which facilitate the taking of their own lives. These fall into four categories: (1) suicide makes it possible for the soul to be transported to another world; (2) the act of suicide can lead others, or a supreme being, to change their views of one; (3) suicide is a way of gaining the positive feeling, the sympathy, of others; and (4) suicide can lead to revenge or aggression against others by making them feel guilty.

Imitation

The role of imitation in explaining behavior has for centuries been a controversial question. In recent decades sociology has paid little attention to imitation. Recently, however, David Phillips conducted studies which indicate a distinct imitative component in suicide.[82] In his initial research, he found that the United States suicide rate temporarily increased by 12 percent for a brief period after a suicide was publicized in the newspapers. The more publicity given the story, the greater was the increase in suicide, especially in the geographic areas where the story was publicized.

Phillips's more recent research concerned the effect of publicized suicides on motor vehicle fatalities in California. Some fatal motor vehicle accidents, especially those involving only one vehicle, are known to have a suicidal component. Phillips found that three days after suicides were publicized in major newspapers, fatal motor vehicle accidents temporarily increased by 31 percent. The more publicity given the suicides, the greater the increase, mainly in the areas where the newspapers were sold. Single-vehicle accidents increased more than multivehicle accidents. Phillips went on to suggest that imitation may serve as a *switching mechanism* which, given conditions of frustration, anomie, and the like, may cause an individual to choose one form of deviance—suicide, homicide, assault, arson, and so on—over another. This is a highly interesting line of research which should be given close attention in the future.

COMMON THEMES

We pointed out earlier that some social integration explanations purport that suicide is a result of extremely low levels of integration while others purport that it is a consequence of very high levels, and still others hold that it is brought about by either extreme. Social disorganization theorists have held that the greater the disorganization, the higher the incidence of suicide. Others have argued that areas which appear to be disorganized and which show high suicide rates may actually be well organized but in ways quite different from the mainstream of society. High levels of role conflict (Gibbs and Martin) and of political power conflict (Thio) have been used to explain suicide. Yet we know that some highly unconflicted societies have relatively high rates of suicide (Sweden and Denmark) while very conflicted societies may not (Ireland, Colombia).

While cultural support explanations have seldom been brought explicitly to bear on suicide, it may well be that subcultures of self-vio-

lence can develop and serve as a generating force behind suicide. Societal reaction explanation clearly has relevance to suicide since society's
members do sometimes tend to react to signals that individuals may be
suicidal by bringing into play social controls (labeling as suicidal) which
may engender a self-fulfilling prophecy. Phenomenological students of
suicide have stressed the importance of cultural and individual meanings attached to killing of the self as determinants of whether suicide
will occur. And there has been a resurgence of an interest in imitation
as a process which may contribute to suicide.

Consider this considerable array of explanations in relation to some
of the major findings about suicide: it tends to be committed by older
persons, by males, by whites rather than blacks in the United States,
by both high- and low- rather than middle-status persons, by socially
downwardly mobile individuals, by those who have suffered severe
losses of loved ones and status, including those who have murdered
others close to them.

Disruption of social relations is a common thread among many of
these explanations and findings. In 1968, several years after the status
integration theory was set forth by Gibbs and Martin, Gibbs wrote of
the importance of disrupted social relations as an explanatory variable
behind suicide. He stated:

> (1) The greater the incidence of disrupted social relations in a population,
> the higher the suicide rate of that population; and (2) all suicide victims
> have experienced a set of disrupted social relations that is not found in the
> history of non-victims. . . . No claim is made that a particular type of dis-
> ruption is crucial. Instead, the referent is all kinds of disruptions, that is,
> any instance where a regular pattern of social interaction between two or
> more people is interrupted. As such, the concept embraces a wide range of
> events—the death of a parent, spouse, or child; separation; divorce; termi-
> nation of employment; some types of residential changes; the termination
> of a love affair; and some changes in employment situations, to mention
> only a few possibilities.[83]

Gibbs did not distinguish between positive and negative disruption of social relations. This is of course difficult to do since what is
defined as favorable and unfavorable change depends on personal and
cultural values. However, it is fair to conclude that loss of culturally
valued roles, through loss of loved ones, loss of job, loss of status, and
so on, is likely to be negatively defined by individuals experiencing
such losses as is the gaining of culturally disvalued roles. Change which
involves taking on of culturally valued roles is likely to be positively
evaluated by the individuals who take them on.

Gibbs's propositions can thus be restated: (1) The greater the incidence of loss of social roles which are culturally valued or gain of social
roles which are culturally disvalued, the higher the suicide rate of that
population; and (2) all suicide victims have experienced patterns of

loss of social roles which are personally valued or gain of social roles which are personally disvalued that are not found in the histories of nonvictims.

This formulation helps to explain the apparent contradictions in social integration explanations, some of which predict suicide when integration is very low and others when it is very high. Individuals have to be integrated into the society to at least some degree in order to experience disruption and loss of roles. When suicide occurs under high-integration conditions, it may well be either because individuals fear losing critical roles (which can be as real a source of frustration as actually losing them) or because some, the suicidal, have lost them although most others have not. When suicide occurs under low-integration conditions, it may be because in general individuals who were socially integrated have lost roles and become disintegrated.

This reasoning seems to explain why high rates of suicide occur in supposedly socially disorganized areas. The inhabitants there tend to be downwardly mobile persons who have lost familial, work, and prestige roles. Similarly, it may explain why suicide rates are high at the lower and upper socioeconomic levels. Very likely it is higher-status people who fear loss of status and of family roles who commit suicide. Among lower-status people, it is very likely the downwardly mobile, those who have had valued roles and lost them, who kill themselves and not those who have always been without valued roles. Similar reasoning leads one to conclude that older people have more valued roles to lose, and can lose them, than younger people. The same is true for whites as compared to blacks and for males as compared to females, although the last is changing as sex roles become more equal in prestige.

SUMMARY

Suicide is the intentional, nonaccidental killing of one's self. Although suicide in some societies has been institutionalized, in most societies it is considered to be individualistic deviance. As a consequence, suicide has often been judged to be a crime.

Rates of suicide around the world vary greatly from over 40 in some countries to a low of less than 1 per 100,000 population in others. Overall the world rate is about 12 per 100,000. Many countries with high suicide rates tend to be stable and technologically advanced. Since 1940 the suicide rate in the United States has been consistently between 10 and 13. Suicide tends to rise during times of economic depression and decline during times of prosperity. Suicide is also highest in the western states and in large metropolitan areas. Males kill themselves two to three times more often than females. Older persons are considerably more vulnerable to suicide than younger ones. On the whole, whites are more self-destructive than blacks; however, young adult black males have distinctly high rates.

With regard to social class, empirical evidence suggests that suicide is more common among persons in lower- and, to some extent, upper-prestige positions and least common in the middle class. Downward mobility has been linked to suicidal behavior. Persons who lose important social roles, particularly job or marital roles, are especially vulnerable to self-destruction.

Socialization experiences of suicidal persons tend to differ from those of other persons. Psychological rather than corporal punishment was used to correct the suicidal person's behavior. Parental affection was withheld: the failures were emphasized and guilt was instilled in the child. As a consequence, the individual tends to blame the self for misfortune and aggression is directed toward the self. Self-destructive persons typically experienced an inordinate amount of loss in their lives. Parents were lost through death, divorce, or separation; marriages failed; and children left home prematurely.

A sense of hopelessness and helplessness characterizes the suicidal personality. The loss of hope involves a loss of competence, or the feeling that one has some control over one's life. Self-destructive persons also tend to set unrealistically high goals for themselves. They rigidly and relentlessly pursue those objectives, blocking out alternate courses of action. Failure is met with an overwhelming sense of despair.

Mental illness is certainly not a prerequisite to suicide. However, former mental patients and those psychologically depressed are high risks for suicide. Neurotic persons may attempt suicide but rarely actually want to die.

Methods of suicide vary widely from culture to culture. In the United States males use guns most often; females rely principally on poisoning and asphyxiation. Other cultures seldom use firearms. Suicide usually takes place at home and on the weekends. Excessive use of drugs and alcohol may accompany the act of suicide.

Attempted suicide is six to 10 times more prevalent than suicide itself. Females are three times more apt to attempt suicide than are males, but males are three times more likely actually to carry out the suicide. And whites are considerably more prone to attempt suicide than blacks.

In the United States those who kill others are less likely to kill themselves than they are in Denmark or England. Murder-suicide usually follows a domestic conflict; the offender is invariably related familially to the homicide victim. Murderers who later kill themselves resemble the general population more than they do other homicidal offenders who do not commit suicide.

A major attempt to explain suicide has focused on degrees of social integration. Social integration refers in a general way to the agreement about basic life values. Three types of suicide are generated by varying degrees of social integration. Anomic suicide is a consequence of sudden decreases in social integration; egoistic suicide occurs when social integration is virtually absent; and altruistic suicide results from excessive social integration. Both extremes of social integration may precipitate suicide.

Social disorganization has also been associated with a high incidence of suicide. Societies characterized by high levels of role conflict and political power conflict may or may not exhibit high rates of suicide. Subcultural expectations for self-violence and societal reactions to potentially self-destructive behavior may bring about suicide. The disruption of social relations, mainly as a result of the loss of social roles, is of central importance in the etiology of suicidal behavior. The actual or threatened loss of social roles significantly diminishes or severely jeopardizes high levels of social integration.

REFERENCES

1. David Horton Smith and Linda Hackathorn, "Some Social and Psychological Factors Related to Suicide in Primitive Societies: A Cross-Cultural Comparative Study," *Suicide and Life-Threatening Behavior* 12(4):195–211, 1982.
2. U.S. Bureau of Census, *Historical Statistics of the United States, Colonial Times to 1970, Part I* (Washington, D.C.: U.S. Government Printing Office, 1975), p. 414.
3. Andrew F. Henry and James F. Short, Jr., *Suicide and Homicide* (Glencoe, IL: Free Press, 1954).
4. Jack P. Gibbs and Walter T. Martin, *Status Integration and Suicide* (Eugene, OR: University of Oregon Press, 1964).
5. *Ibid.*
6. John L. McIntosh and Barbara L. Jewell, "Sex Difference Trends in Completed Suicides," *Suicide and Life-Threatening Behavior* 16:16–27, 1986.
7. Ronald Maris, "The Adolescent Suicide Problem," *Suicide and Life-Threatening Behavior* 15(2):91–109, 1985; and R. H. Seiden and R. P. Freitas, "Shifting Patterns of Deadly Violence," *Suicide and Life-Threatening Behavior* 10(4):195–209, 1980.
8. Evelyn M. Kitagawa and Philip M. Hauser, *Differential Mortality in the United States: A Study in Socioeconomic Epidemiology* (Cambridge, MA: Harvard University Press, 1973), p. 77.
9. Dominigue I. Lambert, Linda B. Bourque, and Jess F. Kraus, "Occupational Status and Suicide," *Suicide and Life-Threatening Behavior* 14(4):254–269, 1984; also, Steven Stack, "Suicide: A Decade Review of the Sociological Literature," *Deviant Behavior* 4:41–66, 1982.
10. Elwin H. Powell, "Occupation, Status, and Suicide: Toward a Redefinition of Anomie," *American Sociological Review* 23(2): 137, 1958.
11. Warren Breed, "Occupational Mobility and Suicide among White Males," *American Sociological Review* 28(2):179–188, 1963.

12. Henry and Short, *op. cit.*
13. Martin Gold, "Suicide, Homicide, and the Socialization of Aggression," *The American Journal of Sociology* 63(6):651–661, 1958.
14. Ian Gregory, "Studies of Parental Deprivation in Psychiatric Patients," *American Journal of Psychiatry* 115(5):432–442, 1958.
15. Theodore L. Dorpat, Joan K. Jackson, and Herbert S. Ripley, "Broken Homes and Attempted and Completed Suicide," *Archives of General Psychiatry* 12(2):213–216, 1965.
16. William A. Rushing, "Individual Behavior and Suicide," in *Suicide*, ed. Jack P. Gibbs (New York: Harper and Row, 1968), p. 100.
17. *Ibid.*
18. *Ibid.*
19. *Ibid.*, p. 101.
20. For example, Norman L. Farberow and Edwin S. Shneidman, eds. *The Cry for Help* (New York: Harper and Row, 1968), p. 100.
21. Gerald F. Jacobson and Stephen H. Portuges, "Relation of Marital Separation and Divorce to Suicide: A Report," *Suicide and Life-Threatening Behavior* 8(4):217–224, 1978.
22. Jack P. Gibbs, "Testing the Theory of Status Integration and Suicide Rates," *American Sociological Review* 47(2):227–237, 1982.
23. Edwin S. Shneidman and Norman L. Farberow, "Clues to Suicide," *Public Health Reports* 71(1):111, 1959.
24. Rushing, *op. cit.*, p. 98
25. For example, Jack D. Douglas, *The Social Meanings of Suicide* (Princeton, NJ: Princeton University Press, 1967), pp. 283–285, 339.
26. M. L. Farber, *Theory of Suicide* (New York: Funk and Wagnalls, 1968).
27. David Lester, *To Kill Themselves* (Springfield, IL: Charles C. Thomas, 1972).
28. *Ibid.*
29. Ronald W. Maris, *Pathways to Suicide: A Survey of Self-Destructive Behaviors* (Baltimore: The Johns Hopkins Press, 1981).
30. Lester, *op. cit.*
31. Karl A. Menninger, *Man Against Himself* (New York: Harcourt Brace Jovanovich, 1938).
32. Herbert Hendin, "The Psychodynamics of Suicide," in Gibbs, *Suicide*, pp. 133–145.
33. Louis I. Dublin, *Suicide* (New York: Ronald Press, 1963).
34. Stuart Palmer, "Characteristics of Suicide in 54 Non-Literate Societies," *Life Threatening Behavior* 1(3):178–183, 1971.
35. Dublin, *op. cit.*
36. *Ibid.*
37. Palmer, *op. cit.*
38. U.S. Department of Health and Human Services, *Fourth Special Report to the United States Congress on Alcohol and Health* (Washington, D.C.: U.S. Government Printing Office, 1981).
39. J. Roizen, "Estimating Alcohol Involvement in Serious Events," in National Institute on Alcohol Abuse and Alcoholism, *Alcohol Consumption and Related Problems* (Washington, D.C.: U.S. Government Printing Office, 1981).
40. Marc Aarens, Tracy Cameron, Judy Roizen, Ron Roizen, Robin Room, Dan Scheneberk, and Deborah Wingard, *Alcohol, Causalities and Crime* (Berkeley: University of California, 1978).
41. C. P. Miles, "Conditions Predisposing to Suicide: A Review," *Journal of Nervous and Mental Diseases* 164(4):231–246, 1977; and U.S. Department of Health and Human Services, *Fifth Special Report to the United States Congress on Alcohol and Health* (Washington, D.C.: U.S. Government Printing Office, 1985).
42. William A. Rushing, "Suicide as a Possible Consequence of Alcoholism," in *Deviant Behavior and Social Process*, ed. William A. Rushing (Chicago: Rand McNally, 1969).
43. Herbert Hendin, *Suicide in America* (New York: W. W. Norton, 1982).
44. Alex Pokorny, "Human Violence: A Comparison of Homicide, Aggravated Assault,

Suicide, and Attempted Suicide," *Journal of Criminal Law, Criminology, and Police Science* 56(4):488–497, 1965.

45. Manfred Guttmacher, *The Mind of the Murderer* (New York: Grove Press, 1962).
46. Cited by Donald J. West, *Homicide Followed by Suicide* (Cambridge, MA: Harvard University Press, 1966), p. 70.
47. *Ibid.*, p. 2.
48. *Ibid.*
49. West, *op. cit.*
50. Marvin E. Wolfgang, *Patterns in Criminal Homicide* (Philadelphia: University of Pennsylvania Press, 1958), p. 273.
51. *Ibid.*, p. 276.
52. *Ibid.*, p. 277.
53. *Ibid.*, p. 278.
54. *Ibid.*
55. *Ibid.*
56. West, *op. cit.*, p. 46.
57. Emile Durkheim, *Suicide*, trans. John A. Spaulding and George Simpson (New York: Free Press, 1966).
58. Powell, *op. cit.*
59. *Ibid.*, p. 139.
60. Gibbs and Martin, *op. cit.*
61. Jacqueline H. Straus and Murray A. Straus, "Suicide, Homicide, and Social Structure in Ceylon," *American Journal of Sociology* 58(5):461–469, 1953.
62. Henry and Short, *op. cit.*
63. *Ibid.*, p. 18.
64. Robert K. Merton, *Social Theory and Social Structure* (Glencoe, IL: Free Press, 1957), pp. 131–160.
65. Maurice Halwachs, *Les Causes du Suicide* (Paris: Alcon, 1930).
66. Ruth S. Cavan, *Suicide* (Chicago: University of Chicago Press, 1928).
67. Calvin F. Schmid, "Suicide in Minneapolis, Minnesota: 1928–1932," *American Journal of Sociology* 39(1):30–48, 1933. Also Calvin F. Schmid, *Suicides in Seattle, 1914 to 1925* (Seattle: University of Washington Publications in the Social Sciences, 1928).
68. Robert E. L. Faris, *Social Disorganization* (New York: Ronald Press, 1948), p. 293.
69. Joan K. Jackson and Ralph Connor, "The Skid Road Alcoholic," *Quarterly Journal of Studies on Alcohol* 14(3):468–486, 1953.
70. Breed, *op. cit.*
71. *Ibid.*
72. Arthur Lewis Wood, "A Socio-Structural Analysis of Murder, Suicide and Economic Crime in Ceylon," *American Sociological Review* 26:744–753, 1961.
73. Walter B. Miller, "Lower Class Culture as a Generating Milieu of Gang Delinquency," *Journal of Social Issues* 14(3):5–19, 1958.
74. Richard Quinney, *The Social Reality of Crime* (Boston: Little, Brown, 1970).
75. Thio, *Deviant Behavior* (Boston: Houghton Mifflin, 1983).
76. Edwin H. Sutherland and Donald R. Cressey, *Criminology* 10th ed. (Chicago: Lippincott, 1978).
77. Albert Cohen, *Delinquent Boys* (Glencoe, IL: Free Press, 1955).
78. Marvin E. Wolfgang and Franco Ferracuti, *The Subculture of Violence* (New York: Barnes and Noble, 1967).
79. See, however, John A. Humphrey and Stuart Palmer, "Homicide and Suicide in North Carolina: An Emerging Subculture of Self-Violence?" in *Violent Crime: Historical and Contemporary Issues*, eds. James A. Inciardi and Anne E. Pottieger (Beverly Hills, CA: Sage, 1978), pp. 99–110.
80. For discussions of the societal reaction approach, see especially Thomas Scheff, *Being Mentally Ill* (Chicago: Aldine, 1966); Edwin M. Lemert, *Human Deviance, Social Prob-*

lems and Social Control (Englewood Cliffs, NJ: Prentice-Hall, 1967); Edwin M. Schur, *Labeling Deviant Behavior* (New York: Harper and Row, 1971).

81. Douglas, *The Social Meanings of Suicide*.
82. David P. Phillips, ps, "The Influence of Suggestion on Suicide: Substantive and Theoretical Implications of the Werther Effect," *American Sociological Review* 39(3):340–354, 1974.
83. Gibbs, *op. cit.*, p. 17.

10
Alcoholism and Drug Use

DEFINITION AND PREVALENCE OF ALCOHOL PROBLEMS

Alcoholism and Alcohol Problems

Billions of people around the world drink alcoholic beverages of one type or another. For most, drinking does not constitute a problem. What are the criteria for alcoholism or, as some professionals prefer, "problem drinking?" Robert Straus argues that problem drinking is the broader term and includes alcoholism. He defines as problem drinkers persons who repeatedly use alcohol in amounts greater than "customary dietary use or prevailing socially acceptable customs"; or in amounts that lead to health problems, interfere with everyday relationships with others, or hamper fulfilling family, economic, and community expectations.[1] The core of this definition has to do with use that is excessive in terms of prevailing customs or injuries to health or disruption of role relationships.

Straus reserves the term *alcoholic* for those problem drinkers whose use of alcohol "is associated with a state of physical or psychological dependence involving often unbearable stress or discomfort or tension."[2] In alcoholism individuals are addicted to alcohol or have a compulsion to use it or in any event cannot control their drinking. The result is impairment of health and social relationships.

Peoples everywhere have access to one or another of the agricultural products for producing alcoholic substances. These can be made from fruits, berries, tubers, and cereals. Alcohol is a sedative, an anesthetic, a depressant. It reduces tension and anxiety. Small amounts of it produce feelings of well-being. Alcohol also impairs sensorimotor coordination. Large amounts ingested quickly can lead to death. Considerable amounts ingested regularly or even occasionally can cause severe bodily disturbance including nausea, hallucinations, and the seizures of delirium tremens, a type of withdrawal symptom.

Wine is usually about 10 percent alcohol, fortified wine 20 percent alcohol, beer 3–6 percent alcohol. Distilled beverages such as whiskey and brandy range from 30 to over 50 percent alcohol. "Proof" is a number twice that of the alcoholic content; 100 proof whiskey, for example, is 50 percent alcohol. In the average person, two cocktails or highballs or glasses of wine or four cans of beer ingested fairly quickly means a 0.06 percent alcohol concentration in the bloodstream. The person is likely to feel relaxed; motor coordination and driving ability are slightly impaired. Four cocktails or highballs or glasses of wine or eight cans of beer lead to a 0.12 percent concentration of alcohol in the bloodstream. Walking is unsteady, there may be considerably exaggerated emotional states; driving is distinctly impaired. In many jurisdictions, a 0.12 percent level of concentration legally constitutes drunken driving. Ten to 20 cocktails, highballs, or glasses of wine or 20–40 cans of beer causes 0.30–0.50 percent alcohol content in the bloodstream. This leads to extreme intoxication. Heart action and breathing slow; coma and usually death occur. The more the drinking of alcoholic beverages is spread over time, the less the intoxication. Alcohol is slowly "processed" by the body. Eating before drinking slows the effects of alcohol as it is absorbed less quickly into the bloodstream than on an empty stomach.

Drinking and Alcoholism in the World at Large

Few societies have been without alcoholic beverages for long periods. In some societies, alcohol is reserved for the few. In others, almost everyone drinks. Among the numerous societies in which the use of alcoholic beverages is widespread, there is great variation in the extent to which problem drinking and alcoholism exist. In certain societies, although drinking is common, excessive drinking is exceedingly rare. In others, alcoholism is rampant.

Alcohol is variously used to relieve pain and tension, to provide a sense of well-being, and to enhance friendship and goodwill. It may be used as a significant element in religious ritual and as a means of celebration. Its distribution and consumption form important segments of many economies.

Donald Horton, who analyzed the drinking of alcohol in nonliterate societies around the world, speaks of the remarkable strength of drinking customs.[3] They have survived in society after society—literate as well as nonliterate—despite, in many instances, concerted efforts to stamp them out. A major reason for this is that alcohol is a quick, inexpensive anxiety reducer which if not overused has few ill effects. It has valuable medical uses, especially as an anesthetic. The judicious use of alcohol lubricates social occasions in hundreds of societies around the globe.

Andrew Poznanski provides a brief history of alcohol[4]: Stone Age beer jugs attest to the use of fermented drinks in the Neolithic period. The ancient Egyptians venerated wine and beer. The use of wine is interwoven in Hebrew ancient tradition. Nonliterates with very simple economies such as the aboriginies of Tasmania have made fermented liquor for many centuries. Alcohol was used in early Roman society and in ancient Greece. Distilled spirits—whiskey, brandy, gin, rum, and so forth—were a later development. The distillation process is believed to have been discovered in the tenth century. That made possible the concentration of alcoholic drinks, allowing for easy transport and quick inebriety.

Craig MacAndrew and Robert B. Edgerton surveyed the effects of alcohol on social behavior in *Drunken Comportment*.[5] While alcohol impairs sensorimotor functioning of people in all societies, the effects on the ways they comport themselves vary tremendously. That is to say, the extent and ways in which alcohol is a "disinhibitor" are greatly different from one society to another. Assumed in Western societies to be a "loosener" of inhibition against aggressive, sexual, and other negative deviance, this is by no means necessarily the case, MacAndrew and Edgerton conclude.

The Yuruna Indians of the Xingu region of the tropical forests of South America are a head-hunting warring group. They drink large amounts of malicha, made from fermented manioc root. They do not become aggressive when drinking; they withdraw into themselves.[6] In contrast, the Abipone Indians of Paraguay are generally grave, gentle, and kind. When they drink, they become contentious and violent.[7]

On the other hand, the Bantus of southeastern Africa show a range of behavior when drinking, depending on the *nature* of the social occasion. MacAndrew and Edgerton report of them:

> There was awed silence on many religious occasions, easy-going conviviality during casual everyday drinking, boisterous hilarity and increased sexual freedom during some of their secular ceremonies. But within the context of traditional practices—and this is the point—their doings conformed to their understanding of what the occasion called for.

In some societies where aggression is common in everyday life, individuals become still more violent when drinking; in many others they become less so. In societies where peacefulness is the rule, that may be continued when individuals are drunk or they may become aggressive. The critical factor, MacAndrew and Edgerton contend, is how the culture defines drinking situations. Some define drunkenness as "time out," as providing "selective immunity," from condemnation or prosecution for aggressive, sexual, and other negative deviance. If so, then alcohol has a "disinhibiting" effect. If not, then alcohol either changes social behavior but little or even has an inhibiting effect.[8]

Alcohol consumption in literate societies around the world varies by the type of drink: distilled spirits, beer, or wine. The United States ranks eighth in the per capita consumption of distilled spirits; twelfth in beer, and 26th in wine. Overall, Luxembourg and France, Portugal and Spain, and the middle European countries are above average per capita consumers of alcohol. Israel and Mexico, however, are decidedly low in alcohol consumption.[9]

There do not appear to be any few characteristics such as technological development, poverty, or internal economic competition which clearly distinguish high and low alcohol-consuming countries. As will be discussed below, customs for drinking and the relationship of those customs to other customs, values, and institutional arrangements of a society have much to do with levels of alcohol use.

Prevalence in the United States

About two of every three Americans drink alcohol at least occasionally. Beer is the overwhelming favorite drink. Americans over the age of 14 consume on the average 36.2 gallons of beer each year, compared to 3.28 gallons of wine and 2.8 gallons of distilled spirits.[10] That means that each person drinks about 320 beers (12-ounce can or bottle), 12.5 bottles of wine, and 10.5 quarts of liquor. If we consider only those persons who drink, we see that on the average 800 bottles of beer, 260 bottles of wine, and 50 fifths of whiskey are annually consumed.[11] However, alcoholics or problem drinkers, 10 percent of all drinkers, are estimated to account for 50 percent of all the alcohol consumed in the United States.[12]

Drinking varies considerably by region of the country and population density. Drinking is most prevalent in the northeast and middle Atlantic states and least common in the South. And drinking is more characteristic of urban and suburban life than that in rural areas.[13]

AGE, SEX, OTHER VARIABLES, AND ALCOHOLISM

Age and Sex

Problem drinking and alcoholism are highest for persons in their twenties and then decrease with age. There are more male than female problem drinkers and alcoholics. This is true in the United States and in many other countries. The National Institute of Alcohol Abuse and Alcoholism finds that 14 percent of males and 4 percent of females are heavy drinkers, that is, they consume one ounce or more of alcohol per day during a given month.[14] Thus three times as many males and females were heavy drinkers. There are approximately five times more alcoholic men than alcoholic women. Almost twice as many females as males drink seldom and little if at all.[15]

The pattern of decreasing drinking with age holds for both sexes. In the same study 54 percent of males aged 18–24 years were heavy drinkers as compared to 21 percent of the females.[16] At age 65 and over, 19 percent of the men drank heavily while only 3 percent of the women did so.

A recent national poll found that 72 percent of men and 52 percent of women in the United States used alcohol.[17] In general it has been found that young adults, age 20–24 years, are the age group most likely to have drinking problems.[18]

Race and Class

Black men and women have had rates of alcoholism two to three times those of white men and women in the United States.[19] Recent national surveys find, however, that a higher proportion of white males and females drink and more whites drink to excess than do their black counterparts.[20] Blacks tend to drink more in public places and are therefore more subject to arrest for drunkenness.[21] Blacks are also more likely to be hospitalized and treated on an outpatient basis for alcoholism.[22]

While American Indian groups differ in regard to alcoholism, in general they have been found to have high rates. "Indians can't hold their liquor" is a common belief. That they become violent or otherwise criminal when drinking is an equally common view. MacAndrew and Edgerton hold that white frontiersmen of the nineteenth century "taught" the Indians to be violent when they drank by providing what amounts to role models for that.[23] The Indians, beset by culture conflict and invasion, also seemed to "use" alcohol as a way of being "excused," at least in some degree, for violating the white man's rules and laws as well as their own.

Findings on social class, drinking, and alcoholism are mixed. In the Boston study reported by Weschler, the percentages of heavy drinkers and of abstainers or infrequent drinkers were found by social class and sex.[24]

The middle class showed the greatest preponderance of heavy drinkers for both males and females. The lower class had the largest percentages of abstainers or infrequent drinkers for both sexes.

Of course, heavy drinking does not necessarily imply alcoholism, although it is quite likely to imply problem drinking. A national survey of male drinking in the United States showed that severe drinking problems were more common in the lower than the middle or upper classes. Thio[25] concludes that a greater percentage of persons in the higher socioeconomic strata drink alcoholic beverages than in the lower strata; but the percentages of problem drinkers and alcoholics are greater at the lower than at the higher levels. He suggests that high-status persons are more likely to use alcohol "as a facilitator of social interaction" while low-status individuals tend to use alcohol in one endless search to solve personal problems. He goes on to suggest an alternative explanation: rates are the same in high as in low socioeconomic strata, but those in the high have more power to hide their problem drinking.

Ethnicity and Religion

The extents of problem drinking and alcoholism in the United States vary considerably by ethnic background. The Irish and French have very high rates. Those of Italian and Chinese ancestry in the United States have low rates. Regarding religion, Jews in this country have low rates of alcoholism. Conservative Protestants (fundamentalist and Pentecostal, as examples) seldom drink; but, if they do, they have high rates of alcoholism. The same is true of Mormons. Other Protestant groups do not generally have high rates. Catholics do tend to have high rates of alcoholism.[26]

Robert Bales writes that the Irish in this country are influenced by the permissive drinking customs of their original culture and suffer from insecurities brought about by low status and culture conflict.[27] Excessive drinking is used to reduce anxiety. In France, where alcoholism is high, children often start to drink at an early age. Among adult males, excessive drinking is seen as indicative of virility. Yet there is ambivalence over the whole matter of inebriation. The French in the United States presumably follow the homeland patterns of copious drinking, retain the ambivalence, and suffer from the effects of culture conflict as well.

In Italy the inhabitants drink as much per capita as the French, but drinking is closely integrated with eating and with the culture generally. They do not associate high intake of alcohol with virility and neither condone nor strongly disapprove of drunkenness. Italian-Americans show higher rates of alcoholism than the people of Italy but their rates are still low for the United States.[28] For the Chinese, in their homeland and in this country drunkenness is disapproved, but drinking in moderation is quite acceptable and is associated with social occasions.[29] Drinking problems among Chinese in the United States or in China are rare.

Drinking is threaded through Jewish culture here and elsewhere. It is integrated with religious ritual and with life generally. The less orthodox the Jewish group, the more tendency toward alcoholism, although for most Jews it is uncommon.[30] Conservative Protestants and

Mormons outlaw drinking. It is not at all integrated with their religion.[31] Those who do drink tend also to violate other customs and taboos of their religion. They experience anxiety and guilt, and this apparently leads to further drinking.

Through these examples of differences in alcoholism and problem drinking by ethnic and religious groups in the United States runs a common theme: the less drinking customs are integrated with the everyday lives, the overall culture or subculture of the group, the greater the predisposition to alcoholism. This is an exceedingly important generalization and will be discussed in the context of explanations of alcoholism later in this chapter.

FAMILY EXPERIENCE, PERSONALITY, AND THE ONSET OF ALCOHOLISM

Alcoholics tend to come from disorganized families and to have had seriously flawed family relationships. Their parents are more likely than those of nonalcoholics to have been divorced or separated.[32] There is likely to have been excessive contention in the families of alcoholics.[33] Those who become alcoholics often had as children and youths hostile relations with their parents and felt alienated.[34] Alcoholics are decidedly more prone than nonalcoholics to have relatives who are alcoholics.[35] The alcoholics in a family tend to be close relatives—parents or siblings—rather than distant relatives. Fathers of alcoholics are especially likely to be alcoholics. Female alcoholics more often have alcoholic relatives than male alcoholics. Moreover, alcoholics have relatives who are alcoholics more frequently than do persons with psychiatric problems in general.[36] Alcoholics themselves tend to divorce more than nonalcoholics. Rates of alcoholism in the United States are greatest for separated persons, next greatest for the single, next for the divorced, next for the widowed, and lowest for the married.[37]

While researchers tend to agree that there is not a single "alcoholic personality," alcoholics are likely to show one or more of a limited number of personality characteristics and conditions.[38] These include neurotic tendencies, depressive disorders, anxiety, hostility toward others or self or both, low frustration tolerance, weak sex-role identity, weak ego formation, and strong dependency needs.

Psychological theories of alcoholism focus on three themes[39]: unconscious self-destructive tendencies, interpersonal problems of dependency and aggression, and either insecurity about power relations or an insatiable thirst for power. Certainly alcoholism is self-destructive physically as well as psychologically. Clearly, many alcoholics use alcohol as a way of attempting to cope with severe dependency and aggression needs. And alcohol may be consumed to excess to provide either the illusion of power for those who lack it or the illusion of greater power for those who, as psychologist McClelland suggests, want more and more power.[40] However, in most cases of alcoholism, in addition to one or more of those conditions, there is exposure to cultural patterns which either advocate heavy drinking or induce conflict between heavy drinking and cultural values approving it.[41]

The Onset of Alcoholism

Jellinek outlines four stages in the development of alcoholism.[42] The *introductory* state involves increasingly heavy social drinking to reduce tension. In the *early* state, the individual drinks excessively, usually sneaks drinks, tends to drink in the mornings to alleviate hangovers, and has blackouts (loss of memory of activities while drinking). In the *middle* state, there is loss of control over drinking. The ingestion of alcohol becomes compulsive. In the *final* or *chronic* stage, there are drunken sprees of several days, fears of being unable to obtain an adequate supply of alcohol, bizarre behavior, malnutrition because of lack of food, and delirium tremens, which often include frightening hallucinations.

The chronic phase is often experienced in the individual's late thirties or early forties, sometimes earlier, seldom later. Precursors are likely to be loss of valued roles[43] or other stressful events including loss of loves ones and/or social supports. Familial and other stressful situations contribute to the anxiety and depression which alcohol is used to alleviate temporarily. Drunkenness in turn creates stress in the alcoholic's family and in his or her other role relations, at work for example. In developing alcoholism, these circumstances are usually accompanied by the presence of cultural or subcultural values which either support excessive drinking or condemn it. If condemning, then the drinker may attempt to alleviate ensuing guilt by more alcohol.

DRINKING IN RELATION TO OTHER PROBLEMS

Alcoholism and problem drinking may result from cultural values and customs which advocate heavy drinking. Often, however, they are symptomatic of stresses generated by social and personal conflict, alienation, and disorganization. These same factors may give rise to other forms of negative deviance. Alcoholics have high rates of abuse of other drugs, crime, homosexuality, suicide, neurotic and depressive mental disorders, and divorce. They also have high rates of unemployment and of accidental deaths and injuries, not necessarily deviant in nature. In some of these associations between alcoholism or heavy drinking and other forms of problem behavior, there appear to be reciprocal effects: each leads to the other. Unemployment and mental disorder, homosexuality, and abuse of other drugs are examples. Also, marital strife and excessive drinking may compound each other and eventually result in divorce. In the cases of suicide, crime, and accidents, heavy drinking appears to precipitate the behavior.

Crime

Criminal offenders have often been drinking at the time of the crime, many of them quite heavily. One United States study reported that alcohol had been ingested shortly before the crime by 64 percent of criminal homicide offenders, 41 percent of assaultive offenders, 34 percent of forcible rape offenders, and 29 percent of other sex crime offenders.[44] Wolfgang found that drinking was more common among homicide offenders who used especially violent means than those who used less violent means: 60 percent of the former had been drinking as compared to 50 percent of the latter.[45] Many other studies show that half or more of criminal homicide offenders had been drinking just prior to their crimes. Victims of violent crimes have also often been drinking.[46]

The consumption of alcohol is often construed to be a mitigating circumstance in the criminal courts. Yet as MacAndrew and Edgerton quite clearly showed, whether alcohol is likely to result in criminal behavior is in great measure a result of cultural values and customs.[47] In violent societies, violent offenders may or may not commonly have been drinking just prior to the crime. In nonviolent societies, alcohol may seem to give rise to violence or it may not. The critical issues are whether the culture tolerates criminal behavior among those who drink. Thus alcohol may or may not be effectively used to avoid prosecution for criminal behavior.

Accidents

In more than half of the 50,000 highway fatalities which occur each year in this country, either the driver or the victim or both was drinking, and in about one-third of the one to two million highway injuries that occur annually, the driver or victim was drinking. Four in 10 pedestrians killed on the highways have been found to have a concentration of alcohol in the blood above 0.10 percent.[48] Drunk driving is the leading cause of death among persons aged 16–24 in the United States. While only 22 percent of the drivers in the United States are between 16 and 24, they account for 44 percent of all fatal car accidents.[49] A majority of those who are arrested for drunken driving have a history of that offense.[50] Alcoholics are more likely to be involved in motor vehicle accidents than others who drink.[51] Approximately 7 percent of drivers who are problem drinkers account for over 66 percent of alcohol-related auto deaths.[52] Drivers who have been drinking account for 700,000 personal injuries of which 74,000 are serious.[53] When a person meets the minimum standards for legal intoxication, he or she is six times more likely to cause an auto accident than drivers who are not drinking.[54]

Alcoholics are far more prone to die accidental deaths from various causes, not only motor vehicle crashes, than nonalcoholics. A San Francisco study compared 1343 alcoholics with the general population, taking into account age and sex. Female alcoholics died from accidents 16 times more frequently than women of their ages in the general population; the male alcoholics' death rate from accidents exceeded their male counterparts in the general population by six times. Male and female alcoholics taken together were 30 times more likely to die of accidental poisoning, 16 times more likely to die of falls, and 4.5 times more likely to die in motor vehicle accidents than the same age and sex group in the general population.[55]

EXPLANATIONS OF ALCOHOLISM

Cultural Supports

Robert Bales proposed in 1946 a sociological theory of alcoholism which draws in part on cultural support explanations.[56] Bales first contended that cultures produce in individuals greater or lesser degrees of tension, feelings of anxiety, hostility, guilt, and the like. Second, cultures induce attitudes and beliefs that alcohol is or is not an effective drug for relieving inner tensions. And third, cultures may or may not advocate other ways of reducing tension such as eating or using drugs. If tensions are great, if alcohol is culturally viewed as an effective tension reducer, and if there are few other culturally prescribed tension reducers, then alcoholism rates are likely to be high in the group.

Harrison Trice proposed a more social psychological theory of alcoholism.[57] He held that certain individuals are vulnerable to alcoholism because they possess "alcoholic personality" traits, notably dependency needs, self-hate, and the need to see oneself as a "man." (Obviously, this explanation is of little relevance to female alcoholics.) In order for a person with these traits to become an alcoholic, he must associate with groups which advocate drinking. Such groups usually equate drinking with "maleness." A further drawback of this theory is of course that it applies only to males in societies where maleness becomes an issue. But Trice does stress the important point that the support of drinking customs and groups is central to the development of alcoholism. And Bales makes the equally important observation that a cultural definition of alcoholism as an efficient reducer of tension is critical to alcoholism.

In those senses, the two theories are in part cultural support explanations of alcoholism. But there are other respects in which cultural and subcultural customs and values play a significant part in whether alcoholism occurs. Those customs and values may advocate abstinence, heavy drinking, or a degree of moderation. They provide guidelines for how to drink—which beverages, how rapidly, and so forth. And they indicate which situations are proper or improper for drinking—before, during, or after meals, only in formal ceremonies or in informal social groups or alone, and so on. Drinking customs and values are in greater or lesser degrees integrated or not with the wider cultural and subcultural systems of values and practices. The less integrated they are, the more they give rise to conflict and tension in individuals. Moreover, cultural customs and values indicate how individuals should behave when they drink and the meaning of that behavior. They set expectations for aggression or demand peacefulness. They allow irresponsibility, in the sense of abrogation of other group norms, or they demand conformity.

Taken together, these aspects of culture exert powerful influences toward the avoidance of alcohol, moderate drinking, problem drinking, or alcoholism. Especially important among these types of cultural prescriptions are drinking customs and values which are in conflict with other cultural customs and values and whether alcohol is defined as an effective tension reducer. Such conflict creates tension in individuals if they drink. And further ingestion of alcohol becomes the culturally approved, temporary solution to the discomfort of tension.

Social Integration

Richard Jessor and his colleagues stress blocked opportunities to success goals as a central cause of alcoholism.[58] This is essentially a version of Merton's goals-means formulation of anomie. Those who are unable to gain the institutionalized means to culturally prescribed success goals, or who have lost those means, turn to alcohol to assuage the pain of frustration. This does appear to have considerable validity in regard to persons who are downwardly mobile, who have, for example, lost prestigious jobs. And it may be applicable in a limited degree to the poor who are blocked from access to the means for achieving success. Yet many of the poor do not even drink let alone become alcoholic.

A related aspect of social integration theory concerns alienation. Individuals who are little integrated into groups tend to quickly become alienated and hostile. Alcohol can be a crutch for reducing anxiety and feelings of inadequacy, and for venting aggression. This connects with the blocked opportunities approach just mentioned. While many who fail to achieve success goals do not feel alienated, others do. When alienation and blocked or lost opportunities coexist, then individuals are candidates for problem drinking and alcoholism. Usually, however, there must be the aforementioned cultural supports. These may take the direct forms of supportive cultural values and customs for heavy drinking. Alternatively, individuals' cultural or subcultural systems may rule out alcohol while their more immediate groups advocate drinking.

Conflict and Social Disorganization

Culture conflict over drinking alcohol has to do, then, with the extent to which drinking practices and values are not integrated with the overall culture or subculture. Orthodox Jewish culture integrates the drinking of wine with religious ritual and other aspects of Jewish life. Conflict is low and alcoholism is rare. In contrast, Mormon culture outlaws drinking. Most Mormons do not drink; but when they do, alcoholism is likely.[59]

A quite different form of culture conflict may also give rise to alcoholism. This is the conflict in a wide range of customs and values, not necessarily having to do with drinking, of two or more cultures. Individuals may have moved from one culture to another or may simultaneously participate in two cultures. Thus the tensions that result from the participation of American Indians in their traditional tribal cultures and in the culture of present day United States society led to severe adjustment problems which they may attempt to alleviate through alcohol.

Thio poses still another form of conflict explanation of alcoholism.[60] Alcoholism is an unprofitable form of higher-consensus deviance and thus is publicly consigned by the powerful to the lower class. The designation of lower-class, powerless persons as alcoholics reinforces the stereotype of the down-and-out person, the "skid-row bum" as alcoholic. Thus attention is directed away from heavy drinking by upper-class, powerful individuals who through the drinking process expedite their business transactions and profit making.

The idea that social disorganization begets alcoholism has long been popular. Since the 1920s, sociologists have investigated the relationship between poverty areas of cities and problem drinking and alcoholism.[61] Without question some alcoholics do congregate in the run-down skid-row areas of cities. This may in good measure be a result of the tendencies for downwardly mobile persons to be alcoholic, without families, and to seek each other out in one of the few places available, the worst "residential" areas of the cities. In any case, skid-row areas are mainly disorganized in the sense that they depart so far from middle- and upper-class standards. They are in fact quite highly organized in that strong cultural patterns exist for derelict inhabitants mutually to support each other psychologically and, to the limited extent possible, economically as well.[62]

Labeling

The labeling perspective has not by any means been a dominant one in regard to alcoholism. However, Trice and Roman,[63] Lemert,[64] and others have focused on this perspective. In the United States, heavy drinking is seen as an escape from responsibility, a violation of the Protestant ethic. Alcoholics are seen as aggressive nuisances as well. They are likely to be excluded from social groups. This forces them into membership in deviant, heavy-drinking groups or into drinking alone. Repeated contacts with police and jailings for drunkenness serve to reinforce the alcoholic identity. Interestingly, alcoholics often have spent their earlier lives in groups which disdain heavy drinking. Societal reaction to problem drinking thus tends to be strong.

In summary of these several types of explanations, lack of social integration and a consequent sense of anomie and alienation set the stage for alcoholism. Customs and values which facilitate drinking contribute to the likelihood of alcoholism. The more these customs and values are in conflict with other aspects of the culture, the more that likelihood increased. Given these conditions, the labeling process may operate to all but ensure alcoholism as an outcome.

CONTROL AND PREVENTION OF ALCOHOLISM

Formal Control

Most states of the United States have laws against public drunkenness. Those laws usually have twin criteria: intoxication in a public place and some degree of disorderly conduct, loudness, or public nuisance. About a third of all arrests in the United States are for public drunkenness. About half of those in local jails are there for that offense. The same individuals are often arrested and jailed repeatedly for public drunkenness.[65] Most are lower-class males, often derelicts. At the same time, two-thirds of the United States public are opposed to arrest for public drunkenness unless the drunken individuals are actually causing trouble.

As Donald Horton, a cross-cultural researcher on alcohol, stated, the use of alcohol has survived countless attempts to stamp it out in numerous societies around the world.[66] Movements to outlaw the use of alcohol began in earnest in the United States in the early 1800s and have continued to the present. The Women's Christian Temperance Union and the Anti-Saloon League were two of the major groups opposing alcohol. Their efforts culminated in 1919 in the Eighteenth Amendment to the United States Constitution (Prohibition). For the next twenty years, in the United States, intoxicating beverages could not legally be manufactured, sold, exported, or imported as a beverage. "Bootlegging" and "speakeasies" sprang up across the country. Illegal drinking, that is, the purchase of alcoholic beverages, became common, chic, and daring. This gross legislative failure was repealed in 1933 by the 21st Amendment.

Ostensibly apolitical movements to outlaw alcohol have in many instances clearly had political ends. The well-to-do use the abolition of alcohol, Prohibition, as an attempt to reduce threats to their power by the "working" and lower classes, especially immigrants. Under the guise of improving life for the poor by removing alcohol, the well-to-do labeled them as "drinkers" who needed guidance and tried to reduce their political influence.[67] One of the reasons Prohibition backfired was the rise of a new middle class that valued the use of alcohol.

Rehabilitation Approaches

Mental and general hospitals, mental health clinics, and social work agencies often refuse to treat alcoholics. They are "difficult" patients and success is poor. This has been changing in recent years. Some hospitals have special wards for the treatment of alcoholics. Occasionally mental health clinics, or segments of them, specialize in treating alcoholism. Much of the treatment for alcoholism has been either by private therapists or by such self-help groups as Alcoholics Anonymous (AA). By most measures, success in the treatment of alcoholism has not been great.

Some psychiatrists and psychologists attempt to treat alcoholism through one-to-one "talk" therapy, often designed to uncover the dependency needs and insecurities presumed to lie behind alcoholism. Others use behavior modification where the individual is rewarded strongly for nondrinking behavior and punished quite severely for drinking. One form of this is aversion therapy in which the patient consumes with alcohol other drugs which cause nausea and headaches. In a variation of this, electric shocks are administered with the ingestion of alcohol. The aim is to associate pain and misery with alcohol to the extent that it is avoided. The conditioning effects of aversion therapy usually wear off in a year or less.

Group therapy is often used in an attempt to treat alcoholics. Alcoholics Anonymous, to be discussed shortly, is in part a form of group therapy. Halfway houses are combinations of group and milieu therapies designed to rehabilitate skid-row alcoholics. Those houses are intended as a bridge between the world of the alcoholic and the everyday world. Patients hold jobs, engage in discussion sessions, and mutually support each other toward the end of reintegration into general society. A major problem is that of weaning the former alcoholic away from dependency on the half-way house.[68]

Alcoholics Anonymous began in the United States about 1940. Today there are 10,000 affiliated AA groups in this and other countries.[69] There are numerous groups in prison, jails, and mental hospitals. Members of AA are all former alcoholics. The basis of "treatment" is informal, mutual support. A new member is assigned a sponsor, a successfully reformed alcoholic, who provides individual support in the early stages. There are usually several evening meetings of the group each week.

Alcoholics Anonymous is religiously oriented in a general way. In the group meetings, 12 steps are taken up in sequence and discussed by the successfully rehabilitated alcoholics and the new members. These are:

Step One: Admitted we were powerless over alcohol—that our lives had become unmanageable.

Step Two: Came to believe that a Power greater than ourselves could restore us to sanity.

Step Three: Made a decision to turn our will and our lives over the the care of God "as we understood Him."

Step Four: Made a searching and fearless moral inventory of ourselves.

Step Five: Admitted to God, to ourselves, and to another human being the exact nature of our wrongs.

Step Six: Were entirely ready to have God remove all these defects of character.

Step Seven: Humbly asked Him to remove our shortcomings.

Step Eight: Made a list of all persons we had harmed, and became willing to make amends to them all.

Step Nine: Made direct amends to such people wherever possible, except when to do so would injure them or others.

Step Ten: Continued to take personal inventory and when wrong promptly admitted it.

Step Eleven: Sought through prayer and meditation to improve our conscious contact with God "as we understood Him," praying only for knowledge of His will for us and the power to carry that out.

Step Twelve: Having had a spiritual awakening as the result of these steps, we tried to carry this message to alcoholics and to practice these principles in all our efforts.

Thus reliance on God, self-examination, making amends to others, and eventually helping other alcoholics are the hallmarks of the AA creed.[70]

When one AA member is in danger of slipping back into alcoholism, another is there to lend support no matter what the time or place. It is this combination of individual and group support by individuals who have experienced alcoholism first-hand that is believed centrally responsible for the considerable success of AA. While the success of AA is difficult to measure accurately, most observers agree that it is more successful than many other approaches.[71] In the process of providing group support and a nondrinking milieu, AA also effectively delabels persons as *active* alcoholics.[72]

Clues to Prevention

Norval Morris and Gordon Hawkins have been among the leading advocates of the decriminalization of drunkenness.[73] It is not a crime in the usual sense. Drunkenness cases clog the courts, and repeated arrests for drunkenness may fix the role of the "drunk" on individuals. Decriminalization can be accompanied by community requirements that chronic drunks make use of detoxification or other treatment facilities.

"Early warning systems" have been established by some employers to detect the beginning signs of alcoholism in employees. The main reason for this is that drinking by employees costs business and industry severely in reduced work efficiency. Mistakes at work, accidents, absenteeism, and certain illnesses can be indicators of incipient alcoholism. Employees are urged to seek psychiatric or other help often at the expense of the employer. This is a form of prevention in the sense that it may prevent the development of alcoholism as opposed to treatment after the onset of alcoholism. Such early warning programs can be broadened from the work setting to the wider community.[74]

A United States government report summarized the characteristics of societies and groups with few drinking problems[75]:

1. Children usually drink highly diluted alcoholic beverages.
2. Alcoholic beverages used by adults tend to be low in alcoholic content.
3. Alcoholic beverages are considered to be part of meals.
4. Parents are role models for moderate drinking.
5. Drinking is considered neither a sin nor a virtue.
6. Drinking is not used to prove maleness.
7. Abstinence is fully acceptable.
8. Excessive drinking is not socially acceptable.
9. There is general agreement among the group's members regarding the ground rules for drinking.

There could be added a tenth characteristic: Drinking is not considered an acceptable excuse for serious negative deviance. And an eleventh: While there may be informal derision of individuals who drink to excess, there is little attempt to label and prosecute formally those who engage in drunkenness per se. (When drunkenness leads to crime, then prosecution is swift.)

It can be seen that these 11 points reflect certain broad theoretical orientations: First, individuals *learn* from others *to drink moderately*. There are *cultural supports* for this but not for problem drinking. Second, drinking practices are *integrated* with the overall culture and practices within it. The process which *labels* individuals as problem drinkers is largely absent.

Notice that two types of explanation for alcoholism are not implied: blocked opportunities in the sense of lack of access to institutionalized means to culturally approved success goals, and culture conflict experienced by individuals because of differing customs and values of two or more cultures in which they have participated. Both so these can be contributing factors in alcoholism. However, their presence does not necessarily induce alcoholism. Some societies with widespread goals-means disparities and some groups characterized by culture conflict do not have significant degrees of problem drinking or alcoholism.

Conditions that in given societies are clearly associated with an absence of alcoholism cannot be transported wholesale to other societies. At the same time, much can be learned about the prevention of alcoholism in our society by analysis of the cultural and social characteristics of societies without this form of negative deviance. If steps are not taken to integrate moderate drinking into the culture, to provide adequate role models for that, and to make socially unacceptable excessive drinking while avoiding the self-fulfilling prophetic effects of labeling, then this socially and individually debilitating form of deviance will continue to be widespread.

NATURE AND EXTENT OF DRUG USE

Definitions and Forms

The remainder of this chapter is concerned with the use of drugs other than alcohol. Drugs are substances not required for the normal maintenance of bodily health.[76] At a particular time in a given society, the use or sale of certain drugs is likely to be illegal while the use or sale of other is not. Some may be controlled in the sense that they can legally be dispensed by physicians or others. The term *drug abuse* is used to refer to the use of drugs which is harmful to the individual or the society. Usually, although not always, such abuse is illegal. *Drug addiction* refers to physical or psychological craving for a drug; deprivation causes acute discomfort. Legal definitions of *drug addict* center on the loss of self-control in the use of "habit-forming" drugs which endanger public health and welfare. Narcotic addiction and narcotic addicts are terms applied to the use of drugs which are physically addictive.

The determination of which drugs are illegal and of what constitutes drug abuse and addiction is in many societies largely a political rather than a scientific matter. The issue is not purely one of health. It is also one of morality. Drugs which are harmless if taken in moderation may nonetheless be defined as illegal and abusive, even addictive. Drugs which are clearly harmful may be excluded from such definitions. Legal definitions have an effect of their own: if individuals use drugs illegally, then they may by others or self be labeled as criminal and hence cast as an outsider.

The variety of drugs is very great. Most fall into one of these broad although somewhat overlapping categories: depressants, stimulants, and psychotropics, the latter being those which cause dramatic changes in how one views the world. Depressants include many narcotics, barbiturates such as Benzedrine, and tranquilizers, as well as alcohol. Major narcotics are opium (from poppies) and its derivatives, morphine, heroin, and codeine. Stimulants are cocaine, made from coca leaves, and the amphetamines (pep pills). Psychotropic drugs include those synthetically produced such as LSD as well as mescaline and peyote from cactus, and marijuana (pot, hashish) from the hemp plant, *Cannabis sativa*. Most drugs can be consumed orally. Some, such as heroin, are often taken intravenously.

Certain of those are addictive physically or psychologically or both; others are nonaddictive. In general the depressants are both physically and psychologically addictive. This applies to opium and its derivatives such as heroin and to the barbiturates and tranquilizers. The stimulants, largely amphetamines, are addictive psychologically but probably not physically. The psychotropics such as LSD may be psychologically addictive but are not physically; the same is true of marijuana.

It is important to understand that wide gulfs often exist between common beliefs and scientific findings about the effects of drugs. For example, many habitual heroin users go through life without ill effects provided they have the necessary funds to maintain the habit and do not resort to crime. Marijuana does not as a rule lead to behavior problems, and it does not "cause" or lead directly to crime. On the other hand, many marijuana users have life styles which are socially disapproved of by the wider society. And some are criminal because of actions other than smoking marijuana. Drugs generally do not generate violent behavior, although the synthetically produced psychotropic drugs such as LSD may on occasion play a part in violence, especially the self-violence of suicide.[77]

Around the World and in the United States

In societies around the world, there are great variations in the extent of drug use in addiction, the types of drugs used, and whether drugs are socially approved or disapproved and are legal or illegal. All societies have access to drugs in the sense that natural substances from which drugs can be made are available. On the one hand, the fact that drugs are obtainable does not necessarily mean that they are used. For example, opium has for many years been plentiful in Yugoslavia yet is little used here. On the other hand, most societies do use drugs of one type or another.[78]

Bourguignon reports that of a sample of 488 societies around the world, 90 percent had institutionalized various forms of altered states of consciousness. Most of those involved the use of drugs and were set in a sacred context.[79] DeRios concludes that when drugs are used ritualistically, usually in a religious context, abuse and social problems seldom arise.[80] The less drugs are integrated in dominant aspects of the culture, the more likely are extreme instances of negative deviance regarding the use of drugs.

Most large countries treat drug use as a medical rather than a legal-political problem. England has been a leader in this with considerable success. Addicts are few and are treated by physicians. Japan and Sweden have had serious epidemics of drug use in recent years, and Israel and Greece lesser ones.[81] Usually epidemics have been preceded by rapid social change, instability, and role strain due to changing role demands, especially on adolescents and young adults. Interestingly, outbreaks of epidemic use of amphetamines (pep pills) appear to occur in countries such as Japan, Sweden, and the United States which stress the moral as well as the economic value of high individual productivity.[82]

Both legal and illegal drug sales are big business in the United States. Physicians write millions of prescriptions annually for barbiturates and amphetamines. Many individuals use these drugs regularly to make themselves "feel better" rather than for specific medical purposes. In general in the United States, it is illegal to possess depressant, stimulant, or psychotropic drugs (except alcohol and tobacco) without a physician's prescription, and physicians are prohibited legally from prescribing certain drugs, such as LSD. Which drugs are illegal has varied greatly over the past several centuries. The result of the present laws which make possession a criminal act is that drug users and addicts are by definition criminal unless they are under medical treatment.

The extent of addiction is especially difficult to determine. In general, it is believed that the United States has a greater drug addiction problem than any other Western country. There are an estimated 3.5 million occasional users of heroin in the United States and 500,000 daily users.[83-84] By comparison there are approximately 400,000 opiate addicts in Iran; 350,000 in Thailand; 80,00 in Hong Kong; 18,000 in Canada; 13,000 in Singapore; 12,500 in Australia; 10,000 in Italy; and 6000 in the United Kingdom.[85]

AGE, SEX, PRESTIGE, AND FAMILY FACTORS IN DRUG USE

Age and Sex

Youths tend to use marijuana and young adults heroin. Both drugs are distinctly more prevalent among males than females in the United States. However, use of prescription amphetamines and barbiturates is greater among females than males. Among youths aged 12–17 years, 27 percent have used marijuana and 12 percent are current users. Among adults aged 18–25 years, 64 percent have tried marijuana and 17 percent are current users; 23 percent of those 26 or older have used marijuana, and 7 percent are current users. Of the youths, 13 percent of the males and 10 percent of the females presently use marijuana. Of the young adults, 36 percent of the males and 19 percent of the females do so. Of the adults, 10 percent of the males and 3 percent of the females do so.[86]

A national survey of 100,000 known narcotic addicts, over 90 percent of whom were addicted to heroin, showed that 9 percent were under 21 years of age; 62 percent between 21 and 30 years; 21 percent between 31 and 40 years; and the remaining 8 percent, 41 years or older. About 84 percent were male and 16 percent female.[87] A different study showed that one-fifth of women in a national sample had used prescription tranquilizers during the previous year and one-twelfth had used stimulants, usually amphetamines. Men were about half as likely to have used one or the other. Tranquilizers tended to be used by older persons and stimulants by younger persons.[88]

Prestige

Use of illicit drugs has been disproportionately high in the lower socioeconomic classes and among blacks and other minorities. An analysis in San Antonio, Texas showed a clear inverse relation between socioeconomic standing and heroin use.[89] One out of 10 black males in St. Louis were found to be addicted to heroin.[90] And blacks are about four times overrepresented among persons treated for drug addiction.[91]

More recently, however, far less disparity in heroin use has existed between the lower, middle, and upper classes.[92] Heroin use has become increasingly common among the economically advantaged.[93] Use of cocaine in particular has become widespread in the United States. It is estimated that 20 million Americans have tried cocaine; 4–5 million use it at least once a month.[94] Each day about 5000 additional persons experiment with cocaine use.[95]

A survey of drug use among physicians and medical students shows that 59 percent of the physicians and 78 percent of the students have used psychoactive drugs at some time in their lives. One out of four doctors report self-treatment with a psychoactive drug, and one in 10 are regular drug users. And significantly greater drug use is reported by medical students than practicing physicians.[96]

The whole issue of "discovery" is of course involved. Prestigious individuals are far more able than others to escape detection for illicit drug use and they are able to obtain drugs without recourse to crime. Physicians in both the United States and England have high rates of addiction to opiates but escape detection. They have the drugs ready at hand, they know how to use them, and they are exceedingly unlikely to be prosecuted. The rates of opiate addiction among physicians in the United States is believed to be 30 times that of the general population.[97] In England, physicians are thought to make up 15–20 percent of all addicts.[98] The legal guardians of drugs tend to be illegal users.

Illicit drug use and drug addiction are concentrated in the urban areas of the United States. Marijuana, heroin, and LSD users tend to be found especially in cities of the western United States. However, the concentration of heroin addicts in New York City is great.[99] On the one hand, urban centers with high concentrations of poor minority, ethnic, and racial groups show high rates of ilicit drug use. On the other hand, so do cities, San Francisco for example, with concentrations of persons who follow counterculture life styles.

Family Experience

An enormous range of individuals use legally or illegally a large group of drugs. Some are addicted psychologically or physically or both; some are not. One could hardly expect to find family and personality characteristics common to all users of drugs. However, it is possible to specify certain familial conditions and personality factors which characterize many of those in the United States who are addicted to "hard" drugs, especially heroin. Heroin addicts are likely to come from broken, unstable, disorganized families.[100] McCord believed that 97 percent of youthful addicts came from families where parents were separated or hostile toward each other.[101] Rosenfeld found that addicts were likely to have been reared in families which were broken or otherwise lacked cohesiveness.[102] Relatively early in life, addicts have suffered a ruptured relationship with their families.[103]

The most striking finding about family experiences and male drug addiction concerns the relationship between mother and son. Numerous studies indicate that mothers of male addicts were possessive of their sons and both overprotective and rejecting of them. They appeared to want their sons to be dependent on them yet were ambivalent about males and unpredictably rejected them. The mothers dominated their husbands, who were passive figures, as well as their sons. The sons had no adequate role models and were unable to develop positive male role identities. The mothers seemed to encourage implicitly their sons' symbolic aggression through illicit drug use against a social system which had been disadvantageous to the mothers. The mothers then disapproved of their sons' deviance. The sons attempted to break away from their mothers in teenage or early adulthood. They married less often than men of their age generally. When they did marry, their wives were often domineering women, not unlike their mothers. Whether or not they married, the male addicts usually gravitated back to their mothers and attempted to reestablish the dependent, ambivalent relationship.[104] Other studies show that addicts tend to be single or divorced. They are not prone to carry on stable family lives just as they were unlikely to have stable family lives as children.

Drugs, Subcultures, and Other Deviance

It is exceedingly difficult if not impossible to become a habitual drug user without interaction with a drug subculture. Where to obtain drugs, how to use them, what sensations to feel, how to cope with stigma and negative identity, how to avoid arrest, and, in the use of expensive drugs, how to obtain money for them—these are all learned in interaction with others who act out elements of drug subcultures.

There are several fairly distinct forms of drug subcultures in the United States. One is the middle-class college drug subculture of the urban slums; marijuana and the opiates are the central drugs. A third, closely related to the second, is the hard drug, mainly heroin, subculture of young and older lower-class adults in the large cities. A fourth form is the professional subculture which includes drug use. In the case of physicians, the professional subculture does not *advocate* that physicians use drugs. However, the knowledge, supply, and protective prestige are all part of the professional subculture. In the case of jazz musicians, customs and values for using drugs may be threaded through the professional subculture. In addition, there are regional subcultural variations, particularly in the South and far West.

Howard Becker outlined in the 1950s three steps necessary to becoming a marijuana user.[105] First, one must learn the techniques to get high, such as inhaling deeply. Second, one must learn to recognize the effects of the drug—hunger, an altered time sense, so forth. Third, one must learn to enjoy the effects of the drug. Defining sensations such as dizziness and disorientation in time and space as pleasurable rather than unpleasurable is the key here. Chein and his colleagues specified four stages of becoming a user of illegal drugs: experimentation, occasional use, regular use, and futile attempts to break the habit.[106] Users may stop at any level or continue on. Heroin users are the most likely to "progress" to the last two stages.

Marijuana subcultures, whether in the college or ghetto scene, emphasize "kicks" and recreational use. They stress a "hang-loose" ethic as opposed to the prevailing "uptight" Protestant ethic of striving for money and prestige. Heroin subcultures are more complex and involve circulatory networks for securing drugs.[107] These include learning who has what drugs and how to obtain illegally the money for them. Heroin subcultures also involve survival networks. These include an ideology that drug use is good, that drug users are positive deviants, that new members of the subculture are to be recruited, and warning subnetworks for avoiding arrest and prosecution.[108]

Contrary to popular belief, most illegal drug users are first introduced to drugs, often marijuana, by teenage friends, not drug peddlers. They may or may not "progress" to use of the opiates. If they do, this too is likely to be a result of interaction with friends. There is no evidence that habitual use of marijuana in itself leads to use of heroin or other hard drugs. Rather, it is the interaction with significant others which is likely to be a critical factor.

Illegal drug use is a common bond among some adolescents, among some college students, and among some adults. It provides a sense of affiliation for a portion of those who feel themselves to be outsiders, to be swimming against the prevailing ethic of the society, and who define adversely the prevailing social system. Exceptions such as drug-using physicians are of special interest because they are unlike their drug-using counterparts in the ghetto and on the college campus. Physicians have the drugs, the knowledge of how to use them and what sensations to experience, the power and prestige to withstand even self-expressed feelings of stigma, and the opportunity for avoiding detection and prosecution. They do not require *interaction* with like-minded others to become drug users and maintain the habit.

Drug subcultures have their own argot, always a sign of a strong flourishing subculture. theirs is a rich vocabulary and a set of distinct role types. A spike is a hypodermic needle; tea or weed is marijuana; scag is heroin; to burn is to cheat in drug dealing or to get another into difficulty. Getting high, kicking the habit, square, and hooked are terms that have found their way into everyday language. Mellow dudes occasionally use marijuana, have control over their lives. Potheads' lives revolve around marijuana. Rowdy dudes will use any drug they can obtain. Cool cats are career addicts who value flashy clothes, are hip, and stress loyalty to other career addicts.

Maintaining the habit of using addictive drugs is extremely expensive. Males commit larceny, burglary, and more and more are turning to robbery in order to finance the habit. Females turn to prostitution and also to theft, especially larceny. Both may become peddlers of drugs in order to supply themselves. Since the possession and sale of so many drugs are illegal and since their use is so widespread in the United States, a significant portion of the crime problem is closely intertwined with the drug problem.

While the relationship between alcoholism and use of other drugs is not clear, some persons obviously use both with the consequence of serious damage to health. Drug addicts usually have poor diets and suffer from a wide range of physical illnesses. They die at a relatively early age. By most standards their mental health is poor. They tend to suffer from depression and severe anxiety. They tend to have strong self-destructive tendencies. Drugs were the cause of death in 31 percent of all officially recorded suicides in 1971 in the United States.[109] Deaths among heroin addicts due to inadvertent overdoses of the drug are fairly common. Often the individual does not know how potent is the drug obtained on the street. All this is not necessarily true, however, of the well-to-do addict who can easily maintain the habit and escape public definition as an addict and negative deviant.

Explanations of Illicit Drug Use

Cultural Supports

There is no doubt that habitual use of drugs, in particular illicit drugs, depends in part on association with others who set forth relevant customs and values. Illicit drug use is an institutionalized form of negative deviance. While Edwin Sutherland did not focus on the use of drugs, his differential association theory is clearly applicable.[110] Individuals learn to procure, use, and gain pleasure form illicit drugs as a result of rewarding interaction with individuals who socially transmit customs for doing so. This is by no means the sole explanation of habitual use of illicit drugs. It is, however, a necessary condition. Even the addicted physician who usually has no contact with the criminal subculture has had prolonged exposure to a medical subculture which can provide the same supports. While the medical subculture does not advocate the illicit use of drugs, it does inevitably advocate the use of drugs as beneficial when prescribed by physicians. And it may be but a short step from legal prescriptions for others to illegal use by self.

In their opportunity structures formulation, Richard Cloward and Lloyd Ohlin directed explicit attention to illicit drug use.[111] They posited a retreatist subculture concerned centrally with the criminal procurement and use of drugs. Those persons who have not succeeded in the legitimate opportunity structures of society and who have been unable to gain entrance to the criminal (theft) or conflict (violent) illegitimate subcultures may seek to become a part of the retreatist subculture. Even here admission may be denied. If admitted, however, the individual gains a form of "success" as a member of an opportunity structure of sorts. This is sometimes termed the "double-failure" explanation since the individual has already been rejected in illegitimate as well as legitimate opportunity structures. While this formulation has merit for explaining some drug use, it is clear that many individuals seek directly to participate in drug subcultures rather than as a last resort after repeated failure to gain access to other illegitimate structures.

Social Integration

Robert Merton's reformulation of Durkheim's conception of anomie has considerable application to illicit drug use.[112] Merton suggested that retreatist deviance is likely to occur when individuals reject both cultural goals and institutionalized means for achieving them. Having been unable to gain the means to the acceptable goals, individuals may give up on both. They become the dropouts of society. It is within the realm of retreatist behavior that illicit drug use is usually located by sociologists. There is some validity to this, for the use of many drugs is a form of escape from the everyday world and drug-using groups are frequently off to one side of everyday affairs.

Yet we know that illicit drug users tend to create countercultures. That is to say, they develop and share customs and values which run counter to those of the prevailing overall culture and social system. They denigrate "square" life in an active, often scornful way. They rebel against a system in which they have been unable to achieve. Up to a point, Merton's rebellious mode of adaptation characterizes illicit drug users as well as does retreat. In Merton's scheme, rebellion consists of rejecting the prevailing acceptable goals and means and attempting to replace them with new goals and means. Illicit drug users do this in a limited sense. They seek to replace monetary success goals of everyday life in the United States with goals which emphasize non-materialism and the pleasures of sensation. They seek to replace the institutionalized means of the Protestant ethic—hard work, deferred gratification, thrift, so forth—with hedonistic activity. Yet they are not truly rebellious, for their rebellion is largely symbolic. Retreatists who have not fully given up, they seek to rebel without actively aggressing.

Charles Winick has proposed a three-part explanation of drug addiction which in some respects combines aspects of cultural support and anomie approaches.[113] He suggests that to become dependent on drugs, the individual must first have ready access to appropriate drugs. This implies participation in a drug subculture. Second, the person must become disengaged from negative proscriptions about the use of the drugs, that is, one must move outside of the mainstream the acceptable culture, as is the case under anomic conditions. Third, role strain or deprivation must be present. Winick defines role strain as difficulty in meeting role obligations and role deprivation as inability to perform a role or part of a role, often because of loss of the role. Of course, everyone experiences such role strain and deprivation at various times. But severe strain and deprivation, often the result of anomic conditions, coupled with absence of felt taboos about drugs and access to them constitute for Winick the necessary conditions for addiction.

Social Disorganization and Conflict

The idea of the Chicago School that the depressed areas of our larger urban places give rise to negative deviance because of social disorganization has frequently been applied to illicit drug use,[114] and it is here that drug subcultures abound in the poverty areas of our cities. Yet as with the skid-row locales of some alcoholics, this can in part be misleading. The neighborhoods of poverty in which illicit drug traffic and use thrive are not necessarily disorganized. They are, however, organized somewhat differently than the more affluent neighborhoods. They are the living results of anomic conditions and, as such, life revolves around coping with anomie. Illicit drug use is one of many coping systems. As noted in the preceding section, drugs can provide simultaneously retreat from the fact of failure and symbolic rebellion against the system which gave rise to the failure.

Thorsten Sellin's culture conflict thesis has limited relevance to illicit drug use.[115] Members of minority group subcultures may find the conflict in customs and values of their ethnic, racial, or religious groups with those of the overall prevailing culture to be severely frustrating. The escape and rebellion of drug use may be modes of adapting to such conflict. But of course to the extent that minority subcultures include strong proscriptions against drug use, modes of adaptation other than use of illicit drugs are likely to be chosen.

Richard Quinney's political conflict formulation of crime holds that those in political control determine what constitutes negative deviance and consign the working class to it.[116] In regard to explaining illicit drug abuse, Alex Thio's power theory runs somewhat along the same lines but is more comprehensive and useful.[117] Thio contends that the youths of the country are powerless and their parents and other adults are the powerful. Adults make wide use of prescription drugs, amphetamines in the main, and alcohol, which are a substantial source of corporate income for the powerful. This is lower-consensus deviance. Parents serve as drug-using models for their children, deny them prescription drugs, and then condemn them for using illicit drugs. Thus the young are forced into higher-consensus negative deviance for which they are disapproved and not infrequently prosecuted.

The problem with power theory applied to illicit drug use in this way is that the parents of young drug users are more often than not powerless themselves. On the other hand, implicit in Thio's formulation is that there is a wide gulf between the focal concerns of youths on the one hand and adults on the other. Adults do largely control the societal reward system; and if the young cannot fit in, then they may be consigned to coping as best they can with the consequent feelings of anomie. Conflict between the adult power structure and the youth culture is a far more important contributing factor in illicit drug use than parent–child conflict.

Societal Reaction

An important explanation of drug addiction is Alfred Lindesmith's cognitive association theory.[118] This is not as such a societal reaction or labeling approach. However, it has close similarities in certain respects. Lindesmith holds that heroin addiction will occur only if the individual perceives that the severe distress of withdrawal from the drug is a result of ceasing to take the drug. If the distress symptoms are seen as due to some other reason—an illness of some sort, for example—then addiction will not occur. The connection to societal reaction theory is in the labeling or defining of the situation by the individual. The society defines addiction as a condition characterized by dependence on a drug and extremely severe symptoms if it is not used. If individuals accept that definition and perceive its application to their own situations, then they become addicts.

William McAuliffe and Robert Gordon take quite a different view.[119] They believe that the pull of the euphoria associated with heroin is the critical factor. The desire to reexperience euphoria and to avoid long periods without it leads to addiction. While not intended as a societal reaction explanation, the McAuliffe–Gordon thesis can be cast in labeling terms. Certain symptoms are defined as extremely pleasurable, as euphoric, and as due to heroin. The threat of withdrawal of that pleasure if the drug is not taken leads to addiction. In any case, the Lindesmith and McAuliffe–Gordon explanations are opposites in one sense and similar in another: Taking heroin may be defined as leading to a euphoric state and avoidance of withdrawal symptoms; abstinence can be defined as leading to frustration due both to the cessation of euphoria and the onset of withdrawal distress.

As indicated earlier, Howard Becker holds that becoming a marijuana user involves learning from others the techniques to get high, to recognize the drug's effects, and to enjoy them.[120] Thus the internalization of a series of definitions, of subcultural labels, is necessary to become a habitual marijuana user. But the central role of societal reaction theory has to do with the fact that illicit drug users are defined and stigmatized as dangerous, as moral lepers, as outsiders. This drives experimenters with illicit drugs to group solutions to the problems of coping with negative identity and the threat and fact of prosecution and punishment. Thus are created and perpetuated drug subcultures which are learning environments for illicit drug use, provide for the circulation of drugs, and serve as protective havens for users.

Edwin Lemert's conception of secondary deviance is especially relevant.[121] Labeled as negative deviants, treated as outsiders, illicit drug users often become careerists in addiction, dependent on one another for physical and psychological survival. This is, as will be discussed, a circular problem in regard to treatment and rehabilitation. Membership in an outsider subculture and the negatively defined role of addict makes reentry into the straight world exceedingly difficult.

In sum, each of the four main theoretical themes found in this book has relevance to illicit drug use and addiction. Cultural supports, learning relevant customs and values from others, are clearly necessary. A condition of anomie, of failure to achieve success in the prevailing social system, is frequently a critical factor. Conflict between that system and the power structure on the one hand and the failed or otherwise stressed individual on the other hand is commonplace. Labeling, definition, is crucial to becoming a drug user and a career addict. Anomie, conflict with the social system, and cultural supports all set the scene for societal reaction to the drug deviant as a nearly irretrievable outsider.

SUMMARY

Alcohol is the most commonly used drug in the world. For the vast majority of persons, the consumption of alcohol does not impede health or social relations. Problem drinkers, however, use alcohol in amounts that are excessive for their culture and tend to suffer adverse medical and social consequences. Problem drinkers who become alcoholics are those whose physical and psychological dependence often involves overwhelming stress and tension. Similarly, drug addiction refers to a physical and psychological craving for a drug. Depressants, stimulants, and psychotropics constitute broad categories of drugs. The depressants are both physically and psychologically addictive. Stimulants and psychotropics, however, tend to be more psychologically than physically addictive.

Patterns of alcohol and drug use vary widely from one culture to the next. Alcoholism is rampant in some cultures, such as France and the United States, and extremely low in others, such as Spain and Argentina. Japan, Sweden, and the United States have recently experienced epidemics in drug use.

Within the Untied States the per capita consumption of alcohol has increased dramatically. About seven of every 10 Americans drink alcohol and about 12 percent of the adult population are considered to be problem drinkers. Most alcohol is consumed in the form of beer and the least as wine.

Drinking maladies are high among persons in their twenties and tend to decrease with age. This holds true for both males and females. Younger persons tend to use marijuana and stimulants, and older persons are more prone to use heroin and tranquilizers. Most research shows that in the United States, blacks of either sex have rates of alcoholism two to three times higher than their white counterparts. Irish- and French-Americans also tend to have high rates of alcoholism, while Italian- and Chinese-Americans do not.

The link between social class and problem drinking is not clear. What is certain is that problem drinkers who come to the attention of society at large are more often drawn from the lower social classes. This is also the case for illicit drug use. It should be remembered, however, that upper-middle-class individuals are considerably better able to hide their excessive use of alcohol and other drugs.

Among religious groups in the United States, Catholics have the highest rates of alcoholism and Jews decidedly the lowest. Mormons and Conservative Protestants rarely drink but are prone to alcoholism if they do. A central explanation of alcoholism and problem drinking among ethnic and religious groups in the United States is that the less drinking customs are an inherent part of everyday life of the overall culture or subculture of the group, the greater is the predisposition to alcoholism.

The family lives of alcoholics and drug addicts tend to be marked by considerable strife, separation, and divorce. Mothers of male drug addicts are likely to dominate their husbands and be overly protective of their sons. The addict aggresses symbolically through the use of illicit drugs. Addicted persons, more than others, commonly have relatives who are themselves addicted. Rates of addiction are highest among the previously married and single and lowest among the married.

Psychological explanations of alcoholism have focused on three themes: unconscious self-destructive tendencies; interpersonal problems of dependency and aggression; and either insecurity about power relations or an insatiable thirst for power. Social integration formulations hold that when institutionalized means to culturally approved goals are blocked or lost, acute frustration may lead to problem drinking or drug addiction. Cultural explanations have contended that if alcohol is viewed as an acceptable tension reducer and if social tensions are great, then rates of alcoholism will be high. In addition, when drinking practices conflict with widely held cultural norms, alcoholism and illicit drug use are more likely. Participation in drug-using subcultures, such as student, urban ghetto, or professional, is vital to learning to use drugs effectively, maintaining access to drugs, and having group support against possible negative societal reaction. Societal reaction theorists point out that if the use of alcohol or other drugs is defined negatively and if the user defines himself as dependent on the drug, then the likelihood of addiction increases.

References

1. Robert Straus, "Alcoholism and Problem Drinking," in *Contemporary Social Problems*, eds. Robert K. Merton and Robert Nisbet (New York: Harcourt Brace Jovanovich, 1976). p. 193.

2. *Ibid.*
3. Donald Horton, "The Functions of Alcohol in Primitive Societies," in *Alcohol, Science, and Society* (New Haven, CT: Quarterly Journal of Studies in Alcohol, Lecture 13, 1945).
4. Andrew Poznanski, "Our Drinking Heritage," *McGill Medical Journal, 1956,* pp. 35–41.
5. Craig MacAndrew and Robert B. Edgerton, *Drunken Comportment* (Chicago: Aldine, 1969).
6. *Ibid.,* p. 17.
7. *Ibid.,* p. 16.
8. *Ibid.,* p. 49.
9. Jack H. Mendelson and Nancy K. Mello, *Alcohol Use and Abuse in America* (Boston: Little, Brown, 1985).
10. *Ibid.,* p. 136.
11. Erich Goode, *Drugs in American Society,* 2nd ed. (New York: Knopf, 1984).
12. Joseph A. Califano, *Drug Abuse and Alcoholism* (New York: Warner, 1982).
13. Patricia Fishburne, Herbert I. Abelson, and Ira Cisin, "National Survey on Drug Abuse: Main Findings, 1979," National Institute on Drug Abuse (Washington, D.C.: U.S. Government Printing Office, 1980); and Judith D. Miller, Ira H. Cisin, Hilary Gardner-Keaton, Adele Harrell, Philip W. Wirtz, Herbert I. Abelson, and Patricia M. Fishburne, "National Survey on Drug Abuse: Main Findings, 1982," National Institute on Drug Abuse (Washington, D.C.: U.S. Government Printing Office, 1983).
14. National Institute on Alcohol Abuse and Alcoholism, "Fourth Special Report to the United States Congress on Alcohol and Health" (Washington, D.C.: U.S. Government Printing Office, 1981).
15. Henry Wechsler, "Epidemiology of Male/Female Drinking Over the Last Half Century," in National Institute on Alcohol Abuse and Alcoholism, *Alcoholism and Alcohol Abuse Among Women: Research Issue,* Research Monograph No. 1 (Washington, D.C.: U.S. Government Printing Office, 1980), p. 12.
16. Wechsler, *op. cit.,* pp. 13–14.
17. Fishburne, Abelson, and Cisin, *op. cit.*
18. Don Cahalan, *Problem Drinkers* (San Francisco: Jossey-Bass, 1970).
19. Lee N. Robins, George E. Murphy, and Mary B. Breckenridge, "Drinking Behavior of Young Urban Negro Men," *Quarterly Journal of Studies on Alcohol* 29(3): 657–684, 1968.
20. National Institute on Alcohol Abuse and Alcoholism, *op. cit.,* 1981; and Fishburne, Abelson, and Cisin, *op. cit.*
21. Marshall B. Clinard and Robert F. Meier, *Sociology of Deviant Behavior,* 6th ed. (New York: Holt, Rinehart and Winston, 1985).
22. Myrna M. Weissman, Jerome K. Myers, and Pamela S. Harding, "Prevalence and Psychiatric Heterogeneity of Alcoholism in a United States Urban Community," *Journal of Studies on Alcohol* 41(7):672–681, 1980.
23. MacAndrew and Edgerton, *op. cit.,* pp. 100–163.
24. Wechsler, *op. cit.,* p. 17.
25. Alex Thio, *Deviant Behavior* (Boston: Houghton Mifflin, 1983), p. 373.
26. For example, Jerome H. Skolnick, "Religious Affiliation and Drinking Behavior," *Quarterly Journal of Studies on Alcohol* 19(3):452–470, 1958, and Steven R. Burkett, "Religiosity, Beliefs, Normative Standards and Adolescent Drinking," *Journal of Studies on Alcohol* 41(7):662–671, 1980.
27. Robert F. Bales, "Cultural Differences in Rates of Alcoholism," *Quarterly Journal of Studies on Alcohol* 6:480–500, 1946.
28. Clinard, *op. cit.,* pp. 153–156.
29. *Ibid.*
30. Charles R. Snyder, *Alcohol and the Jews* (New York: Free Press, 1958). See also B.

278   Chapter 10

Glassner and B. Berg, "How Jews Avoid Alcohol Problems," *American Sociological Review* 45(4):647–664, 1980; and Denise B. Kandel and Myriam Sudit, "Drinking Practice Among Urban Adults in Israel: A Cross-Cultural Comparison," *Journal of Studies on Alcohol* 43(1):1–16, 1982.

31. Snyder, *op. cit.*; also Thio, *op. cit.*, pp. 372–373.
32. H. S. Cutter and J. C. Fisher, "Family Experiences and the Motives for Drinking, *International Journal of Addictions* 15:339–358, 1980; T. L. Napier, T. J. Carter, and M. C. Pratt, "Correlates of Alcohol and Marijuana Use Among Rural High School Students," *Rural Sociology* 46:319–332, 1981; and H. Wechsler and D. Thum, "Teenage Drinking, Drug Use, and Social Correlates," *Quarterly Journal of Studies on Alcohol* 34:1220–1227, 1973.
33. R. Zucker, "Parental Influence on Drinking Patterns of Their Children," in *Alcoholism Problems in Women and Children*, eds. M. Greenblatt and M. A. Schuckit (New York: Grune and Stratton, 1976).
34. Wechsler and Thum, *op. cit.*
35. Nancy S. Cotton, "The Familial Incidence of Alcoholism," *Quarterly Journal of Studies on Alcoholism* 40:89–116, 1979; and George E. Vaillant, *The Natural History of Alcoholism: Causes, Patterns and Paths to Recovery* (Cambridge, MA: Harvard University Press, 1983); and B. A. Christiansen and M. S. Goldman, "Alcohol-Related Expectancies Versus Demographic Background Variables in the Prediction of Adolescent Drinking," *Journal of Consulting Clinical Psychology* 51(2):249–257, 1983.
36. Cotton, *op. cit.*
37. For example, David J. Armor, J. Michael Polich, and Harriet B. Stambul, *Alcoholism and Treatment* (Santa Monica, CA: Rand Corp., 1976); and Margaret B. Bailey, Paul W. Haberman, and Harold Alksne, "The Epidemiology of Alcoholism in an Urban Residential Area," *Quarterly Journal of Studies on Alcohol* 26(1):19–40, 1965.
38. Gordon E. Barnes, "The Alcoholic Personality, A Reanalysis of the Literature," *Journal of Studies on Alcohol* 40(7):571–634, 1979.
39. See Thio, *op. cit.*, pp. 382–384.
40. David C. McClelland, Willian N. Davis, Rudolf Kalin, and Eric Wanner, *The Drinking Man* (New York: Free Press, 1972).
41. For a related view, see Bales, *op. cit.*
42. E. M. Jellinek, "Phases of Alcohol Addiction," *Quarterly Journal of Studies on Alcohol* 13(4):673–684, 1952.
43. L. R. Bellwood, "Grief Work in Alcoholism Treatment," *Alcohol Health Research World*, Spring 1975, pp. 8–11.
44. *Fourth Special Report to the United States Congress on Alcohol and Health* (Rockville, MD: National Institute on Alcohol Abuse and Alcoholism, 1981).
45. Marvin E. Wolfgang, *Patterns in Criminal Homicide* (Philadelphia: University of Pennsylvania Press, 1958), p. 166.
46. University of California at Los Angeles, Center for Disease Control, *The Epidemiology of Homicide in the City of Los Angeles, 1970–1979*, Department of Health and Human Services, Public Health Services, Center for Disease Control, 1985; and P. W. Haberman and M. Baden, *Alcohol, Other Drugs and Violent Death* (New York: Oxford University Press, 1978).
47. MacAndrew and Edgerton, *op. cit.*
48. National Institute on Alcohol Abuse and Alcoholism, NIAAA Information and Feature Service, March 3, 1983, IFS No. 105, p. 4.
49. John A. Volpe, "Alcohol and Public Safety," in The American Assembly, Columbia University (Englewood Cliffs, NJ: Prentice-Hall, 1984).
50. Thio, *op. cit.*, p. 368.
51. Straus, *op. cit.*, p. 208.
52. Volpe, *op. cit.*, 1984.

53. *Ibid.*
54. *Ibid.*
55. Berthold Brenner, "Alcoholism and Fatal Accidents," *Quarterly Journal of Studies on Alcohol* 28(3):517–528, 1967.
56. Bales, *op. cit.*
57. Harrison M. Trice, *Alcoholism in America* (New York: McGraw-Hill, 1966).
58. Richard Jessor, Theodore D. Graves, Robert C. Hanson, and Shirley L. Jessor, *Society, Personality, and Deviant Behavior* (New York: Holt, Rhinehart and Winston, 1968).
59. Snyder, *op. cit.*
60. Thio, *op. cit.*
61. Joan K. Jackson and Ralph Connor, "The Skid Road Alcoholic," *Quarterly Journal of Studies on Alcohol* 14(3):468–486, 1953.
62. Stuart Palmer, "High Social Integration as a Source of Deviance," *British Journal of Sociology* 24(1):93–100, 1973.
63. Harrison M. Trice and Paul M. Roman, *Spirits and Demons at Work: Alcohol and Other Drugs on the Job* (Ithaca, NY: State School of Industrial and Labor Relations Paper, Cornell University, 1978).
64. Edwin M. Lemert, *Human Deviance, Social Problems, and Social Control* (Englewood Cliffs, NJ: Prentice-Hall, 1967).
65. President's Commission on Law Enforcement and Administration of Justice, *Task Force Report: Drunkenness* (Washington, D.C.: U.S. Government Printing Office, 1967).
66. Horton, *op. cit.*
67. Joseph R. Gusfield, *Symbolic Crusade* (Urbana, IL: University of Illinois Press, 1963).
68. Jacqueline P. Wiseman, *Stations of the Lost* (Englewood Cliffs, NJ: Prentice-Hall, 1970).
69. Harrison M. Trice, "Alcoholics Anonymous," *Annals of the American Academy of Political and Social Science* 315:108–116, 1958; and David R. Rudy, *Becoming Alcoholic: Alcoholics Anonymous and the Reality of Alcoholism* (Carbondale, IL: Southern Illinois University Press, 1986).
70. *Alcoholics Anonymous* (New York: Works, 1939), pp. 71–72.
71. Harrison M. Trice, "The Affiliation Motive and Readiness to Join Alcoholics Anonymous," *Quarterly Journal of Studies on Alcohol* 20(2):313–320, 1959.
72. Harrison M. Trice and Paul M. Roman, "Delabeling, Relabeling, and Alcoholics Anonymous," *Social Problems* 17(4):538–546, 1970.
73. Norval Morris and Gordon Hawkins, *An Honest Politician's Guide to Crime Control* (Chicago: University of Chicago Press, 1970).
74. Paul M. Roman, "Secondary Prevention of Alcoholism: Problems and Prospects in Occupational Programming," *Journal of Drug Issues* 5(4):327–343, 1975.
75. National Institute of Health, *Alcohol and Alcoholism* (Washington, D.C.: U.S. Department of Health, Education, and Welfare, 1967).
76. Erich Goode, *Drugs in American Society*, 2nd ed. (New York: Alfred A. Knopf, 1984).
77. Louis A. Gottschalk, Frederick L. McGuire, Jon F. Heiser, Eugene C. Dinovo, and Herman Birch, *Drug Abuse Deaths in Nine Cities: A Survey Report*, National Institute on Drug Abuse Research Monograph 29 (Washington, D.C.: U.S. Government Printing Office, 1979).
78. For a useful review, see Gregory A. Austin, Mary A. MacAri, and Dan J. Lettieri, *International Drug Use* (Rockville, MD: National Institute on Drug Abuse, 1978), pp. xvii–xxv.
79. E. Bourguignon, *Religion, Altered States of Consciousness, and Social Change* (Columbus, OH: Ohio State University Press, 1973).
80. Marlene D. DeRios, "Man, Culture, and Hallucinogens: An Overview," in *Cannabis and Culture*, ed. Vera Rubin (The Hague: Mouton, 1975).
81. Austin *et al.*, *op cit.*

82. E. H. Ellingwood, "The Epidemiology of Stimulant Abuse," in *Drug Use: Epidemiological and Sociological Approaches*, eds. Eric Josephson and Eleanor E. Carroll (New York: Wiley, 1974), pp. 303–329.
83. U.S. Bureau of Census, *Statistical Abstract of the United States, 1986* (Washington, D.C.: U.S. Government Printing Office, 1985), p. 118.
84. Arnold S. Trebach, *The Heroin Solution* (New Haven, CT: Yale University Press, 1982).
85. *Ibid.*
86. U.S. Bureau of Census, *op. cit.*, p. 118.
87. *Ibid.*
88. Glen D. Mellinger, Mitchell B. Balter, Hugh J. Parry, Dean L. Manheimer, and Ira H. Cisin, "An Overview of Psychotherapeutic Drug Use in the United States," in Josephson and Carroll, *op. cit.*, pp. 333–336.
89. Lawrence J. Redlinger and Jerry B. Michel, "Ecological Variations in Heroin Abuse," *Sociological Quarterly* 11(2):219–229, 1970.
90. Lee N. Robbins and George E. Murphy, "Drug Use in a Normal Population of Young Negro Men," *American Journal of Public Health* 57(9):1580–1596, 1967.
91. Carl D. Chambers, "Some Epidemiological Considerations of Opiate Use in the United States," in Josephson and Carroll, *op. cit.*, 1974, pp. 65–82.
92. John A. O'Donnell, Harwin L. Voss, Richard R. Clayton, Gerald T. Slaten, and Robin G. S. Room, *Young Men and Drugs: A Nationwide Survey* (Springfield, VA: National Technical Information Services, 1976).
93. *Newsweek*, August 10, 1981.
94. *Time*, April 11, 1983.
95. *Ibid.*
96. William E. McAuliffe, Mary Rohman, Susan SanTangelo, Barry Feldman, Elizabeth Magnuson, Arthur Sobol, and Joel Weissman, "Psychoactive Drug Use Among Practicing Physicians and Medical Students," *New England Journal of Medicine* 315(13):805–810, 1986.
97. *Modern Medicine* 25:170–191, 1957.
98. Lawrence Kolb, "The Drug Addiction Muddle," *Police* 1:57–62, 1957.
99. William H. McGlothlin, Victor C. Tabbush, Carl D. Chambers, and Kay Jamison, *Alternative Approaches to Opiate Addiction Control: Costs, Benefits, and Potential*, U.S. Department of Justice (Washington, DC: U.S. Government Printing Office, 1972).
100. Isidor Chein with the collaboration of Daniel M. Wiher, *The Road to H* (New York: Basic Books, 1964).
101. William M. McCord, "We Ask the Wrong Questions about Crime," *The New York Times Magazine*, November 21, 1965.
102. Eva Rosenfeld, "Teenage Addiction," in *Problems in Addiction*, ed. William C. Bier (New York, 1962).
103. Nathan E. Seldin, "Mother of the Young Male Drug Addict," unpublished paper, cited in Nathan E. Seldin, "The Family of the Addict: A Review of the Literature," *International Journal of the Addictions* 7:97–107, 1972.
104. Seldin, "The Family of the Addict," *ibid.*, pp. 98–101.
105. Howard S. Becker, *Outsiders* (New York: Free Press, 1963), pp. 42–58.
106. Isidor Chein with the collaboration of Daniel M. Wilner, *op. cit.*, p. 149.
107. Seymour Fiddle, "The Addict Culture and Movement into and out of Hospitals," in United States Senate, Committee on the Judiciary, Subcommittee to Investigate Juvenile Delinquency, *Hearings* Part 13, September 20–21, 1962 (Washington, D.C.: United States Government Printing Office, 1963), p. 3156.
108. *Ibid.*
109. Louis A. Gottschalk, Frederick L. McGuire, Jon F. Heiser, Eugene C. Dinovo, and Herman Birch, *op. cit.*, p. 105.

110. Edwin H. Sutherland and Donald R. Cressey, *Principles of Criminology* (Chicago: Lippincott, 1939).
111. Richard A. Cloward and Lloyd E. Ohlin, *Delinquency and Opportunity* (Glencoe, IL: Free Press, 1960).
112. Robert K. Merton, *Social Theory and Social Structure* (New York: Macmillan, 1968).
113. Charles Winick, "A Sociological Theory of the Genesis of Drug Dependence," in *Sociological Aspects of Drug Dependence*, ed. Charles Winick (Cleveland, OH: CRC, 1974), pp. 3–13.
114. On social disorganization, see Robert E. L. Faris, *Social Disorganization* (New York: Ronald Press, 1955).
115. Thorsten Sellin, *Culture Conflict and Crime* (New York: Social Science Research Council, Bulletin No. 41, 1938).
116. Richard Quinney, *The Social Reality of Crime* (Boston: Little, Brown, 1970).
117. Thio, *op. cit.*
118. Alfred R. Lindesmith, *Addiction and Opiates* (Chicago: Aldine, 1968).
119. William E. McAuliffe and Robert A. Gordon, "A Test of Lindesmith's Theory of Addiction: The Frequency of Euphoria among Long-Term Addicts," *American Journal of Sociology* 79(4):795–840, 1974.
120. Becker, *op. cit.*
121. Lemert, *op. cit.*

Index